# Nobody's Business

## The Aran Diaries of
# ERNIE O'MALLEY

*Edited by* CORMAC O'MALLEY
*and* RÓISÍN KENNEDY

*Afterword by* LUKE GIBBONS

THE LILLIPUT PRESS | DUBLIN

First published 2017 by
THE LILLIPUT PRESS
62–63 Sitric Road
Dublin 7
www.lilliputpress.ie

A CIP record for this title is available from
The British Library.

10 9 8 7 6 5 4 3 2 1

ISBN 978 1 84351 715 3

Set by Marsha Swan in 10.5pt on 14pt Sabon
Printed in Spain by GraphyCems

# Contents

# Illustrations

Ernie and Cormac O'Malley on Inishmore, 1954. Photographer Jean McGrail. Courtesy of Cormac O'Malley. (Cover)

Ernie O'Malley on Inishmore, 1954. Photographer Jean McGrail. Courtesy of Cormac O'Malley. (p. viii)

Elizabeth Rivers in doorway of Man of Aran Cottage, Inishmore, Aran, c. 1940. Photographer unknown. Courtesy of David Britton. (p. 5)

Pat Mullen. Photographer unknown. Courtesy of David Britton. (p. 7)

Sean Keating, *Launching a Currach*. Charcoal drawing. Private collection. Photograph courtesy of Adam's Fine Art Auctioneers. © Seán Keating. All Rights Reserved IVARO, 2017. (p. 14)

Irish Dancers in a cottage on Inishmore [Bridget Johnston, on right Sonny Hernon], March 1952. Photographer George Pickow. Ritchie-Pickow Collection – James Hardiman Library – National University of Ireland, Galway. © National University of Ireland, Galway. (p. 32)

Charles Lamb, *A Quaint Couple*, 1930. © Crawford Art Gallery, Cork and Laillí Lamb de Buitlear. (p. 45)

Elizabeth Rivers, *Loading Cattle for Galway from the Aran Islands*. Wood engraving. Courtesy of David Britton. (p. 59)

Annie Hernon knitting close to a cottage hearth, 1952. Photographer George Pickow. Ritchie-Pickow Collection – James Hardiman Library – National University of Ireland, Galway. © National University of Ireland, Galway. (p. 70)

Seán Keating, *Two Girls waiting by harbour for hooker*. Charcoal drawing. National Museum of Ireland. Photograph courtesy of Adam's Fine Art Auctioneers. © Seán Keating. All Rights Reserved IVARO, 2017. (p.76)

Maurice MacGonigal, *Unloading Turf, Kilmurvey Pier, Inishmore*, c. 1954. Private collection. Photograph courtesy of Adam's Fine Art Auctioneers. © Estate of Maurice MacGonigal, by permission of Ciaran MacGonigal. (p. 79)

Elizabeth Rivers, *Seaweed Harvest, Aran Islands*. Wood engraving. Courtesy of David Britton. (p. 84)

A young woman spinning, Aran Islands, c. 1952. Photographer George Pickow. Ritchie-Pickow Collection – James Hardiman Library – National University of Ireland, Galway. © National University of Ireland, Galway. (p. 87)

Seán Keating, *Self-Portrait*. Drawing. Private collection. Photograph courtesy of Whytes.com. © Seán Keating. All Rights Reserved IVARO, 2017. (p. 116)

# PREFACE: ARAN ON HIS MIND OR 'NOBODY'S BUSINESS'[1]

## Cormac K.H. O'Malley

My father, Ernie O'Malley, had the Aran Islands on his mind on and off for almost forty years. The islands represented a special place for him, an intellectual getaway, a place where he could have 'peace and freedom'. This relationship was not critical to his life or career, but his reflections on Aran in his diaries and in other writings tell us much about himself as a nationalist, a long-suffering patient, art critic, archaeology buff, folklorist, military organizer, parent, wanderer and writer.

In his youth my father summered around Clew Bay, Co. Mayo, and retained vivid memories of the local boats, islands, islanders, fishing, fishermen, stories and folktales, and he wrote of these nostalgically in the first chapter of his memoir, *On Another Man's Wound*.[2] Thus when he first went to Inisheer, the smallest of the Aran Islands, in spring 1919, with Peadar O'Loughlin of Clare, to help start a company of Irish Volunteers there, he would have been familiar with some of the rural island traditions of storytelling and their way of life. Father was not an affable, easygoing young man who could sing a song or tell a ballad easily; in fact, he was a relatively shy introvert, who could never speak well in public. However, when required in the evening time sitting around a turf fire on Inisheer, he drew upon his resourceful memory to relate to the islanders some seafaring stories such as those of Till Eulenspiegel, Hakluyt's sea tales, 'Bricriú's Feast' and 'The Story of Burnt Njal'. Since he could not speak Irish, no doubt, Peadar in translating his tales for the islanders must have added some engaging language, and they in turn apparently 'rocked with delight'. Sadly for him from the perspective of his immediate mission, no Volunteer company was organized, and he comments on that in his later diaries, but at least his tales were remembered after he left. Folklore remained an interest throughout his life, and he wrote up tales and folk traditions when he travelled later in New Mexico and Mexico.

*Ernie O'Malley on Inishmore, 1954.*

Father took about ten years off after being released from his military internment camp just before the start of the *Tailteann* Games in mid July 1924. He first went to Europe to recover from his ill health and wounds after his eight years of military activities. When he returned to Ireland in autumn 1926, he found he could not concentrate on his medical studies and by autumn 1928, he went off to the United States to raise funds for the founding of the *Irish Press*. When that campaign ended, he remained there and wandered around the United States and Mexico – writing his memoir, principally in New Mexico and New York. It was there he met my mother,

Helen Hooker, an American sculptor, artist and photographer, and fell in love. When he returned to Ireland in 1935, one of the places he wanted to go to get away from his own family's domestic life in Dublin was to the quietude of the West. Having lived in such relative isolation during his travels perhaps returning to the centre of his parents' family home was too much, and soon after arriving home, he wanted some solitude. He would also have encountered many people who still wanted him to be as he had been in his activist nationalist days, whereas he had moved on and wished not to be thought of in that heroic light. As in his days on the run, he took off to wander around Ireland to see archaeological sites and monastic ruins. He went to Clare and Galway, and it is thought that he went on to Aran. By that September he had married Helen Hooker, settled down in Dublin where he returned to his medical studies, and started to prepare his memoir for publication in early 1936. Their first child was born in July 1936, and while Helen's American family visited in Dublin, my father once again sought out peace and quiet and headed to the Aran Islands.

It must have been quite a surprise when my father landed in Kilronan on Inishmore and met Barbara MacDonagh, daughter of the 1916 executed leader, Thomas MacDonagh, who was there on her honeymoon with her husband, Liam Redmond, and had rented McDonagh's hotel in Kilronan for a few weeks that August. There were plenty of unoccupied rooms there, and he was invited to stay. Despite his good intentions to be isolated, no doubt, he was interested in meeting up with young people who knew of nationalist politics, literature and theatre. Barbara was studying Arts while Liam was doing Medicine at UCD, and both were involved in the Dramatic Society, which father had helped found in 1926. There would have been great chats, and father would have met Dr John O'Brien who became a great source of friendship and information for years to come.

After his respite in Aran father returned to Dublin and continued his medical studies, but my parents spent more and more time on excursions around Ireland photographing archaeological and medieval Christian monastic sites. After father lost a libel suit on his memoir in 1937, my parents decided in 1938 to live in County Mayo where eventually they settled in an old O'Malley home at Burrishoole Lodge, near Newport.[3] There they started an almost self-sufficient farm during the Emergency years, but also spent time photographing rural Western Ireland. My mother took a special interest in fixing up the farm buildings and continuing her sculpting, while my father collected extensive folklore tales from around Clew Bay and started to research and write on local history.

In the autumn of 1941 when father wanted to avoid some unannounced guest at their home and to take a break from his farm responsibilities, he wandered off once again, this time towards Galway. When close to Galway he remembered Aran and went by the steamer, *Dun Aonghus,* out to Inishmore. He might have heard talk in Dublin from his friends in the art world that Elizabeth Rivers, an English artist, had moved to Inishmore in 1935 and was supporting herself by running a small boarding house for like-minded paying guests in Robert Flaherty's former Man of Aran Cottage.[4] He arrived there in Kilmurvey unannounced, settled in for a few weeks and felt content to be able once again to write, talk and walk without domestic interference or responsibilities. The fruit of those writings is published here for the first time, though only three of his 1941 diary notebooks have been located.

After a few weeks, father returned to Burrishoole to continue supervising the farm during the day and to write and read in the evenings. Before the end of the Emergency, the family moved back from their relative isolation in Mayo to Dublin to place their children in schools there. They both became involved in various aspects of the arts: mother continued her sculpture and helped found the Players Theatre with Liam Redmond, who then lived next door in Clonskeagh; father became more involved in artistic and literary matters as the books editor of *The Bell* and writer of art criticism. By mid-1948 their marriage had become dysfunctional and father took the three children, Cathal, Etain and myself, back to Burrishoole. All of us children had contracted some form of tuberculosis in Dublin though only my brother and I were confined to bed. Father, in effect, homeschooled us for a period. In 1950 my mother returned to Ireland and without consulting my father took or 'kidnapped' my brother and sister from their Irish-speaking boarding school, Ring College in Dungarvan, thus contradicting father's specific orders to the school. Father's plan for our education was for us to become proficient in Irish and for the boys to have a Benedictine education in Ireland and then to go to Ampleforth College, a Benedictine boarding school in England. After spring 1950 father kept me on a tight leash during the summers when I stayed with his close friends; I was moved frequently from house to house and was placed in boarding school but under a veil of secrecy so no one knew where I was except one other person.

Almost thirteen years after father's 1941 visit to Aran, he returned there, but much had changed in his life. His wife had left him. Two children had gone. He had suffered setbacks in his health with heart attacks in 1952 and 1953, had been told to stop living by himself in his beloved Mayo home and had had to move to a Dublin apartment where he would not have to climb stairs. He also had the dual challenge of making sure that I was not kidnapped by my mother and taken to America and of getting me to speak Irish before going to Ampleforth in 1956. His plan was for us to spend the month of August on the Aran Islands for at least three years. Accordingly, in the summer of 1954 we spent July in Burrishoole packing up his books, furniture and paintings and drinking off his wine cellar in preparation for our move to Dublin, and we passed August in Kilmurvey House in Kilmurvey, Inishmore.[5] After the month of work in Mayo my father was quite exhausted and by staying in an Aran guest house, we did not have to bother with shopping and cooking as three meals a day were provided. My recollection of Kilmurvey is that there were not many children in the vicinity with whom I could play and so my learning of Irish was quite minimal that summer. However, father and I explored the ruins of forts, castles, churches and houses as well clambering over stone walls and spent much time with colourful Dr John O'Brien.

For the summers of 1955 and 1956, my father decided that we should go to Inisheer, which was a smaller community; it had guest houses for outsiders and more children for me to play with and thereby learn Irish. Father always brought along books to read and notebooks to write in. Writing a diary was a mental exercise for him, a way to keep his writing in shape. He assiduously counted the number of words he wrote each day, and occasionally reread his diary and made minor corrections. Unfortunately, his 1954 diary has not been located though it may turn up yet. The short diary from 1955 and a longer diary from 1956 were found among his papers when he died, but had never been transcribed until the last few years after they had been donated to New York University Library.

These Aran diaries relate my father's immediate reactions and reflections as to what he saw, felt and experienced; they were not studied, reviewed and restated. He titled his 1956 notebook 'Nobody's Business'. On a few occasions he contradicted an earlier comment and wrote his new insight on whatever page he was writing at the time, but did not bother to go back and change his original thought. When reading the diaries one feels that one is right there listening to the actual conversations or watching the windswept landscape. One senses the aches in his back as his rheumatism pained him and he searched for relief from the occasional sunshine. Father wrote these diaries in the same manner as his first published memoir with good, detailed descriptions of landscape and seascape including animals, birds, fish, fauna and local occupations. He included his characteristically brief but adroit character analysis and dramatic dialogue, which allows one to 'hear' better what is being said in a particular accent or dialogue. It is interesting to note that although he himself did not know much Irish, he insisted that his three children learn Irish fluently, and yet in his diaries he expresses some ambivalence towards time spent by islanders learning Irish in the Aran schools. He also picks up on the resistance by the islanders and others to the 'official' form of Irish, which was then being taught. His interest in folklore comes through as he relates the local lore and history. In short, he delivers a vivid slice of life in the world of the Aran Islands during those years – though, of course, his writings reflect only his own immediate perceptions and do not attempt to give an overview of life on Aran, and are also clearly once again, like many others, the observations of an outsider.

A quick note about editing my father's extremely difficult handwriting. In some places ellipses have been used for limited deletions – where words were indecipherable, wording confusing or incomplete or for other reasons.

# INTRODUCTION

## *Róisín Kennedy*

Ernie O'Malley's diaries were never intended for publication. As noted in the preface, two of the later diaries are labelled 'Nobody's Business'. They record observations and private conversations made on his visits to Inishmore and Inishmaan in 1941 and to Inisheer in 1955 and 1956. O'Malley's constant curiosity and concern with art and material culture run throughout their pages. In 1941 he stayed in a cottage rented by the artist Elizabeth Rivers where he and the other guests shared an interest in theatre, books and painting. While in Inishmore, O'Malley also met the painter Charles Lamb who was based in Connemara and with whom he conversed about some of their mutual acquaintances in the Dublin art world.

The Emergency was an exciting time for art in Ireland, and O'Malley later recognized its significance.[1] While there was a lack of art materials and other restrictions, the war forced more adventurous artists, collectors and critics to return from abroad to live in the neutral Free State. The lack of international travel ironically assisted in the development of an already embryonic gallery system focused on modern Irish art. In 1943 Victor Waddington opened a new gallery in Dublin specializing in modern painting. In the same year the Irish Exhibition of Living Art was founded as an alternative annual exhibition forum to the Royal Hibernian Academy, rapidly outdoing its rival in popularity and quality. However, in 1941 when O'Malley was chatting with Rivers and Lamb about Irish art, he had yet to develop his later positive views on its progress in the Emergency period. The diary records several negative comments on the lack of quality in Irish art, the lack of commitment by artists and gallerists and above all the general lack of taste and awareness of artistic matters in Ireland.

O'Malley married and settled in Ireland in 1935 with his wife, the American sculptor Helen Hooker, after a seven-year period in the United States and Mexico. Partly through Helen's involvement in the art world and partly through his own networks, he developed friendships and associations with many modernist artists in Dublin. He began to assemble an impressive collection of modern Irish art that came to include eight major paintings by Jack B. Yeats. He also collected work by Louis le Brocquy, Evie Hone, Mainie Jellett and Norah McGuinness among others. From the mid 1940s O'Malley, who had by then developed a positive attitude towards this cohort of Irish artists, was closely involved in promoting their work, which he believed could form the nucleus of an expansion of modernist Irish art internationally.[2]

When he returned to the Aran Islands in the mid 1950s, O'Malley's material circumstances had altered dramatically. Helen had closed their home in Clonskeagh, Dublin, and returned to the United States in 1950 and divorced him. He had in effect abandoned his home in Burrishoole, near Newport, Co. Mayo and was living in Dublin. He was in poor health, having suffered a series of heart attacks. O'Malley and his son, the youngest of his three children and the only one not taken by Helen back to America, stayed in the guesthouse run by the Colman Conneely family in 1955 and at the guesthouse run by Marie Flaherty O'Donnell in 1956. On the more isolated island of Inisheer there was not the same mix of creative types that Rivers' home had provided. But O'Malley sought and befriended a young Danish artist, Orla Knudsen. He also came into regular contact with another visitor to the island, Seán Keating, the leading academic painter in Ireland. A difficult character, he was often at loggerheads with the liberal art world with which O'Malley was aligned. Unsurprisingly the two men, despite their shared interest in art and nationalism, had a distinctly frosty relationship.

While the later diaries make reference to the ways in which the Aran Islands were being affected by emigration and changes in established farming practices, the art field continued to be of central concern to O'Malley. This was also changing. Despite the apparent advances of the foundation of the Cultural Relations Committee in 1949 and the Arts

Council of Ireland in 1951, the wartime optimism associated with the art world was diminishing. There was a decline in one-person exhibitions and a slackening of art sales in Dublin in the post-war period. Victor Waddington moved his art gallery to London in 1957. He was undoubtedly helped in making this decision after the Irish government introduced a 60 per cent levy on artworks being imported into the country and a 40 per cent levy on art materials in 1956.[3]

O'Malley was a dispassionate observer of all things and people that came into his notice. As a consequence his account of the Aran Islands is remarkably unsentimental and devoid of the kind of rhetoric normally found in visitors' memoirs. He does admit to having an affinity with the place in the 1941 diary: 'A strange place, this Aran. I have settled down here as if I had lived here for a long time and as if I could stay a long time.' Elsewhere it is evident that his feelings stem as much from the freedom from domesticity and the leisure to read and to write that his stays provided rather than from any attachment to Aran. While his earlier stay enabled him to discuss and consider the state of art and culture in Ireland generally, his later visits prompted him to look more closely at the islands as a microcosm of Irish culture, one that was being undermined and eroded by economic turmoil and official neglect but above all by what O'Malley considered to be the inherent suspicion of intellectualism amongst Irish men and women.

In his 1941 diary O'Malley laments the general lack of engagement with the arts and culture by the Irish. This he attributes to economic factors and by extension to the legacy of colonialism: 'Art needs money necessarily for its development. It needs leisure, and we share neither so far, but might have both eventually … Leisure for sport most people seem to have in this country, but not leisure to read or to look at pictures.' Introspection and a lack of knowledge or curiosity about the outside world have also had a negative impact on the Irish. The diaries consider the role of colonialism in this process: 'At one time the Irish were open to every idea, and when their best work in manuscript and metal work was being done they were able to keep abreast of every foreign idiom in their work and to absorb or to change it. Conquest shut them off from the outside world. Then journeying was restricted and finally stopped altogether.'

'"Things get so bad at times in the country," I said, "that I feel like putting up a notice which would read as pure snobbery, *people with creative tendencies welcomed*,"' O'Malley records in his diary. But even if the level of creativity was to increase, the Irish, unlike people of other countries, according to O'Malley, have no sense of how to appreciate art: 'Abroad there are certain indefinable standards in creative work. Certain looks, a piece of sculpture, a picture, a concert have a quality which people understand. They are sound constructively and creatively. You haven't to explain them every time you come across them, or to defend them against the resentment of people who cannot see the work.'

The low level of engagement in the arts in mid-twentieth century Ireland was exacerbated by the conservative education system that was run almost exclusively by the Catholic Church. The learning of Irish was the overriding priority of the Department of Education at the expense of other subjects, including the teaching of art and drawing.[4] The latter was dropped from the primary school curriculum in 1922. To add to this the introduction of censorship of film (1924) and of literature (1929) discouraged the development of an informed and engaged understanding of contemporary European cultural issues by large swathes of the population. Those in the, know – through elite education, family connections or exceptional circumstances – were able to access forbidden literature and avant-garde art and cinema through travel, membership of private clubs and societies or through the British media. Most of these channels were not available to the less fortunate citizens of Ireland. As a result a two-tier system of engagement with arts and literature developed in the country that is evident in the diaries. For example, it is clear that interaction with modern literature, film and art did not pose any difficulties for O'Malley nor for the privileged guests with whom he mingled on Inishmore.

Aside from the world of high art and books, the diaries also refer to a much wider sense of culture; the buildings, monuments and objects of the past and present. The dramatic juxtaposition of the ancient past and the contemporary found in the Aran Islands offered O'Malley a unique context in which to observe the impact of the forces of historic and contemporary attitudes on the indigenous design and architecture of Ireland. The diaries note how on Aran the professional middle classes – the priests and teachers – differentiate themselves from the other islanders through the gentrification of their houses. These 'show their authority'. The schoolteacher in Kilronan lived in what O'Malley describes as a 'fine unisland house'. He admits that it is unrealistic to expect such people to live in a 'cabin' but he feels they should set an example through their choice of architecture. Instead they build 'as a townsman would'. This is particularly lamentable as regards the priest because the Catholic Church, which wields such power amongst the islanders, allows convents, chapels and houses to be constructed without consideration of local traditions. He concludes by making the broader point that as most Irish people originate in the countryside they presume to understand country ways, without in fact having any appreciation of the uniqueness and the inherent symbolic value of vernacular design.

The Church comes in for other criticism, most notably in the high-handed attitude of the parish priest of Killeany towards the ancient monuments of Aran with which he does what he pleases. The local doctor, Dr O'Brien, shows O'Malley how at the remains of the monastic site of St Enda's at Killeany on Inishmore three fragments of a high cross had been cemented together by the priest. O'Malley had previously advised the doctor to guard the pieces. He believes that the fragments came from different crosses and he criticizes their placement in the interior of a building, against a wall, which prevents the surfaces from being properly seen. To O'Malley's amusement, the priest had also removed various stones from the Cromwellian fort of Arkin to make an altar at the site. This provides a perfect example of the circular nature of Irish history as played out in its monuments. Arkin was built in the seventeenth century from the ruins of a fifteenth-century Franciscan abbey and now it is being mined to recreate part of a church. But at another level the actions of the priest reinforce the misunderstanding of the significance of these fragments by the very people who should be educated and aware of their aesthetic and historical value.

Later in his stay on Inishmore, O'Malley comes across another priest, Fr Quinn, who has a much more serious interest in archaeology. He has marked the surfaces of a number of Early Christian crosses with chalk to bring out their forms in his photographs. The priest is researching the function and iconography of the crosses, but unlike O'Malley, he is not interested in their aesthetic content. He does not recognize them as pieces of sculpture, to O'Malley's evident disappointment. For O'Malley the aesthetic and the functional aspects of the object are integral.

The diaries also consider the attitude of the Catholic Church towards modern art. O'Malley's fellow guests admire the work of the modernist painter Jack Hanlon, a priest, but fail to understand his unswerving loyalty to the church. According to O'Malley the Irish Church considers that art 'sidetracks you from their idea of how you should worship God, and it introduces ideas'. He did not believe that the church would ever take a lead in artistic matters in modern Ireland. His view is at odds with the Celtic Revival's conviction that the decoration of new churches by Irish artists would provide vital patronage of Irish art and visually educate the Irish people.[5] The Revival was still continuing this project in the 1940s at Loughrea Cathedral in Co. Galway and arguably in the work of stained-glass artists like Evie Hone, whom O'Malley greatly admired. But unlike many influential contemporaries in the Irish art world, O'Malley saw a fundamental division between the aims of modern art and that of the Church.[6]

There was a good deal of debate about the Church's role in visual art in the 1940s. While individual clerics were supportive of modern religious art, the vast majority were indifferent. This attitude stemmed, according to O'Malley, from the colonial suppression of the Catholic Church in Ireland: 'You can't expect to compel a people to do without churches and their decoration for over 200 years, do without rich vestments, ritual, choirs and sing the richness of ceremonial in their church and state, and expect people and clergy not to suffer for it. When their churches begin again there is no standard of taste.' But since emancipation a lack of proper instruction of priests in the role of aesthetics and art had compounded the general ignorance of religious art. O'Malley suggests that 'they begin a Chair of Ecclesiastical Art in Maynooth, which if they should, art may develop, but I see no hope for it, whatever'. The same suggestion was made by Dermod O'Brien, the President of the RHA, the following year.[7] No chair was inaugurated.

While the negative impact of the Catholic Church on architecture and design is foremost in O'Malley's concerns, other conversations with O'Brien reveal more sinister interventions. The doctor speaks of collusion between the medical profession and the Church in the taking of the illegitimate babies of young Connemara women to the now notorious mother and baby home at Tuam. Both men appear sympathetic to the plight of these women but the real implications of this practice are not recognized.

Like many other visitors to Aran, O'Malley was drawn to the distinctive appearance and customs of its inhabitants in which issues of art and design became part of daily life. Such observations are reminiscent of those made in his journals of his time in New Mexico and Mexico in the early 1930s. Indeed, there are several points in the Aran diaries in which O'Malley is reminded of these earlier encounters with non-European ethnic groups. His conversation with Rivers about the behaviour of children leads to a comparison with Aran children and those of Native Americans. The low doorways of the houses on Inishmaan remind O'Malley of houses in New Mexico. The Aran diaries contain dispassionate, almost ethnographical accounts of the women in particular. O'Malley notes their beauty and attractiveness where relevant, but he is not in any way troubled by the limitations placed on their lives either by traditional island life or by the increasing interference of the new state. Their peculiar dress is of recurring interest and on his visit with Dr O'Brien round the houses of Inishmaan, he carefully notes their costumes: 'The women wore black and white shawls, red petticoats, two, I could see and three, I suspect, as they belled out from the waist ... Even the married women wore plaid, so it was hard to pick the unmarried from the married. All wore pampooties and all had red save a few in black.'

Later in the 1950s O'Malley notes the absence of women in public view on Inisheer: 'Only occasionally does one see a red skirt, that of an elderly woman, when the steamer comes in on a Wednesday or Saturday. Occasionally a few girls of about 15 or 17 sit on the strand but only when the boat is due. A few young girls normally wander about the strand ... and an odd woman may bring down an ass for turf to the pier, but the bulk of women are absent save at Mass on Sunday.' This suggests that the earlier political drive as exemplified in Article 41 of the 1937 Constitution to keep women within the home was actually affecting their visibility in rural Ireland. Equally it reflects the demographics of the Irish population where young women were emigrating in large numbers to seek work abroad.[8]

O'Malley was equally interested in their homes. The diaries record the interiors of the cottages on Inishmaan: 'All the dressers are nicely painted here and many of them are full of delph. In two houses were cradles of basket work with two pieces of board underneath which made them rock gently. The child lies on straw, clean and sweet with a blanket above that.' O'Malley expresses a rare sense of humour when he sits with the doctor in the idiosyncratic home of the shrewd businesswoman Moya Flaherty who served them tea on Inishmaan: 'The room was a repository for religious emblems. "I must count them," I said. "I have never seen the like of this."' There were eleven large pictures, two small pictures, and two tiny pictures, five large statues, three small statues, five crucifixes and three medallions. That was indeed a record.' The peculiar position of Mrs Flaherty, whom O'Malley considered to be enterprising and different from the other islanders, is expressed through the objects that she collects. Given to her by the parish priest, the plethora of religious kitsch ironically indicates her special standing, separate from her fellow islanders.

The Aran Islands had an exceptional place in Irish art, especially in the work of Jack B. Yeats and in the paintings of Maurice MacGonigal and Seán Keating. The uniqueness of its geography, archaeology, language, dress and customs provided artists with new and exciting material from which to create an alternative vision of modern Ireland. The islands were particularly popular with nationalist students in the Metropolitan School of Art in Dublin. In the 1910s and 1920s MacGonigal, Keating, Charles Lamb and Harry Clarke spent their summers sketching there, away from the monotony of the east coast.

But this cult of the West, typified in representations of the glorified male Aran islander, was breached during the Emergency when O'Malley's diary recorded his visit to Inishmore. The subject matter of the West of Ireland peasant, treated in an academic realist style in mid-twentieth century Irish art, had by that time become stultifying. It appeared to be not only at odds with the realities of the lives of contemporary Irishmen and women, including the islanders themselves, but its domination of the exhibitions of the country's major annual exhibition of art, the RHA, threatened the development of more modish types of subject matter. More tellingly the realist style associated with depictions of the West was seen to inhibit the progress of more innovative approaches.

While on Inishmore in 1941, O'Malley stayed with Elizabeth Rivers. She was a rare artist in that she made the Aran Islands her permanent home for a number of years rather than being a visitor for a few weeks in the summer. Having trained in printmaking in London and as a painter with André Lhote and at Gino Severini's École de Fresque in Paris from 1931 to 1934, she visited the Aran Islands, returning and settling on Inishmore in 1935. (Rivers was to return to London in 1943 two years after O'Malley's visit to work as a fire warden and play her role in defending her native city. But she came back to Ireland after the war.)

Aran was then internationally fashionable as an unusual destination for those seeking a primitive location. Robert Flaherty's 1934 film *Man of Aran* was a major enticement to visitors looking for new horizons, as had been the 1931 *National Geographic* article 'The Timeless Arans' that encouraged the director to make his epic in the first place. Upon Rivers' arrival she rented the traditional Irish cottage that had been constructed especially for the shooting of the movie. She took in paying guests as a way of subsidizing her income. In 1942 these were to include Kenneth Hall and Basil Rákóczi, the two founding members of the White Stag group, who relocated from London to Ireland in 1939.[9] Other visitors to the cottage were the painters Hilda Roberts and Phyllis Hayward amongst many others. In addition to mainlanders, as S.B. Kennedy has written, Rivers 'joined in the life of the islands, her cottage becoming a sort of open house for those who wished to call.'[10] O'Malley himself turned up without warning on her doorstep and was offered accommodation straight away. Rivers was, according to Rákóczi, a Bohemian at heart[11] and gained a lasting notoriety by being reprimanded by the parish priest on Inishmore for wearing trousers. The attitude of the priest towards Rivers was widely perceived by the islanders as a personal vendetta that extended beyond concerns over the wearing of trousers to the more subversive influence that a young single female artist with unconventional ideas might have on the locals.[12] The irony of this is that Rivers was in fact deeply religious, converting to Catholicism in later years.

Unlike the older generation of Irish artists who painted Aran subjects, Rivers came to the location without any particular interest or knowledge of the established identity of the islands in Irish nationalism. She was advised to go by an English friend who had honeymooned there and by the director of the Lefevre gallery in London, Alexander Reid, who suggested to the young artist, 'go away and find yourself a definite locality for subject matter'. Rivers later admitted: 'I knew nothing about Ireland I went straight to Aran.'[13]

Despite being based on Inishmore, Rivers succeeded in integrating into the growing Dublin art world. Her evident ability at networking would have appealed to O'Malley. An exhibition of her Aran scenes held in London in 1939 was opened by the Free State High Commissioner, John Dulanty. She played a role in the move of the White Stag group to Ireland in this period. She and Kenneth Hall along with the Irish artist Norah McGuinness were members of the art dealer Lucy Wertheim's Twenties Group in London in the 1930s.[14] Rivers also knew O'Malley's friend, the writer Frank O'Connor. He opened her second one-woman show at the Contemporary Picture Galleries in Dublin in 1942. O'Connor had come to know Rivers' work through his job as an editor for the Cuala Press. The two collaborated on *A Picture Book,* a travel book with text by O'Connor and fifteen illustrations by Rivers, published in September 1943.[15]

Rivers' exhibitions of her stylized paintings and woodcuts of the Aran Islands in London and Dublin received positive reviews. One critic commented that her paintings of the Aran Islands 'gives us pictures which have strength, character and truth, rare in subject matter of this kind'.[16] In 1946 her refreshingly direct account of her experiences amongst the islanders in Inishmore, *Stranger in Aran*, was published. Rivers had probably completed the text of this book around the time that O'Malley stayed with her in 1941.[17] Illustrated with her sparse line drawings, one reviewer described it as 'showing no trace of condescension or patronage'; being humorous, tender and dark it was 'almost entirely objective'.[18] Ultimately inspired by J.M. Synge's seminal *Aran Islands* (1907), the book weaves stories of the islanders' lives, with illustrations of the daily activities in a factual and sympathetic account.

Rivers took an active interest in the crafts of the islanders, which she saw as intimately linked to their resourcefulness and self-sufficiency. *Stranger in Aran* makes reference to the constant creativity of her neighbours, recounting their cultivation of the land, gathering of kelp, spinning, knitting, *crios* (traditional woollen belt) making, basket-weaving and production of flannel. Rivers' earliest exhibition after settling in Inishmore was a collaborative venture, shown in the Daniel Egan Gallery in Dublin in 1936. The exhibition consisted of a series of three-dimensional vignettes of island life, with sets made by Rivers and puppets by the Dublin artist Violet M. Powell. Dara Dirrane, Rivers' neighbour in Kilmurvey, made the doll of Sebastine, a fairy protector.[19] Powell went on during the war to stage lectures and presentations of these vignettes in several cities in the United States. According to the diaries, O'Malley had bought one of her dolls. They also reveal that the dolls' clothes were made by Naneen Mullen, who lived at Eoghanacht and was one of the island's most celebrated knitters. But Rivers tells O'Malley that when Naneen came up to Dublin for the exhibition, the city 'people all around talked as if she wasn't there and said her costume was a fake and wasn't worn at all ... Naneen was very ashamed and wanted to come back home.'

Powell encouraged islanders like Naneen to consider selling their knitwear. This practical attitude towards the continuation of indigenous craft plus the desperate need for income amongst women living in rural Ireland was recognized by several enterprising women in Dublin in the 1930s and 1940s. Muriel Gahan's Country Shop on St Stephen's Green was the first commercial establishment to commission sweaters and *criosanna* from women in Inishmore. Gahan visited the island in 1931, immediately identifying the potential of its indigenous arts, which had, as she defined it, the three principles governing country crafts: necessity, economy and beauty: 'The Aran Islands are a perfect illustration for our three principles, with their boat builders, their basketmakers, their weavers, their knitters, their blacksmiths, their carpenters – every kind of craft you can think of ...'[20] She encouraged the knitters to make adult-sized versions of the white Holy Communion jumpers, which had previously only been made for children, thus instigating what would later be termed a design classic.[21]

Gahan wrote of her experiences of visiting craftsmen and women in Mayo, Connemara and the Aran Islands in the early 1930s. The 'sad part was that nobody took the slightest interest in them, with the result that they took no interest in themselves. They didn't realise that they were doing something very valuable. People looked down on people who worked with their hands. All that mattered was if you were a priest, or if you were a poet, or if you had a job in an office, but never, never if you were turning out the most beautiful crafts ...'[22] Elements of this attitude are still evident in O'Malley's diaries where despite his recognition of the ubiquity of design he nonetheless separates high art produced by professional writers and artists from the handiwork of ordinary men and women.

Being himself not well off for much of his career as a writer, O'Malley was sympathetic and aware of the financial difficulties for artists in contemporary Ireland.[23] But, perhaps realistically, he brings hard economics to bear on his appraisal of the Aran Islanders and the position of their goods on the open market. He discusses the high price of Aran sweaters with Rivers. It is noted that London shops pay 25 shillings per sweater to Aran islanders as opposed to 8 to 10 shillings to Scottish Highlanders for a similar product. Elsewhere O'Malley calculates that an Aran girl making socks out of machine spun wool for the army 'could make 30/- [£1.10.0] a week ... working from 10 am til about 11 at night, with intervals I expect'. The high cost of the Aran sweaters reflects the fact that they were entirely home-produced but more significantly the unique quality of the product, not to mention the skill of the craftswomen who had made it. The travel writer Clara Rogers Vyvyan, who stayed with Rivers in the late 1930s, saw the artistic aspects of the Aran sweater in unequivocal terms:

> They knit or weave and fashion their own woollen and homespun garments for themselves and their menfolk, but for all the simplicity of their needs and of their material, they execute their work with the devotion of an artist ... There are circles and ellipses and zigzag lines and dots like a chain of pearls, and loops and lovers' knots and lines like rippled water. These garments are like Gothic architecture that combines with simplicity of form a lavish richness of adornment on capital and column, on architrave and transom. Like those medieval craftsmen, those women put their own personal ideas in to their work, so that no two jerseys are alike.[24]

When O'Malley is charged 6 shillings for a *crios* in 1941 he refuses to pay, partly because it is made from shop wool. O'Malley also refers to what he considers to be the jealousy between the knitters, rather than recognizing it as the pride that they took in their own individual patterns and skill. When O'Malley returns to the Aran Islands in the mid 1950s, he pays more attention to the wearing of traditional dress by boys and men, noting that they have on new homespun sweaters at Mass and the fact that they are made of a finer material than that of his son's. The diary notes elsewhere that the women on Inisheer are now making bright blue sweaters.

It is also revealing that in the mid 1950s the *crios*, a piece of traditional costume, was being made by a Danish artist who had settled on Inisheer, and was now a fashionable item of contemporary craft. But while traditional crafts were succeeding on the level of trained middle-class designers and artists, they were being undermined by official government policy and by the mechanisms of a competitive market. Government initiatives in design in the post-war period focused on industry rather than handmade objects. In the 1950s the newly founded agency for development of the Gaeltacht regions, *Gaeltarra Éireann*, sought to use cheaper materials and to have the jumpers made for less money on the mainland. It set up knitting factories where machines were used to produce sweaters more quickly and homogenously. In 1956 in the face of such action, the Country Shop introduced the 'Handmade in Aran' labels as proof that their goods were not mass-produced. Only sweaters and *criosanna* made on the islands were sold in the shop for all the years of its existence between 1931 and 1978.

Rivers was an important conduit between the Country Shop and the craftswomen of the Aran Islands as goods were packaged and posted from her home in Kilmurvey to Dublin. She knew the knitters and *crios*-makers well, visiting them and recruiting new ones when needed. A set of her drawings of the craftspeople of the Aran Islands hung prominently in the Country Shop from 1943.[25] In 1951 Victor Waddington commissioned a set of wood engravings of the Aran Islanders from Rivers. Her work, more than that of any other modern artist, had an affinity with the islanders. These engravings and others of her woodcuts can be found in several homes on Inishmore, and she was invited to design the covers for books written by islanders.[26]

Former neighbours on Inishmore continued to correspond with the artist years after she had left the island.[27] O'Malley notes in his diary that 'Rivers has great feeling for the people and great sympathy with them.' The diaries suggest that O'Malley, by contrast, was never completely at ease with the islanders. He chose as his principal companion and guide to the islands the educated professional Dr O'Brien, rather than a fisherman or driver. The visit to Inishmaan in the company of the doctor gave O'Malley the opportunity of observing the islanders without the need to engage with them directly. Another reason for his reliance on O'Brien, with whom he shared a medical background and a liking for travel and literature, was O'Malley's deficiency in speaking Irish, which he found a handicap in his dealings with the locals. Other accounts of O'Malley's personality suggest that he was more comfortable in the company of middle-class professionals and visitors. In his earlier dealings with fellow members of the IRA during the Civil War it has been noted: 'Even in prison he preferred the company of the cultured and landed gentry.'[28] However, in a letter written on his return from Aran in 1955, O'Malley tells his correspondent: 'I had a wonderful holiday in Inisheer ... the people themselves were an added attraction. They were simple and unspoilt.'[29]

While O'Malley obviously had high regard for Rivers, he is scathing in his accounts of other artists he encountered, or discussed in his diaries. His remarks, never intended to be publicly aired, highlight both his own prejudices and those of the wider artistic community in Ireland. Artists are condemned for their lack of commitment, their laziness or neglect of their talent, and their tendency to drink excessively.[30] The artist and writer Cecil Salkeld, whom Charles Lamb discusses with O'Malley, was later notorious in Dublin literary circles for failing to live up to his potential.[31] A child prodigy, he had studied at the Metropolitan School of Art before attending academies in Kassel and Düsseldorf in the early 1920s. His familiarity with German modernist art including the Neue Sachlichkeit movement was highly unusual amongst Irish artists (with the exception of Stella Steyn, who studied at the Bauhaus). Returning to live in Dublin in 1925 with his German wife, Salkeld wrote criticism and poetry as well as producing paintings and illustrations. In fact, Lamb's suggestion that Salkeld was feckless seems at odds with all that he achieved in these years. In 1937 Salkeld set up the Gayfield Press. He participated in the Living Art exhibitions from 1943 to 1949, was elected an Associate member of the RHA in 1946 and held one-man shows at Victor Waddington's gallery in 1945 and 1946. His acclaimed play *A Gay Goodnight* was performed in Dublin in 1943 and in 1942 his triptych of the *Triumph of Bacchus* was completed in Davy Byrne's pub, off Grafton Street.[32] Perhaps Lamb was referring to an underlying tendency of Salkeld's that eventually surfaced in the late 1950s when he took to the bed.

O'Malley regarded Salkeld highly as a painter, including him in his 1945 shortlist of promising Irish artists whom he intended to promote.[33] Academic painters such as Lamb, Keating or MacGonigal did not feature on this. He later acquired two works by Salkeld, *Late for Tea* (1945) and *Malin*

*Town, Co. Donegal* (c.1945, both in the Irish American Cultural Institute's O'Malley Collection at University of Limerick). He referred positively to Salkeld's ability to capture the 'atmospheric softness' of the Irish landscape in the work through his combination of academic draughtsmanship and his surreal handling of paint.[34] In the diaries, O'Malley challenges what he considers to be Lamb's conventional appraisal of Salkeld by declaring: 'We are too set in ours [ways], to opt out by what we consider normality.'

Lamb's time at the Dublin Metropolitan School of Art (1917–21) overlapped with Salkeld's. Both were students of Keating's in the School of Painting. Like Keating, Lamb pioneered the development of the West of Ireland genre. Both Lamb and Keating wanted to produce art that revealed the economic and social conditions of life in rural Ireland and especially in the Gaeltacht areas of Galway, including the Aran Islands. Early in his career Lamb created a number of large and ambitious paintings that reflect these ideas, most notably *Dancing at a Northern Crossroads* (1920, private collection) and *Pattern Day, Connemara* (1936, NUI Galway). His focus of interest was the area around Carraroe in Connemara where he lived permanently from 1935, having spent his summers there from the early 1920s. One of his best-known paintings, *Quaint Couple* (1930, Crawford Gallery of Art) had been presented by the Haverty Trust to the Crawford Gallery after its exhibition at the RHA in 1931. It depicts an elderly Aran couple silhouetted against an expanse of sky. Drawn to the peculiarities of the local costume, which also intrigued O'Malley, Lamb portrays the man wearing a homespun jacket and his wife with a *séalta mór* (large shawl) around her shoulders.

O'Malley's diary reveals him to be extremely unsympathetic towards Lamb. His problem with the artist was that he 'never talks about painting … He seems to have no interest in its intellectual side'. The idea that Irish art lacked a theoretical basis is echoed in a more general statement by Rivers. Irish artists, she tells O'Malley, 'dab at it, feel sensuously in terms of paint but they paint with their bodies. The quality of mind that goes into good French painting is lacking here. I suppose we haven't got that quality of mind.' The painter David Hone, a cousin of Evie, later wrote that Lamb's 'approach was strictly objective and non-intellectual and he had little interest in developments in painting after French Impressionism'.[35] But others have argued that Lamb was strongly influenced by the 'intellectual ferment' of Dublin in the post-1916 Rising era, after he moved from Portadown to study painting there in 1917. His first visits to Galway were encouraged by the poet Padraic O'Conaire. He was, according to the writer Arthur Power, determined to express nationalist ideas in his art. He idealized the people of Connemara and the Aran Islands, believing them to be pure, unspoilt and devoid of social snobbery.[36] His efforts to learn Irish and to integrate with the locals are evident from his exchange with O'Malley. While their conversation roamed across a range of topics including boats, fishing, vegetables, neutrality, porter, Salkeld and the RHA, it remained stilted. O'Malley concluded his account of their meeting: 'Anyone I have talked to here is more interesting than he is.'

O'Malley was not known for his ability to engage in small talk. In a later diary, thinking of his talkative wife Helen, he wrote: 'When one does not talk much, save of necessity, then a gush of talk all the time is strange and one stands outside to judge.' To some, O'Malley's reticence reflected his intolerance 'of anyone who did not come up to his almost impossibly high standards of valour or endurance' or in this case understanding of art.[37] For others, O'Malley's brusque nature was the result of an innate shyness.[38] The diaries suggest that the former interpretation is the more likely.

The conversation between Lamb and O'Malley is surprising given that both men had been profoundly influenced by the events surrounding the founding of the new Irish state in the years 1916 to 1923. While Lamb might have been reluctant to discuss his practice as an artist, he had strong reasons for his choice of subject and his approach. He also had interesting connections with art circles in Dublin and wider afield. His father-in-law, as O'Malley knew, was the distinguished British novelist Ford Madox Ford. As the diary makes clear, O'Malley had read Ford's memoirs with great interest. But while both men had chosen to live in the West of Ireland and were part of the same community of artists and art lovers, there seems to have been little to connect them ideologically or emotionally.

A similar impasse is evident in O'Malley's meetings with the painter Seán Keating who he encountered on Inisheer some fifteen years later. Keating was a more verbose figure than Lamb. The 1941 diary records that both Rivers and O'Malley found him an interesting talker and in the later diaries Keating's anecdotes and observations recur. However, O'Malley also makes reference to the artist's aloof personality, which he attributes partly to his frustrations at having to teach rather than being able to concentrate full time on his painting. The 1956 diary notes:

> Seán Keating was going away, and I know he is sad when he leaves so he was more taciturn than usual. He had a defeated tinge to him, maybe because he has not made more a success of himself as an artist, somewhat because he has to accept a job other than painting to enable him to live.

... although he knows, and everyone on the island knows him, he visits no house, and he speaks to very few people ...

O'Malley also notes that Keating 'does not like anyone I know of, is a confirmed misogynist and disturbing in his pessimism'.

1956 was a difficult year for Keating. He had retired as Professor of Painting at the College of Art in 1954 without a pension and moves were afoot to move his studio space out of the premises.[39] Furthermore Keating, then in his late sixties, was beginning to suffer from failing eyesight. He privately admitted that from this period onwards he would concentrate on Aran 'pot boilers' rather than paintings taken from life.[40]

The type of academic realism practised by Keating continued to be deeply unfashionable in the 1950s at a time when the quality of his work was also declining. In 1948 O'Malley described one of Keating's works as 'a rotten portrait painted ... from a photograph',[41] echoing Mainie Jellett's dismissal of Irish academic art as appearing like 'complacent colour photographs of cottages'.[42] Keating used photography extensively in his paintings of the Aran Islands. He had based some of them on photographs of the filming of *Man of Aran* that had been given to him by Flaherty, with whom he was friendly. In 1939 he acquired a cine-camera and created his 'Aran Series' of paintings based on footage taken with this.[43] O'Malley was extremely interested in photography as an art form in its own right and as a method of documentation. He and Helen had used the camera to record medieval monasteries and sculpture scattered across the Irish countryside. But he considered that painting should produce more than factual records and that it was an innately different art medium to photography.

Keating, like Lamb, had a political agenda in his approach to painting and in his choice of subject. The depiction of the men and women of the Aran Islands was central to his vision and construction of Irish identity. Surprisingly, given his background as a revolutionary figure, O'Malley's diaries reveal that he did not approve of using art to project ideology. This is evident in his appraisal of the work of the academic painter and Keating's successor as Professor of Painting, Maurice MacGonigal. O'Malley tells Rivers that he knew and liked MacGonigal, but 'not as a painter. He mixes a kind of nationalism with paint.'

Keating and O'Malley also differed strongly in their ideas on modernism. Keating disliked what he considered the elitism and the lack of craftsmanship associated with the movement. But he was also wary of the growing influence of critics and bureaucrats involved in its promotion. Connected to this his writings and broadcasts show that Keating was clearly disturbed by what he perceived to be the growing dilettante nature of art production in Ireland in the mid twentieth century. O'Malley would certainly have concurred with at least some of Keating's reservations in this regard, as the derogatory comments in the diary on the self-trained artist Eugene Judge suggest. From the 1940s onwards the authority of the RHA, of which Keating became president in 1950, and the National College of Art, where he was Professor of Painting from 1937 to 1954, was superseded by the new art institutions such as the Exhibition of Living Art, the Arts Council and the Cultural Relations Committee. Keating's attitude to the new art type of art worker is summarized in his declaration that 'the artist is pre-eminently a specialist and will not waste his time or his gifts on anything that savours of highbrowism or 'polish or mere instructions in Aesthetics'.[44] Unlike Keating, who believed that only artists could comment on art, O'Malley was keenly aware of the dynamics of the modern art world. In this fast-developing field, the dealer, critic and collector played as crucial a role in the cultivation and dissemination of art and in the creation of the canon as the artist. O'Malley was himself an active promoter of artists whose work he admired through his friendship, patronage and advocacy of their work in his writings and in his networking with international curators and critics. But for Keating, O'Malley was, at some level, what the artist pejoratively referred to as an 'elaborator'.[45]

1956 was also a difficult year for O'Malley. The nucleus of artists that he had championed in the 1940s had now largely dispersed. Jellett died prematurely in 1944. McGuinness took on her mantle as president of the Living Art and spent much of her time battling against continuing prejudice towards modern art at the Dublin Municipal Gallery and at the National College of Art. Le Brocquy had settled in London and become part of the British art scene. Evie Hone, one of the artists most respected by O'Malley, died in 1955. His last major art project was the instigation of a substantial retrospective exhibition of her work, which was eventually staged in Dublin and at the Tate in London in 1958. O'Malley was still in contact with Jack B. Yeats. The artist, now in his eighties, ceased painting in 1955 and was to die three days after his much younger and dear friend O'Malley, on 28 March 1957.

A poignant connection back to the Aran Islands is found in a letter from the artist Margaret Clarke to Elizabeth Rivers written after O'Malley's death, when Rivers was based in Dublin. Clarke tells Rivers that her daughter-in-law Sunny, an acquaintance of O'Malley's, had been visiting the West of Ireland and had called to see Burrishoole, the Mayo home of the O'Malleys, which was no longer lived in. 'They peeped through the windows and she saw one of your framed works still hanging in the hall,' Clarke tells Rivers. The now neglected artwork evokes a moving image of their departed friend and perhaps for Rivers, a memory of O'Malley's sudden appearance on Inishmore and the conversations and speculations that they shared all those years ago.[46]

*Nobody's*
*Business*

# I

# Inishmore, Aran Islands, September–October 1941

**Monday**[1]

'Had you any other ideas of showing paintings,' Phoebe [Keats] asked.[2]

'Yes, I had,' I said. I knew Roisin Walsh, a girl in charge of the Dublin [City] Library.[3] I offered her to collect pictures for a loan to libraries provided she would give space for them to hang. A great number of people use libraries in Dublin, and in this way pictures, especially contemporary pictures, would be seen by a great number of people. Notices of current exhibitions could be put up in the Hall and so people would be led on to indulge themselves in art.

'And what happened?' asked Mrs Keats.

'Nothing. I could not get her to move although she is usually very lively and a splendid librarian. She has an easy way of working with people. She does not lose her temper nor try to push things yet things happen when she begins to work, but she is a wreck with unnecessary work.'

'That's too bad,' Mrs Keats said.

'Yes. It was a disappointment because I thought she would work with me. She also turned down a music library, which I wished to start. It wouldn't have cost the City of Dublin much as I could have collected fifty volumes of records as a beginning and probably a hundred people saw the scheme beginning the work.'

Mrs Keats seems to feel the emptiness of Ireland in creative work or in an appreciative reception. 'I didn't want the girls to risk the bombing and have to pay that price for their education, but Tony [Keats] said, "I don't mind in the least, mother, as long as I get a half an hour's sleep before the raids begin."'[4]

Ireland is a hopeless country to foreign creative people. They can't find people to speak their own language. That is the hardest part of life here. Abroad there are certain indefinable standards in creative work. Certain looks, a piece of sculpture, a picture, a concert have a quality, which people understand. They are sound, constructively and creatively. You haven't to explain them every time you come across them, or to defend them against the resentment of people who cannot see the work. By seeing I mean complete understanding [of the work]. Fourth- and fifth-rate minds attack aspects of creative work, which they do not understand. When they do not understand, the work is bad, silly, 'it doesn't mean anything' [or] 'he's trying to play a joke'. They think the creator is insane or is laughing up his sleeve at them. They do not like the 'ugliness' of it. 'I can't see what he means.' They never put themselves in the position of the artist. He must have meant something. He couldn't always paint or write for a joke or because he is mad. Their limited experience is used as a criterion against a man whose work is his whole life, who, for thirty years perhaps, has been writing or painting and thinking in terms of his art.

Art needs money necessarily for its development. It needs leisure, and we share neither so far, but might have both eventually. Our country people have leisure, but they have no money. Our middle class in professions and trade have some money, but they haven't enough leisure. Leisure for sport most people seem to have in this country, but not leisure to read or to look at pictures.

Lunch came. It's a nice room to eat in. We eat at two tables separate, Mrs Keats with me. There is a sense of humour in her face. I have heard her tease the eldest, Phoebe.

All morning gulls have been squawking outside, diving and sitting in a mass. Mackerel fry must be outside in the bay. It is hard to fish with a line when fry are abundant as the mackerel will not take. One has then to wait until dark to short one's nets. Porpoises had been playing around. They jumped right out of the water. They followed each other in file, they twisted and splashed each other. They have a sense of humour, porpoises, and try [to] give the impression of enjoying life.

*Elizabeth Rivers in doorway of Man of Aran Cottage,*
*Inishmore, Aran, c. 1940.*

'When do the shark come here,' I asked Rivers.[5]

'From March to May, the Bay is then thick with them; they are going North.'[6]

Rivers has deep brown eyes, black, rather curly hair, grey a little on her temple and a slow, reflective manner of speaking. A delightful drawl, good teeth and a pleasant smile. Full of poise and happy, I thought, looking at her across the table.

'I met Julian Huxley in London, and he wanted to come here to make a film of the basking shark.[7] This Bay is full of them in Spring. They cruise along with an upright triangular fin, looking like a destroyer.'

'Did they think of catching them for oil this year,' I asked.

'No, none of them considered them from that point of view.'

'I wish someone would take a film of porpoises,' I said. 'They have a sense of humour that is refreshing. Julian Huxley is director, I think, of the London Zoo. He seems a pleasant fellow from what of his work I have read, less willing to annoy than his brother, Aldous, who has a worm in his brain.'[8]

'Have you read much of Huxley?' Rivers asked me.

'A little,' I said, 'but not recently. *Beyond the Mexique Bay* was interesting, unsound in spots, but a fresh point of view and very understanding of Indians and mestizos.[9] *Point Counter Point* I liked best of his books.'

'That was simply amazing,' said Rivers.

'But he has a queer perverse streak in him. He likes to torture his characters and at times he goes out of his way to shock.'

I was sitting near him once in the Queen's Concert Hall, and I thought he looked most peculiar; his long narrow face. Then I thought of what the Hon. Dorothy Brett had once said to me in New Mexico.[10] 'I was coming downstairs at a reception with a psychologist,' she said, 'and I saw Aldous below me coming upstairs. "Who is that man," the psychologist asked. "Aldous Huxley," I said. "Well, whoever he is, he has a worm in his brain. I can clearly see that," said the psychologist.'

I walked towards the West in my nailed boots, but it was hard enough to walk on the rocks. The boots slipped on rounded stones, which tended to rock and roll under foot. On a rock near the shore, forty or fifty shags were standing looking towards the West. Nearby rocks were crowded with grey and ... with white gulls. A few hundred yards out seals rolled voluptuously, red-legged, small black and white birds swept out in groups of fifteen from under the cliffs and kept me at my distance ... On the shore wrack lay in small heaps. Further up on a foundation of stones were two round cocks of dried seaweed.[11] A large rake with a handle, sixteen feet long lay beside one head. Suddenly a group of cormorants took flight. They flew out South East towards Connemara, clear in the distance now tipping their wings in on the sea water with a clapping sound. After one hundred yards they lifted themselves a foot above the water and swung back South in slow curve. Finally group by group, about a hundred cormorants followed at quarter of an hour intervals until the rock was bare. Gulls joined in. Out to sea six currachs were casting nets and birds were squawking with a clattering din. Seagulls must make noise when they are busy.

Just now taking up a copy of *The New Statesman* of 9 September 1941. I read an essay on Arnold and the influence of his Cornish mother, a Penrose, Mrs Humphrey Ward written by his brother, Thomas, and himself.[12] 'Imaginative rebellion against fact', spirituality, a tendency to dream, unworded lines, the passionate love of beauty and charm, ineffectualness, in the practical competition [of] life – these, according to Matthew Arnold, were the characteristic marks of theft. [In] his *Study of Celtic Literature* – certain qualities which the Celtic people possessed in a high degree, instinctive tact and grace, delicacy of feeling, a natural concern for things of the mind. I have never read Arnold's *Study of Celtic Literature*, but extracts from it I have read. They show the Celt as visionary, a kind of misty temperament and leave out the bad practices [of the] unessential Celt.

*Pat Mullen*

After tea Pat Mullen[13] and James Johnston came in for darts.[14] There must be a certain way of holding a dart as all weapons are used in a technical way, only a natural expert can evolve a method that neglects the ordinary method or methods. Everyone seemed to throw [darts] according to their own sense of throwing. Mullen, tall, 6' 2" at least, holds his dart on high, arm outstretched and got it in. Johnston leans forward from the mark, bending as if he world topple over. Tony [Keats] holds it carefully poised at the level of her breasts if she has any breasts. Rivers throws in an out-arm way with her left hand. She broke her right arm not so long ago. I slash it from the height of my eyes or so I think. The game was introduced by [Robert] Flaherty so that Mullen has close on nine years' experience.[15]

The radio is turned on at 10.[16] I can't listen to it. The Irish radio is not well-written or so it seems or I would listen. The English radio is better, better put together somewhat. P[at] Mullen laughs at the Irish speaker on the radio.[17] 'He can't speak Irish. His voice goes up and down.' The people here can't understand Irish on the wireless.

To bed early. I read Hemingway *For Whom the Bell Tolls*.[18] It's now suppressed[19] as is *Fiesta*.[20] It is a good book. It grips you. The Spanish idiom I do not understand. I mean his introduction of it for his characters. Robert Jordan, the American, speaks it also.[21] Now he is a lecturer in Spanish. He knew Spain and Spanish well. Therefore, he is not slow in his understanding of Spanish idiom. The Spanish naturally know their own language yet it comes over in the book as a kind of literal translation. The only reason for such writing would be if Jordan did not know Spanish well; then his interpretation of it would be halting, and he would lumber in mind over their words, and yet the rockiness of the words by their transposition create a kind of excitement. The book deals with an attempt by Jordan to blow up a bridge, [a] few days before the actual demolition. Into this period Hemingway has telescoped his knowledge of Spanish psychology and of the Spanish war, for he was there. It is absolutely impartial.[22] The weakness and aimlessness of the bicyclist guerrillas and regulars are shown with deadly aim, the point of view of the Francoites is kept. The book shows great balance for Hemingway's emotions were definitely bicyclist.[23] I have a candle, and so I read quietly and go to bed at 11 o'clock.

**Tuesday**
Tomatoes fried and fried brown bread. I don't like fried brown bread. The two grown girls have been out early hauling in P.J. Mullen's nets. P.J. is Pat's son.[24] A curly-haired boy with a rather red lined face. What age he

is I do not know. The girls follow him faithfully for he is directing their fishing. He orders them about, and they carry out orders. In a boat this is always the case, I find. Pat MacIntyre orders me about in a boat.[25] He has an abrupt way of talking, rough and sharp. He had a loose pendulous lip, loose cheeks and a rather sallow skin, brown eye and a green suit on holidays. That gives his face a more than swarthy look. Josie Gill[26] also orders me about sharply enough. I have to learn my job and take [it] as the girls are now taking it.

'I don't now believe anything P.J. says,' said Phoebe [Keats]. 'I believed everything at first, even that midges could be made into soup.[27] You soon learn not to believe what he says.'

She is mistaking a kind of Irish factwariness for truth. It is peculiarly Irish quality by which for fun a man will pervert his imagination to the simple trusting and continue to pervert it. One advantage is that even if he speaks the truth no one will suspect him. Perhaps this was a defence mechanism against oppression to hide their serious talk so that it should not reach the enemy. Perhaps it's an attempt to make a man out to be smarter than you think he is in an attempt to impress you. This aspect of imagination is used mostly for foreigners.

Phoebe was knitting a ... wool net. 'P.J. taught us,' she said. She uses a stitch for repairing nets and a small needle or whatever it is called. Certainly P.J. has helped her to spend her time here related to the sea, rowing with blisters on her hands, fishing with a bent pin, cutting fish, pulling in nets. All of them knit. Mrs Keats knits but hates it.

'Then why do you knit,' I asked.

'Oh,' she shrugged her shoulders, as if to say, 'I have to do something.' She has a ... melancholy. Young Tony knits also, but Phoebe [knits] nets for hair.

'I do all their clothes,' Mrs Keats said, 'and my own. Tony's blue ensemble was marvellous, and now I am going to make a trousers for my husband.'

'But I thought a trousers is very difficult indeed to make,' I said. 'Tailors seem to think so and I think so also.'

'Oh no. I don't think they're difficult at all.'

I started off with oil skin coat and sou'wester for Kilronan. Miss Rivers called me back to give me something to carry for food. 'I don't like to eat,' I said, 'for they won't eat, I know.'

'But you had better bring something for you'll be hungry before evening. When will you be back?' she asked.

'I don't know,' I said, 'that depends.'

'Well, I'll expect you when I see you.'

Mrs Keats had wanted to come with me when she heard that the doctor was going to use the needle, but I had to steer her off.[28] 'I'm a good friend of the doctor,' she offered in extenuation. But I was not going to take a woman.[29] I was going to the island to talk to the doctor not to have to pay courtesies and be held up by the physical difficulties of a third person.

The day was hot, and I sweated along the hill road as I climbed. I left Phoebe, Phyllis, P.J. and Tony fishing at their ease from the edge of the pier and envied them.[30] The teacher had a fine garden, shrubs, trees, plants, vegetables, a red gate of iron; one of the few gates in the island.[31]

The gap principle is always used here [in walls] away from houses. Stones are piled up to fill a gap, torn down when a beast passes through, then built up again. The fields are too small for gates, and there is not enough wood to use for a gate-fence. Some of the stone building is magnificent in their walls. They place sometimes large slabs upright instead of cross-ways. Some walls are light-shot and give a delicate lace pattern especially at twilight or sunset.

The school house is nearly occluded from light by reason of trees close to the windows. Trees can be grown on the island as is shown by the trees in the hollow of Kilronan.[32] When the height of the ridge is reached the down drop begins to the [Kilronan] harbour. The Middle and South Islands, [and] bits of Connemara coast show up with a white glean of houses close together as if a Greek-island city was hidden there. Then the sun passed, and there was no longer a glint or a house. The cement and base stone look glum and miserable in sun and in rain. The houses thus built are … cold, unbeautiful. The sun and elements (rain) do not help them. They remain forever miserable housing for decay.

Liam O'Flaherty's sister is married to a schoolteacher.[33] They have a fine, unisland house…[34] … The schoolteacher builds as a townsman would. He breaks tradition. Priests err in a similar way.[35] Their houses show their authority. They [do not] centre the lives of the people in their building. 'That is easy talk,' my conscience says. 'Do you want priests to pull down their fine two-storeyed houses and build a cabin?'[36] 'No, I don't, but when they have to build a convent, chapel or house, they should build it as the country man does if they live in the country. There is no use in crying "back to the land" if people of intelligence build suburban houses in the heart of the country, equip these houses with suburban taste, and then expect to stop the retreat to the city. First, they have to understand, but that needs great understanding, sympathy and thought. It's the very well-educated and the deeply taught or the untaught creative worker who can understand [the rural] people. They are really difficult to understand. One must be educated to them. The Irish approach is to consider that "we come from there, and, of course, we understand them". That is completely wrong. We are not detached enough even to see them, not alone understand them. There's a wisdom of the heart for your own family, but I doubt that there's a wisdom of the heart for you own nation, when your mind is not stocked and thoroughly equipped. The Irish have a definite facility, but their drawback is that they think they know things and that most of them are experts.'

Dr O'Brien was serving a pint to a man and pulling off his pampooties to put on shoes.[37] He wears a khaki shirt principally, I suspect, because it does not show the dirt, but it is dirty enough. His coat is well frayed at the edges, but today he put on an attractive blue coat and a good pair of flannel trousers.

'You'll have tae [*sic*.] on then,' I thought, 'when you get out of the currach.'

We made for Killeany, for the far end of the island.[38] That shortens the journey, but lengthens the talk. He did not salute any of the people save an old woman who dipped her knees as he passed.

'Do you see that old woman? Well, she gave me a hell of a fright one night. She was having a baby and instead of a breech presentation the baby showed his backside. At last I got him out, and he weighed fourteen pounds. Look there he is.'

A boy of about 21 or 22 [years] was in a field nearby. He was over 6' 2". 'How old do you think he is?' he asked me.

'About 21.'

'No indeed. He's hardly 17.'

'I live by myself,' he said, 'and I like that. I can get a good feed for myself whenever I want to, but I can do all day without a meal.' 'Twas well I knew he could go without food. Many is the sick headache I have had from him. 'My sister lives with me, but she doesn't like me. We're a queer family. We're half mad.' The doctor talks like a Russian at times.

'I was sorry to hear of your mother's death,' I said. 'Did she die suddenly?'

'No, indeed, she died slowly and in great agony. It was the awfullest thing I ever had to put up with. She broke her hip bone, and she wouldn't let me send her to hospital. She was in terrible pain.'

'Why didn't you give her morphine?' I said.[39]

'She didn't want to take anything, and my sister would [not] let me give her a drink or anything in the line of medicine. My sister thought I was going to poison her. She had that queer thought in her head all the time.'

'Families are strange in Ireland,' I said. 'They hate each other so thoroughly, often. When I was coming here I dropped in to see a Miss Gill outside Westport.[40] I was talking of the Spanish civil war. She had no emotion about that fight, no more than it was a local cock fight.'

'Why are they so bitter in a civil war,' she said. Previously she had been talking about her husband's family and her own.

'Well, don't you remember what you said about your two families,' I replied. 'They behave like guerrilla bands who have no mercy, no understanding, and whose ambition it is to land a good shot whenever they get the chance. They are bitter and heartless, and yet they know each other, and if they wanted to, they could well understand each other. That is like civil war. Now do you understand civil war?'

'Oh, Yes. I do now,' she said.

We were talking of Frobisher,[41] Drake, and pirates as we walked along.[42] The doctor has read a great number of sea books. 'A book I read recently mentioned putting in at Galway, that was in Elizabeth's time,' he said, 'but I don't know whose voyage it was.'[43]

'You may be right. The Irish harbours were of use to them on account of contrary winds,' I said.

'The Irish were very cruel to the Spaniards then at the time of the Armada,' he said.

'They were,' I said, 'but they were forced into it. Bingham, President of Connaught, issued a proclamation, I believe, for I never have seen a copy of it, promising death to all who harboured Spaniards.'[44]

'The O'Flaherties killed a lot of them,' he said.

'No, I think that is correct. A boat was wrecked off Bofin and the O'Flaherties tried to keep the Spaniards until forced to give them up. Even then, six years or so later, Bingham was trying to get hold of Spaniards in Morrough and Doe O'Flaherty's country.[45] Many an Irishman had his lands confiscated and lost his head as well for their sake.'

'I'm very glad to hear that,' he said. 'There's a whole school of English writers and historians who write of the wild Irish tearing Spaniard to bits, thus they avoid their own guilt. Masefield mentions them in his poem, "King Philip".'[46]

'In *Drake and the Tudor Navy* there is mention of the Irish and so on.[47] None of them ever mention the fact that the great majority of Spaniards were executed by the English or that massacres were carried out by their orders. I saw a synopsis of a letter from Clancy, High Sheriff of Thomond, to the Lord President, I think it was, telling him that Spaniards had come ashore near Lahinch.[48] I wish the State Papers had given the letter *in extension*. Evidently he received an order back to get rid of the Spaniards. Yet he is blamed as if he carried out the massacre on his own authority.'

'Yes,' he said, 'I heard of the Clare killing of Spaniards. The O'Malleys killed them on Clare Island, and I have not heard that they even received an order to kill them.'

'Here we are on pirate ground almost as we're talking. So, you see that castle – Arkin's Castle.[49] In the English civil wars there were five or six ships of pirates there. They built a castle. Come along here, I'll show you.' On the sea was a strong wall. It ran all along the sea though there are only bits of it now in place. 'Do you see that gate [that's] blocked up now? Well, at full tide a small boat could sail in to the inside.' There was good water outside, I could see but not very much shelter for a large boat. Now there are bullet-shaped piles of stone, six or eight of them, marking the passage to Killeany. Cromwell besieged them, but they surrendered and were allowed to walk out with honours of war drums beating and so on. I have a small cannon back in the house I found there and I'll show you it, some day.'

He stopped a few boys to ask them about currachs, but their people's currachs were at sea and beyond the sound to the ocean-side. The doctor talked on about recent visitors and Land C.B. inspectors.[50] ... All seemed to have served in the European war. 'One man, McCourt, the Irish amateur golf champion, a very nice fellow, was buried by a shell, and he didn't remember anything when he woke up, [nor have any] of his sensations where he was hit. He had to be taught slowly to walk again and later to become a great golfer.'

Walking on sand, we pass the graveyard, now partially covered with sand.[51]

'Why don't they plant bent?'[52] I said.

'The sand will soon sweep over it. They did plant bent, but they must have given it up,' he said. He is a great believer in old customs, in old ways of doing thing; sailing ships, hard work, and resents the merchant's approach.

### Inishmaan Trip

A currach was carried down by three men. The doctor sat in the bow. I got in second last into the stern and sat on my waterproof as I had bad memories of tar. The last man walked out in his pampooties in the sea water. They all wore caps and homespun waistcoats. There was not much current today for there is [usually] a strong current in the Sound. The Middle Island seemed less than a mile, but when we were close to it, I looked back. The Big Island then looked its proper distance, about two miles.

*Seán Keating,* Launching a Currach

They row with an easy stroke, always in time. A pull, then a sudden dip of the oar and a strong heave backwards, about twenty-five strokes to the minute. Close in shore they give a slight dip of the oar. We landed on a stony beach. The big stones are curved. Close by the cliffs of stone had fallen in. Some pieces must have weighed forty or fifty tons. They would have been the pride and joy of Dolmen builders.

Walking on the rounded stones was very difficult with nailed shoes. If they had been slippery with water or with draft weed, they would have been dangerous to walk on.

'Up here,' said the doctor, 'is the scalp.[53] It was through here the Playboy came. He was an O'Malley from Connemara. He killed his father with a loy in a sudden rage, not meaning to do it.[54] Then he came to the Middle Island for shelter, and they put him up, but the police heard of it, and they raided the Middle Island.[55] O'Malley was in a house here, and a brother of the house ... rushed out the opposite door, but one of the police knew O'Malley, but he never said anything.'

'That was decent of him.'

'Ah, he was a decent man,' said the doctor. 'The boy pretended to be O'Malley. Now wasn't that smart of him, but the [RIC] found out the cheat, and they spotted the other man, O'Malley, making for the shore. They rushed after him, but he turned off here and went down through this scalp to the shore and got away. He went to America and came back over to Galway as a mate on a big ship, and he must have been a smart man.'

There's little tillage ground on this island as one climbs up the road.

'Over there is Synge's Chair,' said O'Brien. ''Twas there he used to sit and write or look out to the sea.' There was a new red-tiled house, the only one on the island. 'I don't like the red tiles,' said O'Brien.

'Neither do I, but what can you expect. The LCB has never employed an architect.[56] They make use of contractors, and so Ireland is an abomination of desolation of bad taste when it could have lead Europe in its new types of cottages, but there is neither understanding nor imagination at the head. This present crowd want practical things, and they forget that beautiful objects are the most practical that they can be.[57] Taste is being debased, but the people are not to blame for they don't know, and nobody had analysed for them the great beauty of their own straw-roofed white-washed cottages.'

'Up there, you see,' he said pointing to a group of dour-looking slate roofs, 'that's Joyce's village. A captain called Joyce was walking through the streets of London when he heard of an island for sale. It was the custom in them days to auction islands, that would be about 150 years ago, and he bought a bit of this island, and he had his ship. And he left some children behind him, by-blows or love children.'

'I always liked the word "love child", that best describes it, and there is no stigma attached.'

'Yes, so do I,' he said.

We met a group who sat on the walls expectantly. They wanted to talk. 'Have you any news?' one of them asked.

'No.' The doctor has no news. The Russians were still fighting the Germans. They hear of the war by rumour, and they spread it by talk. By the time a Connemara man meets a man from Inishmore and the Inishmore man passes it on to the Middle Island, and the Middle Island propagates it amongst themselves, there is very little left of the original news, but it is then more of a story to suit themselves.

I followed the doctor into every house. 'You might as well come in and see their houses,' he said. They shook hands with him after their *Dia dhuit* and brought chairs forward for him.[58] In the first house the doctor went into an inside room to examine a woman who had cancer. They spoke Irish to me until I told them my Irish was very bad. Over the fireplace were very dried fish, outside on the walls split fish were yellowing in the sun. The hearth was narrow enough and the chimney out thrust came low. All the doors were low and a danger to the head, as in New Mexico.

One of the girls was using a machine for making stockings. She could either work there or at the factory. A long snake of wool, cheap wool at that, supplied by the Government, was spun; later on the girl cut off the necks and finished the toes [of the socks]. For this work she could make thirty shillings a week. She made about two or three dozen stockings a day working from 10 [am] til about 11 at night, with intervals I expect. That works out at twelve dozen a week and three pence a sock. The socks are sent to the Army.

On the hearth was a small pot of oil from fish. This they were going to use for light. They boil down fish livers, instead of putting them out for the sun to act on them. They ladle the oil out into a broad scallop shell.

'What about tea, doctor,' they asked hopefully, when he came up out of the room.

'No tea,' he said, 'only the ration.'

'We haven't any tea for two weeks here,' said the man with the white specks of beard, 'and half the island hasn't any tea.[59] They don't get it in the shop, and we haven't any salt. Wow, what are we going to do.'

'I don't know,' said the doctor. 'There's no sign of any more tea and salt is scarce.'

'It sells for twenty-five shillings for ten hundredweight [per] bag in some shops in Galway and that's a shame.'[60] I said. It's bad enough to see it being sold here for a pound a ten stone.[61]

We left the house. 'They'll shake hands with you,' he said, 'if they think you're a relative of mine.' He called in to chat in another house. The women wore black and white shawls, red petticoats, two I could see and three, I suspect, as they belled out from the waist. The waists were of flowered pattern as were half their sleeves. Even the married women wore plaid, so it was hard to pick the unmarried from the married. All wore pampooties and all had red save a few in black.

Four red-haired women in succession, deep rufous, the colour in Northern Scotland, which I am told is Scandinavian, as is the word pampooty.[62] The women have a virginal simplicity, the young women especially. They seem only a little shy, but then the doctor is there as a centre of interest. One woman gave suck openly and quite naturally.[63] The small girls have a piece of ribbon on their hair, which is tied on top. Their dresses reach to their ankles. The high waist emphasizes the length of their dress and gives them a quaint look, quaint is not the word, grown-up look is better, more of woman in them than their sisters of short skirts, and perhaps they tend to become more of womankind also. Boys wore caps at an angle and in some houses petticoats.[64]

Fish stank the air about their houses. Irregular stones in backyards gave a sense of building as if of composition so that the barrenness of the house against stone or sky was relieved. One old man called us back to the house. His wife produced a box of what looked like butter. O'Brien and I tasted it in turn. It was butter.

'Oh, butter. That's good, and there's nothing wrong with it?'

'Nothing whatever wrong with it,' said the doctor. She thanked him gratefully. They had been afraid to touch it. In the winter they are scarce enough of butter and in the summer also. Hardly any of them have two cows as the grass is sparse. Government milk cannot be given to them and so they receive cocoa instead.

We looked for Faherty. He had written *Riders to the Sea* in Irish.[65] Someone had given him a translation said the doctor, but it's himself wrote it. He was a good writer, so the doctor said, but he was not at home. They had a fine painted dresser in their house, decorated in red and blue. All the dressers are nicely painted here, and many of them are full of delph.

In two houses were cradles of basket work with two pieces of board underneath, which made them rock gently. The child lies on straw, clean and sweet with a blanket above that. One child had a hydrocele of the testicles.[66] The young mother, a charming black-haired girl, showed his testicles without any embarrassment. Above the chimney was what I took to be *bán*.[67] Actually it was conger eel, yellow conger, which is best when old. Black conger is not good, they say, but yellow conger is lovely. Their faces lit up as if they were having a good feed.

The nurse was a fine red-haired, Co. Mayo girl, married to the young schoolteacher.[68] Her house was carelessly kept for all her nursing training. Untidy, scattered, nothing of beauty. Possessions made a conglomerate unlike the tidy economy of their kitchens. She did not know that the birth of her baby should have been registered. 'She's only a maternity nurse,' O'Brien said. ... She was very pleasant and good-looking, however.

O'Brien showed me a well-slated house which had [been] built to the West.[69] Two of the brothers went mad, one went to an asylum and two of the children had club feet. They pulled down over four feet of the house.[70] It's unlucky, of course, to build to the West.

'The clergy don't seem to mind these superstitions, isn't that strange?'

'No, it isn't,' I said, 'for the people are used to the other superstitions of the clergy, and, I suppose, the clergy must give them some leeway.'

'Take the question of not fishing on Saturday, Sundays and holidays. All Catholic fishermen fish on these days, and you can't be a fisherman unless you fish every day according to the run of the fish.

'Yes, they could stop that if they wanted for it has nothing to do with religion,' he said. 'They [clergy] have great power, and they abuse it.'

We came to the new church. 'What do you think of it?' he said.

'I think it's terrible,' I said. 'It has no relation to the people, and it is built as if it was determined to stress that point. There isn't a particle of sympathy with the island people. It's vulgar, assertive and smells of power. Its outside cemented wall is the only cemented wall on the island, and it looks blatant.'

'I know,' he said, 'why can't they build something that suits the land-scape.' That cost over £2000. A returned Yank here gave £1000, and the people gave close on £1000 and yet there is a debt on it.

As usual O'Brien began telling yarns. When I mentioned French men, he thought of … He was a great, big, tall man, and one day he was on the cliffs when he heard French men lifting their lobster pots underneath. It was just at dawn. He crept close to the cliff and let fall a big stone. Away it went, but he didn't see how close to them it was, but they moved away out in their boats, and when they reached their big boat one of them took out a gun and fired a shot … could see the puff of smoke, but he was hidden behind rocks, and it could do no harm to him.

Another day near Kilmurvey the Connemara men were gathering [kelp] with large poles. The Kilmurvey men threw stones at them but without any result. At last they took up a stone and skied it.[71] It struck one of the pots on the deck of a boat; the pot, they had a fire in, and the boats went further out. Their kelp used to be sold across in Connemara, and the factor if he had his knife in, you wouldn't buy an ounce of kelp even though its quality was the best.[72] [An Aran man] went over to Connemara, but he couldn't sell any kelp. He went up to a house to have a drink, and when he got inside there sitting on a stool was the very man whose pot he broke. He stood back thinking they were going to make an attack on him, but the man came over and held out his hand. 'What'll you drink,' he says to him. 'That shot of yours was the best shot I ever did see,' and they sat down and drank.

There's an island near the Hotel of the Isles, which O'Brien once visited and wants to go back to.[73] The first time he tried to go there, no one would bring him across from the mainland to the island. 'Perhaps they were making poteen,' he said.[74] The next time he came there with a doctor who examines people all over Ireland. 'The women have never worn boots,' he said. 'They walk fine and straight, and I like them well.' We arranged to hire a boat sometime next week, but we would have to return that same day as the doctor cannot be away for any length of time.

Men were thatching houses with rye, but when I examined the ears more than half the rye was yet in them. They do not use a flail on Middle or North Island.[75] They put a stone up and bang the sheaf against it. Then they throw the straw in the air and collect the grain. All through the North Island today men had been thatching. In the gardens their cabbages grow very high. 'That's because we thinned them late,' said a man. 'The stalk was four times the height of an ordinary stalk.' Yet on the Big Island [there] are two men and a woman, an agricultural instructor and a poultry instructress, and another expert. There's really nothing much for them to do on an island like this save waste their time and other people's money except they are staying here for a month or two at a time.

We stopped in at … Moya Flaherty's, for tea on our way back having first visited the pub, but the doctor took a drink and then no more. We were served full of energy. She tried hard to keep children from peering around the doorway leading to the kitchen at us, but without success.

Moya Flaherty was shrewd enough. She wore a heavy shawl, but above it was the black and white scarf. Red scarves are also worn, ending by being tied around the waist. She looked shrewd also. What does business do to people that you can quickly recognize it in their faces. Here were two business people, Flaherty and the small tidy pub, and they both looked different to the other people I had seen. The men were more shrewd looking, a few with a devil in their eye, and that was good to see. 'The women here have the name of being good looking,' O'Brien said. Certainly I saw three good-looking women today and five or six young girls.

The tea had been drawing on the turf ash perhaps for an hour, perhaps more, so it tasted. I ate two mackerel whilst the doctor ate an egg. The room was a repository for religious emblems. 'I must count them,' I said. 'I have never seen the like of this.' There were eleven large pictures, two small pictures, and two tiny pictures, five large statues, three small statues, five crucifixes and three medallions. That was indeed a record. When I had checked she, herself, came in to the room to show me what Fr O'Malley had sent her as a present – two missals and a work on Blessed Oliver Plunkett.[76] Evidently Fr O'Malley knows that she is a collector. The doctor, when she left, looked at me with an amused smile. I suppose they could … be symbolic of your inner state of piety, but they need not be.[77]

Fr O'Malley, they all liked. He minded his own business. He had a currach fitted up with an outboard engine, and to everyone's surprise he was not drownded [*sic*]. He fished at leisure and enjoyed himself. This kind of out-of-doors priest is required here. The people understand such a kind, and above all, he was not Puritanical. The Irish speaking district needs such priests. Most Irish priests are extrovert, about 80 per cent, I would say. Therefore [they] pick men with a sense of life for people who believe in a heroic life. A scholar they might respect on the mainland where he would be always at his books. They would have a certain pity for him as if he were an invalid. Fr O'Malley is now chaplain to the nuns at Kylemore Castle.[78] 'He is a friend of the Bishop,' O'Brien said. They have a boarding school there, and he will have a double orbit of adulation.

O'Brien has never lost a delivery, I believe, and he has been eighteen years on the island. That must be a record, I thought. 'Have you ever had a caesarean?' I asked.

'No,' he said. 'I have been lucky – never.' His vaccination today was easy enough. He scratched away with a pin, which he then stuck in his lapel, then blew from a phial and rubbed it in with the pin, which again returned to the back of the lapel to rest securely in diseased germs.

One house had a red-haired woman who suffered from epilepsy. Her second child had a great burn across the top of its head, running on to the forehead. 'That's when she dropped the child when she had a fit,' he said, 'but the hair will cover it in time.' It must be hard on the children to see their mother have a fit and be helpless to do anything, and it must produce terrible memories for them.

Another woman was really beautiful. She had a baby of about four months in a wicker cradle. She was strongly sun-burned, and between her colour and a slight blush, her beauty was enhanced. The people had begun to shake hands with me on leaving as I said *Dia dhuit* when I came in the door.

'She is beautiful,' I said. 'Would you tell her that I think she is the most beautiful woman on the island, but say it carefully so as not to embarrass her.'

'You should have seen her three years ago,' he said. 'She has lost two children, and she has only the baby now, and the loss tells on her. She had beautiful eyes, and she was unselfconscious of her beauty.' But the doctor didn't give her my message.

It was late now about 6.30 when we went back along the road towards the landing place. 'There is a very rare herb found on this island,' said the doctor. '*Astragalus danicus*, I think the name is, and it is found in [the] Burren near Ballyvaughan and in a few other districts.'[79]

'I had a book once on the botany of Aran.'[80]

'I have it myself,' I said.

'Lent to me, and I copied it out in two nights. Then a man named O'Conner came here, and he was collecting everything old and not paying for it. I lent him my copy, but he went away with it and never gave it back to me.' The doctor is very decent about offering books. He has offered to lend him me several books when we were out in the open, but I notice he does not repeat his offer on the inside nor has he ever shown me his books.

Under a quiet sky we rowed back. The tide had dropped a good deal. Fishing boats had come in with their loads. I saw a lobster on the strand. 'I'd like a lobster,' I said to O'Brien, but he [the lobsterman] wouldn't take money. We ended by walking away with two lobsters and a good crayfish.

'I'll keep the crayfish,' he said.


## Inishmore

At the graveyard I stopped to see what the priest had done to a cross.[81] He had set it up facing North East, cementing three pieces of cross together. Two pieces the doctor had when I was here years ago. One of them he used to tie down his haycock. He had then promised me to guard it and not allow anyone to interfere with it or to try to assemble it. But the Parish Priest had prevailed on him, then the teacher in Killeany had contributed part of another cross. The Parish Priest cemented them together. The central cross has a horse and rider and on the reverse, the West side, are the legs and dress of a person but it is broken or torn. The cross is close to the wall so that its west side cannot be photographed. The altar is also due to the Parish Priest. At the East end he has erected on stones a piece of Arkin's Castle, a kind of corridor with two standing stones with crosses on them at either side. Arkin either restored or built his Castle in Cromwellian times using stones from a Franciscan monastery of the fifteenth century, and so Arkin's Castle has been plundered now for the sake of the church.

Pat Mullen had been upset with O'Brien a few nights ago. Today, when the doctor and I met him, Pat had said, 'Good morning, kindly,' to me but had not spoken to the doctor. Now as we spoke of Pat, the doctor said, 'I had a row with him, you know. I was going to that island I told you of near the Hotel of the Isles, and I had engaged a boat overnight for another doctor and myself. Pat Mullen in the night saw the boatman and arranged to bring out a fishing party from Miss Rivers. Now that would mean they would have to stay out all day in [Galway] Bay and fish, and it would be a chance that we'd [not] reach our island. So I refused to allow the boatman to take them, especially as Pat had abused the other doctor and the boatman. I heard him on the quay leaving his curse on the boat in Irish, and I said, "You needn't try to lay your curse on me, Pat, for I won't take it."'

And so another enmity begins on an island that already has well more than its burden of ill-will.

'I heard a good story,' O'Brien said as we reached his house. 'You know that on the mainland they are buying up every kind of an old hen. Well this buyer was buying them by weight so this Mayo man filled the inside of the hen in some way with water and sold his cargo to the buyer. That was a good one.' In kelp they used that trick throwing in sand and stones to the molten kelp to increase its weight. In turf they use it bringing bad turf and small badly packed carts at that. Yesterday I had seen a hooker loaded with turf set off from Kilmurvey.[82]

'That's hard on the Connemara men,' I said to Rivers. 'They have to sail across here, then maybe they can't sell their load, and they have to go to Kilronan or even to the South Island.'

'I know,' she said, 'but when you order turf, you are sold bad turf so that it's not actually a better way for buying turf to have them come on chance. There's only one or two of them you can trust.'

'You know what they call each other in Aran when they want to insult each other, "You Connemara Bastard."'

O'Brien wanted me to stay upstairs. 'I don't know what the room is like. It's untidy, I think.' If O'Brien thought it was untidy, then certainly it was untidy. He is spring-cleaning, as he calls it, slowly. One room, a litter, is slowly getting colour on its walls and will be in shape in about two weeks' time, but really what deterred me was a dread of fleas. 'The dog has fleas,' O'Brien said. 'He took them from the cat, and he'll give them to you. I have fleas also, but I don't mind them.' We were seated at the table and I tried to shove the dog away, but the dog was playful and generous and was determined to give me his fleas. Soon I found myself covered with fleas. It was partly my imagination I knew from experience, but it is very hard to distinguish between a flea and an imaginary flea.

My feet were swollen from heat, tight socks, and lack of use. Rivers had remained up when I arrived shortly after half-past 12. Anne Kelly was up also. Whilst we boiled the lobster our talk ran on ghosts and fairies.

'You know you really believe such things here,' Rivers said, 'and why shouldn't you. I lived in Norway for a time, and these beliefs have been driven to the outer fringes.' I knew that the outer fringes of the world still carry the old beliefs. The people there have been driven out and out by pressure from more pushing and what is called civilized people. She had not heard of phantom ships, which I had heard of over twenty-two years ago on the South Island.[83] There were stories here of people being changed to seals but none of mermaids though Mrs Kelly said she had heard of mermaids on ... Island near Roundstone [Galway]. The seals, Rivers did not know of either. In Clare when a member of the family is dying or about to die, the mother hears herself called normally three times, and then if her son is in Australia she is prepared for the telegram or the letter to come. They have no set opinion on drownding [sic.] boats either, which they used to set adrift near the West road coast. 'Oh, yes, I know of boats being "a killer",' she said, 'but that is completely different. Such a boat kills or injures someone when it is being launched. But in the dangerous boat the builder knows when he begins to cut a certain timber with an adze if the shaving flies the other way. That boat will drownded [sic.] people, he thinks, and it should not be gone on with.'

Josie Gill didn't want me to buy Willie Kelly's boat on Islandmore [Clew Bay]. 'It drownded [sic.] two boys,' he said, 'two good sailors too, and I wouldn't have you do anything with it.'

In this dim fantasy of belief and half belief and superstition, we sat up in friendly company. Rivers has great feeling for the people and great sympathy with them. She sees their faults. Like ourselves at home, she has to constantly check in the kitchen to see that things are done properly or to see that instructions are carried out. 'They simply will not learn,' she says, 'unless you get a very young girl who delights in keeping herself clean when she has been taught about it.' It's a question always with me, I fear, of my standards or theirs. It's like neglected land. It slips easily back to rushes and heather, and I know if I let things slide soon, I would be like them. ... Casualness, easy-going, always avoidance of rows by not telling you about things broken or out of order, allowing you to find out for yourself when things are wrong, failure to carry out instructions so that the onus of having them carried out is always on you. She had gone through the same stage. 'It seems a pity to interrupt their charm by harping or to hurt them by calling attention to their own deficiencies, but I can't live life this way in my own house,' I said.

## Wednesday

This morning there was a tap at my window. P.J. Mullen was calling me quietly for last night he had promised to bring me out fishing. The false dawn had come by the time he and his team, Phyllis and Phoebe, had had their tea and by the time we had carried down the two-man currach, it was close on six o'clock. There were three nets down in the angle of the bay. P.J. was in the stern. He pulled them in, the fishes jumping and moving whilst a wooden bowl served to bail out the boat from the water brought in by the nets. Mackerel and pollock. Mackerel gleaming green and blue pollock, a dull brown-blue with dull cod-fish eyes. Pollock don't evidently salt as well.

Soon the three nets were in the boat, the catch estimated at 200 or so, not a bad catch they all thought. Others' boats, five or six, were away out. They only came in while P.J. and his girls were picking out fish from the nets. It's hard enough to free some of the fish as they get thoroughly tangled turning back again to get out. Sharks had been killed by being hit hard on the gunnel of the canoe but they were only a few feet long.

There was a large crab in one net. 'Spit in its eye,' P.J. said. He spat in the crab's eye, but the animal did not take any notice. It still held on tightly with its claws. I tried again to spit, but I had no success. Slowly it released one claw, then after a long time when I put the tail of a mackerel across its eyes.

We were to breakfast without fish I found until I asked P.J. for fish; then he brought us up a few. They were not nearly as good as the mackerel which I ate in Clew Bay. But these mackerel here would have been close on twelve hours in the net but I doubt if they were all dead. They had a dull flat taste. Hake was caught also, about four or five of them, but I did not see any of them in the house.

Mrs Keats is farming near Boyle [Roscommon]. She was willed a house which she used in summer. Now she lives there the whole year round.

She talks about farming in a weary way. 'I didn't know anything about farming, but I got great help from instructors. I asked them questions and found out as much as I could.'

'What about the Department Pamphlets?'[84] I said.

'We found them very useful and very good.'

'Very few people in our parts use them,' I said. 'I tried to get a few people around me to buy them, but the effort is too great. At Kilmeena the Parish Priest announces them from the altar and sells them after Mass.[85] That is the right way to sell them. But I don't see why the Department does not have a stall at fairs and markets where they could give information, show charts or drawings and give advice generally. The information is not brought to the people.' The people of course don't want the information. They think, I am sure around me, that no one can teach them anything about farming – that paper talk can never be any good.

'And did you grow much wheat,' she asked.

'About six and a half acres in all,' I said, 'between wheat, oats, rye and barley.' It's strange what a conditioned world a little farming opens up. Here am I able to talk in a conversational way about crops as if I were deeply interested in them, or as if I knew much about them. She had grown three acres of potatoes.

'That must have been hard work,' I said.

'Yes,' she said. "The weeds here are terrible. They took so much help to weed, and finally we had to leave them.' Yet her three acres could not have been as hard to dig as were my one and a half acres especially that three-quarters of an acre in the Castle field where the men had to use pickaxes and crowbars. Nothing could have taken more labour than that work, but we had no weeds to contend with.

'Skin ground does not produce weed, that is lea land. It would be a good thing to change round potatoes each year then to save yourself from weeds.'

'Yes, except for fencing.' I had forgotten that, yet fencing on an acre and a half wouldn't be such a terrible chore provided, of course, you could take the barbed-wire from a previous patch of potatoes.

'Have you any hens?' she asked.

'About forty or fifty,' I said.

'Oh, well that's not so bad. I have hundreds.'

'And they're frightful beasts and so stupid,' Phoebe said, her face getting slightly red with hate. 'When we change a house round they would stay out all night rather than look for the door round the area. They're really frightfully stupid. And they're dirty also. We can't keep them clean.' I thought of our hens before enough barbed wire was put up … Hens hopping out of unexpected corners, trying to lay in flower beds and insisting on coming to the flower garden to lay when their own nests were ready waiting for them. But that was after their houses had been changed to the belt of wood in front of the house, and they did not know their surroundings.

'Hens refuse to recognize change,' I said. 'They're conservative.'

Then they both spoke badly of hens with real relish. I could see that they had made misery in Mrs Keats's life and in Phoebe's. They are an incalculable force, hens, the most annoying of all farm creatures. Uncertain in movement and devilish save when completely enclosed by wire, but then few people will go to the expense Helen was at [war] with them.

The farm had got on Mrs Keats's nerves and the house. 'The house is too big, and there are people we couldn't do anything with. A gardener who was old and married and to whom we gave a house, milk and vegetables, and £85 a year, but luckily he bought a farm, and we were relieved.'

A house can destroy you. It's the worst of white elephants. It makes you slave for it, and yet it has no return. Our house, for instance takes extra girls to help to run it, but it has no friendly feel for people who would not dare to drop in unless they knew us well. A long cottage, the kind of house Helen and I planned years ago, would have been best.[86] She could have designed things for it, but Burrishoole [Lodge] can't be designed for – with its dark pine walls. It has a brooding sense that heavy furniture only fills. Here in Rivers' there is simplicity, the absence of things. Nothing to get in your way or set up a barrage between you and thought. Actually my room should be barer. I should have a library all to itself and have a bed room with few things in it, where I could sleep and work.

They must have a good deal of land, as land and more land crop up at every sentence. Sheep on pastures and pigs and a certain number of cattle. 'Tony Keats is really very good,' said Mrs Keats. She knows all the men and talks to everyone about cattle. 'When the last cow was calving, the help said the cow's time was due in two days, but Tony came in that evening and said, "I think she'll calf in two hours or so, and so she did."' She knew all about the bones softening.

'And at the fair one day, Phoebe said, "Mammy how much money have I now? Could I have £5 please, I want to buy some pigs." She went around and examined all their teats, a thing I could not well do and bought the bonnons with the most teats. An instructor a year later said they were a pair of the best pigs he had ever seen.'

I talked about a silo with which we had experimented.

'We had one too, but we made a cock out in the open last year, and this year we weighted it down with limbs.'

'And it was successful?' I asked.

'Yes, very. The cows loved [the silage],' she said. That cock idea is wasteful, of course, but it's the lowest step in silo production.

The talk switched to painting either through Phoebe or Mrs Keats. Phyllis doesn't talk at all. Precise in speech and slow smiling, her time seems to be taken up with P.J. and fishing. They set nets at night, take them in in the morning, collect the fish, eat their breakfast, cut, gut and salt the fish before dinner [at noon], and between that and tea collect the nets and put them out in the Bay. She is interested in ballet and writes poetry, but that was an accidental shot of mine. Louis MacNeice's last poems, 'Plant and Phantom' which I lent her, she did not like.[87] I was not able to question her about individual poems as I had only read a few myself. She had never heard of Rilke so I gave her a selection of his poems, translated.[88]

Both Phyllis and Mrs Keats knew Fr Jack Hanlon and evidently liked him.[89]

'What I can't understand,' Mrs Keats said, 'is his attitude. He accepts the judgement of the Church on art, and yet he is a painter. I don't understand that. I'd have to live what I believed.'

'I understand,' I said, 'for him his priesthood is the most important thing. He has his own ideas about art, but he would throw his art to the winds in the morning. He is a priest first of all, and there is his allegiance.'

'Well, I don't understand it,' said Mrs Keats. 'What is the attitude of the Church to art?'

'[For] the Irish Church, I would say that art is sin. It sidetracks you from their idea of how you should worship God, and it introduces ideas. But the Church used not believe that about art,' I said. 'I know, but then everyone that is now their opposition was Catholic ... so they could afford to be more lenient, as it were with their own children. In Ireland there has been a complete break in artistic tradition. You can't expect to compel a people to do without churches and their decoration for over 200 years, do without rich vestments, ritual, choirs and sing the richness of ceremonial in their church and state, and expect people and clergy not to suffer for it. When their churches begin again there is no standard of taste. They have imbued some of the Presbyterian Puritanism and all have combined both to go against the nature of the people and to kill art strivings.'

'And what do you think can be done with the Church?' she asked.

'Nothing in so far as art is concerned. Leave it alone. If they begin a Chair of Ecclesiastical Art in Maynooth, which they should, art may develop, but I see no hope for it, whatever.'

Anne Kelly came out of her room, fed up with working, I suppose. She has a white face, her eyes look at you wide-eyed as if they did not see. She has a very soft voice, diffident as if she hesitated to speak. She did not like Kilmurvey at first. 'I always hated the country and country life, and I thought it would be like country life when I came here first but now I love it.'

'Do you know Máire Scully?' she asked.[90]

'I do,' I said.

'What do you think of her singing?'

'I like it, but it lacks something, sex I suppose, but she is the best singer in Irish now recorded, though I have heard better singers over the radio.'

'Máire doesn't want to have children,' she said. 'She's afraid it will interfere with her singing.'

'Nothing could perhaps improve her singing more than to have a love child,' I said, 'or to let herself go.'

'Foley is better," she said, "and has a much better voice.'[91]

'Do you know Máire Scully's records?' I asked Mrs Keats.

'No,' she said, 'what does she sing?'

'She sings in Irish,' I said, 'sings better than anyone so far recorded, and you should get some of her records.' She did not seem to take any interest perhaps because it was in Irish, perhaps because being a singer herself she should knew who are the really good singers. She talks about a big studio in London, but I have never heard of her work. That would not be hard for me for I don't know those who are famous as singers, not liking singers in fact.

Mrs Keats at times becomes diffident when she thinks she has broached any difficult subject such as the Church. There are many things I feel she would talk about if I were not present: the war and why Ireland doesn't contribute; Germans and the Nazi creed; the conduct of the war; the sins of this present Government; the running of the war.[92] She knew Douglas Hyde and seemed to be impressed by him as an institution whereas no Irishman is impressed by an institution.[93] Hyde is Hyde who did good work on the [Irish] language. We seem to reserve our own admiration for race-horses, visiting movie actors and people like Mrs Kiernan, the singer of ballads which they like.[94]

Tinkers were introduced [to the conversation] for no reason that I could think of. 'I like tinkers,' said Anne Kelly, 'tinkers and Aran men. The Aran men do all the buying in the shop, and they do not bargain. They are not like the country people who spend an hour over a shilling trying to make you reduce it.[95] An Aran man will pay if he likes something, and a tinker will pay at once also.'

'I always wanted to get their travel routes,' I said, 'where they come and go to, their halting plans, and the roads they move on from one province to another. They must follow old routes at times but perhaps they don't.'

'I don't know anything about them,' said Anne, 'but I could find out for you, and I'll find out also if there are any people who would be interested in having an exhibition and had asked in Galway.' I had mentioned an exhibition and had asked if anyone there was interested in painting.

The evening was warm I found when I went up at the hill towards Dun Aengus.[96] The walls here make for irresolution. You think you are going to cross a wall at one point, then find it is too steep or the stone work on top looks a bit flimsy. You search around for another spot to cross then change your mind and are left in a fog of indecision. When this happens in field after field you have to train yourself to make a quick decision.

A man and a young fellow were trying to corner a calf, but the calf had a mind of his own. He dodged behind rocks and boulders, was caught, twisted loose and leaped away again. After a hide and go seek of twenty minutes, the calf was cornered in an angle. The man built up a wall again and at racehorse speed the calf dashed away for the village.

'They do be very wild,' the man said to me. 'They are used to the one little field for months, and they go wild when they get out of it. We feed them on new milk,' he continued. 'I don't think they do that on the mainland save in Connemara, and they do be very big and strong.'

'I feed mine on new milk too,' I said.[97]

'For how long?' he asked.

'For three or four months,' I said, 'maybe longer.'

'I didn't think they did that,' he said, 'save in Aran and in Connemara.' He seemed disappointed that what was unique in his country should happen anywhere else.

Climbing quickly I was soon within Dun Aengus. It had been repaired by the Board of Works and looked very different now to the ... sketch in the *RSA Journal*.[98] Then there were toothed gaps in the inside now; now the inside wall is level on top.

I lay at ease and read Lermontov's *A Hero of Our Times*, an extraordinary hero who worked hard against his own grain hiding carefully his love emotions.[99] It was an unexpected piece of writing and very good. Russians from the beginning of the career as novelists did not accept the expected.

Their characters do not accept conventional laws. They are as they are, all are when we do something we want, laws unto themselves.

There was a wind in on top of me, and I fell asleep on the level floor of the fort. I awoke cramped. There is a feeling of peace up there with the light sound of wind and the distant sound of sea breaking against cliffs to the West. This was a calm day, there was a light haze on the water and I could not see far out.

After tea there was a quiet lull whilst we sat and talked around the fire. The fireplace belonged to another house and was removed here. Robert Flaherty yet hopes to return to Aran. He lived here two years spending the winters here. He liked the place, and the people … [they] in return were fond of him. He did not have much luck with his Indian picture.[100] The British Raj did not approve of his outlook on its subject people; his sympathy lay with the Indians, and he must have showed it. The film was cut. Englishmen with ridiculous malplaced faces acted as natives and spoke broken English in cultured tones. That must have cut Flaherty in two as he was the first to use the native people alone. He did not believe in actors. Later the Russians either thought the matter out for themselves or they copied him.

'He seems to have been pursued by bad luck,' Rivers said. 'Nothing he tried to do seems to have worked out as he intended it.'

'A friend of mine, Paul Strand, had bad luck also,' I said.[101] 'He took what is admitted to be a very fine film in Mexico – *Redes* or nets, the life of a Mexican fishing village and the exploitation of their work by a middleman.[102] Anyhow it was said to be a magnificent camera work. The Mexican government at the end wouldn't let the film out of Mexico, and I think it had to be changed then.'

'It's tragic,' said Rivers, 'what happens to really good workers, sincere workers, in the film industry.'

Darts began again as Tony insisted in his eager way. Today Mrs Keats had a letter from her herd giving her all the information necessary about the animals in her absence. Phoebe does not talk about the farm although she has been given twenty acres as an experiment by her mother to show her how difficult it is to run a farm. 'She is now £60 in debt,' Mrs Keats said, 'although we lend her machinery and the land is rent free. The Department of Agriculture estimates that it costs £20 to produce an acre of your own potatoes, that is rent free, I presume.'

James Johnston teased and barracked when anyone else played darts.[103] He kept up a running commentary about nothing. He has an impish sense of humour and a capacity for reaching people in their sore spots. I'm sure he often touches Pat Mullen on the raw. Pat is serious enough despite his sense of humour. The Church is a mania with him. He never seems to let go of it, and it has been mentioned every day since I have come here. Evidently he hasn't been able to work the Church out of his system, but that would be hard enough, for here he alone of his class and type, stands out against it. Yet one can see the struggle he has had, and is having. He sounds at times like a small boy in a rage. But he is kindly and understanding. Every evening he drives over on his outside car to raise 'hell and devilment' as he says himself.[104] His bad language does not vary. I wonder does he think that frees him in the minds of people, gives him a tough outlook also. I don't know. Then when darts are over, he drives home again to the other end of the island in the dark. He never presumes, never throws his weight around.

Darts I find difficult, but I am sure I could pick it up quickly enough especially if I watched a really good player. None of these people are good, however, and I get bored watching them, or playing draughts. Phoebe plays with Miss Rivers, a game I can't follow sufficiently to interest myself.

**Thursday**
Hazy again the day but fine. The wind keeps coming from the same point all the time. There's not much wind but enough to bring the hookers across from Connemara. Some evenings I have seen them use an oar to help them into the harbour here. There is a fine ring of sand below the rocks on which seven or eight currachs are kept. The currachs must be great boats in a bad sea. About five or six hookers were anchored this morning off the pier. Later I saw four start at intervals, one after another, and cross to Connemara. The main sail is not hoisted until the boat is well underway.

A strange place, this Aran. I have settled down here as if I had lived here for a long time and as if I could stay a long time. Actually, the time goes fast. This is now Wednesday, and I am writing of what has occurred last Thursday. In the morning I write. At first I used to stay to talk around the fire after breakfast with Mrs Keats or one of the girls, but I saw I was giving too much time to talk. The girls were not interesting as girls but as people; now they are too busily engaged with fishing to take notice of anything else. So, I can get up earlier and have my breakfast at 9 and be ready to begin writing at 9.30, come up for air for a few minutes at 1 and then continue until 1.30. Often it doesn't seem of the least importance save as a symbol to get oneself back to what one wants, to write again, but I expect if I could keep writing for a few weeks, I might break myself into something worthwhile. Otherwise I am only fooling myself as I could easily be cut in the opening.

Jane, the younger child of two, walks about the place. She has slashing eyes half closed. She comes to me now, talks away rapidly at times with words whose meaning I do not know.

*Irish Dancers in a cottage on Inishmore [Bridget Johnston, on right Sonny Hernon], March 1952.*

Aran, I had begun to say, grips you. I don't seem to have any sense of responsibility about home, for if I went back there I could not write. The house and all its pomp, proposed farm buildings, and the getting in of crops can all go up in smoke as far as I am now concerned.[105] If I can't write at home I must write somewhere, and if I find a place in which I can write, then it is best to settle down there.

Mrs Keats and the two girls originally came for two weeks. They are now here seven weeks, glad enough to allow the farm to run itself with a boy named David in charge. David is the girls' tutor. He is an Oxford boy who doesn't want, I presume, to return to England [during the war]. He helps at other things in the interval. Her husband, Tony, had been in the British army and had served in India. At least she had been in India and Kashmir. The husband had been a prisoner of war in Turkey. 'Many of them went mad there,' she said.

'Were the conditions as awful as that?' someone asked.

'They must have been,' Mrs Keats said.

Now conditions in Turkey were hard, but they were never as bad as conditions in British jails. 'It was worse for the rankers,'[106] I said. If they escaped and were recaptured, they could be sent to the salt mines as punishment, but officers were not made to suffer severely. Some were, when they became incessant escapees, sent to a certain old fortress as a punishment.

'He speaks Turkish, but he is not now interested in the war,' said Mrs Keats.

'He was at first,' said Phoebe, 'but not many are now.'

'Are they seeing war through the glass of Ireland?' I asked.

'Here we don't sense the war because we have withdrawn ourselves from it.'

'But what about the rest of the Anglos. Perhaps they too are bored by the war?'

'Among civilized races the love of trees is probably even wider spread than that of animals. Uncivilized people delight in destroying trees, with the exception of specially selected ones which are believed to shelter ancestral spirits. This destructive propensity is not however due to wantonness but to the desire for access to fresh areas of virgin soil wherein to plant crops,' – a review of a book, *Men of the Trees*.[107] Certainly Irish peasant people love to destroy trees. Willie Walsh and Pat Clarke have spoken to me about the patch of wood on the South side of our small inlet.[108] They would love to clear it out, I know. Here there is hardly a tree. There are a few plantations of sallies which grow well but only in gardens are there trees of any size and back at Kilronan.[109]

'Why are Irish country marriages always arranged?' Mrs Keats asked.[110]

'It seems to work out well,' I said. 'You see the Irish family is a unit, not a collection of individuals. If the oldest boy in the family marries the dowry brought in with the wife helps to marry the next sister.'

'But is it always so practical as that? Do [they] not fall in love with one another before they marry?'

'Only a few of them as far as I can see. Romantic love does not exist for it means poverty and too much sufferings. The couple seem to like each other more and more as they grow in children and often love each other sincerely. A woman who comes to slit potatoes for us, a very fine woman, told me she never saw her husband but once before she married and that she was very happy.'[111]

'I often advised young girls,' she told me, 'that made matches are best for everyone in the long run.'

'But do they not believe in natural selection?' she asked. 'Think of the children. Children of a love marriage are always the best.'

'Love marriages, I expect, are determined by economics,' I said. 'I don't approve of the made marriage, but due to a deeply religious acceptance of the *tribes* of this world, they seem to work out fairly well.'

'And why can't I find in people's expressions what they are saying when that speak Irish?' she asked. 'In French and German or Spanish I would know whether the speaker is angry, or sorrowful, or something of what he felt, but here I don't find out any clue?'

'Well you may know a little of French or German and that helps. But there is no stress in Irish and no such thing as the modulation of the voice which you get in French. The emphasis in Irish is given by the position of the word in the sentence. If you want to say "I am going to town", you can emphasize the "I", then "going" or the "town". We are horrified when English people stress words like ghastly — pronounced *gast-lee* — with a terrific stress, but it affects our ears as a punch under the chin.'

Irish would make a grand secret language if that is how it affects an outsider.[112] The enemy would not know from people's faces what emotions they were having. However, I think the Irish are too excitable a people to be able to conceal their emotions as completely as that. Could their secrecy of living have destroyed their intonation? They are so sensitive to criticism that our house at times becomes like a conspiracy. Helen talking in her high pitch, my voice more than ordinarily lowered so that any reflection on them or any talk about the doings of the staff will not be carried back. With English people the discussion would probably be carried on in loud voices. That to us is the signal mark of the English, a discussion on intimate family details carried on at 'full throttle', oblivious of conversations round about, which beat vainly for a bearing against this heavy artillery. The Irish on the other hand have an almost conspiratorial talk, very difficult at times to hear, and probably annoying to English and to Americans. I suppose really there is not enough energy left to those on the West coast to talk at full lung strength. The American crescendo is nerve tiring and dangerous for people who suffer nervously.

Here in Aran if they try salute at all it is with a good show. Previously that was my difficulty in Aran. The one of *Dia dhuit, beannacht Dé art …* seemed to lie on the stranger. I remember setting out from our guest house one day counting salutes. They were slow in coming, some people would not reply. As I went over west I was met with a sturdier lung. At last I made up a game with myself trying to shout out *Dia dhuit* (*guish*, they say) before they were able to say it.

Outside today the house is being thatched by two men. The wheat was lying on the ground loosely.[113] I picked up a handful. The grains were yet in the wheat, almost half full of grains, yet that was being put on top of the house as thatch. That waste seems wasted now in a bad year. I spoke to Rivers about it.

'Yes, I know,' she said, 'but I think they may confuse it with generosity. It is not good to take the last bit out of anything. They waste food for that reason for they do not want to be thought mean.' That is where a sense of hospitality becomes uniform. They are lavish about milk, butter, bacon, cabbage. At home if I need a sauce for myself, Julia will supply enough for eight or ten, when it becomes cold they are wasted. Even now after careful training in such waste, she will slip back into her own ways. In the kitchen for their own meals … she can do as she likes. 'They like pure food also,' continued Rivers. 'They don't like sauces or anything mixed with potatoes, vegetables, fish, meat.'

'They probably think you eat very indecently,' I said.

She nodded. 'I suppose they do.'

'They won't eat scrambled eggs,' I said, 'that they consider turkey food, for they give it to young or to ailing turkeys, and so it is relegated to a lower order.'[114] Soups, I couldn't get the staff to eat at home, but rice, macaroni with cheese, and various succulent puddings, they would devour at least. Macaroni was very difficult to break them in on, and so was rice, but rice became scarce, and it was withdrawn from the menu. Cheese, I had to cut down on for they ate too much of it. They even ate the cheese reserved for grating until cheese was put off the menu for a time.

'It's a wonder they eat fish here,' I said.

'They have to or they wouldn't,' she said. 'They rarely have meat, maybe once a year or so.' That was the old Irish custom, butcher's meat on Christmas Day only.

Near Murrisk I don't know if they now eat fish regularly.[115] Once they ate fish, winkles, shell fish, practically all the time.[116] A Murrisk man, who seems to be in charge of a portion of the fishery there, said to me, 'The Frenchmen are very dirty eaters. They'd eat anything.'

'What do they eat anyhow?' I asked.

'Oh, all sorts of fish, fish we wouldn't touch and shell fish. They mix them all together and throw them into a big pot and make a soup with them.'

'But the French are the best cooks in Europe,' I said, 'and they know a great deal about food. Did you ever taste their food?'

'Indeed, and I did not. I wouldn't be seen near it.'

'Well, you have a lot to learn,' I said. 'Fish soup is the best way to eat fish and is really wonderful. What do you eat anyhow when you are on board?'

'Bacon and eggs.'

'Bacon and eggs! Do you eat bacon and eggs all the time at sea?'

'Oh, yes,' he said, 'it's good food. We like it.'

Our people don't seem to absorb lessons learned abroad. Here, around me [in Mayo], all men who have worked in England, Scotland, Jersey, America, a few have served abroad I'm sure in the British army, in India or Egypt, and yet when they come home, all that experience lies fallow within them. They are afraid of their neighbours' criticism if they introduce anything new. There will be the usual oracular decree, 'it's no good trying that'.

'It would not work in this soil' or 'man dear, what are you trying to do?' They are shamed out of activity, not by this direct speech but by an indirectness in tittering laugh, innuendo and stories, which would show that the innovator is trying to make a big fellow of himself, trying to show off what he knows. Ideas, here, are met with criticism and closed minds. There is no intellectual generosity. Their famous hospitality is personal and spontaneous. Ideas are something else, foreigners to be viewed with suspicion.

Was it conquest brought this suspicion? At one time the Irish were open to every idea, and when their best work in manuscript and metal work was being done, they were able to keep abreast of every foreign idiom in their work and to absorb or to change it. Conquest shut them off from the outside world. Then journeying was restricted and finally stopped altogether. In Elizabeth's time no one could go abroad without a permit; capture meant death or imprisonment or confiscation.[117] The wealth and learning destroyed meant no patronage, no money to adventure. Foreign armies absorbed the youth where foreign universities and churches once took them in. Then a lull until the new adventuring began, this time in the British army or as immigrants without money or political refugees who could never return. There is a great deal of experience here if it could be rationalized. But you can't expect a people who have no real higher education to produce thought. The energy here goes first into the Church, and so the Church would have to direct any activity. But the Church has a zest for power, and it never thinks abstractly or disinterestedly. Always they are churchmen first. They can't discuss ideas for that reason for if you prove them wrong, they suddenly remember their Roman collar and become annoyed.

Next their energy goes into business, any kind of business. This they love in a small way as it satisfies their love of talk and gossip. It brings them in contact with the outside, and they are able to make money, to change their standard of life from what they know and understand to something that is [a] better structure but which brings a surroundings that they do not understand.

Lastly professions: solicitors and barristers. Both satisfy a certain quickness in the Irish mind, a kind of thought that develops from speech. In the country there is a great reverence for the barrister. The better the speech, the better his knowledge of law. The court house satisfies this eagerness for drama, which they produce quickly in talk about events. The sparring invective and oftentimes sonorous long rolling words delight and impress them. It is a fight which they understand, but too few of them realize that it is a mock fight in which participants of the Bar abuse, storm [and] castigate in a purely dramatic manner. The only angry fellows are the plaintiff and defendant, both of whom think their counsel are ready to lose their lives for them. If they could hear the repercussions of their case at a Bar dinner later, they would understand more about law. That would be a good broadcast. First a case in court, then the aftermath. Defendant and plaintiff discussing the case in local pubs, the Bar laughing over the case at a Bar dinner in the local hotel.

Doctors (1), dentists (3), veterinary surgeons (2) in their order of merit. Doctors have nearly as much influence as a priest, and yet they must cooperate with the priest. The priest expects to know if there is anyone having an illegitimate child. He then takes the matter in his own hands, says

Dr O'Brien. There is rarely an illegitimate child on the islands, but it is common in Connemara. 'The girls go out to service in Galway and other places. They are very innocent, for their parents don't tell them a thing. Then they are seduced before they know what it is all about. I know of a family in Connemara where there were three sisters, and the three of them brought back babies in their bellies.'

'And what happens to the babies?' I asked.

'They are sent to a home near Tuam,' he said, 'run by sisters.'[118]

The doctor abuses his power for he has little human sympathy with his dispensary patients. The solicitor appears a kind of a God-like man to the countryman who hangs on his word and thinks he is full of knowledge as a blackberry bramble is of thorns. I expect the older type of solicitor is decent to his poorer clients, but he should dissipate the awe and talk more in terms of a human being.

The army is left as a profession, but there is little respect for it. In this country a standing army has been looked upon as an expensive luxury. It has, up to this war, been staffed with the civil war officers, many of them incompetent and uneducated.[119] They don't study their profession. They are lazy of mind, without ideas and hang on to draw their pensions. Nothing in thought can be expected from such an army.

The universities are not staffed by live professors. Ideas are not encouraged. Coffey, President of the National, said to me once when he was suggesting plays for the University theatre, 'I would like to see plays produced which would be an adjunct to the arts course – a play of Shakespeare or a play of Molière, for instance.'[120]

'But that is not the dramatic approach,' I said. 'A play must have intrinsic merit in itself, and contemporary plays must be presented for they try to solve contemporary problems.'

'A study has nothing to do with ideas,' said Coffey. That should be written in gold over the portal of the National University, or rather, to be correct, the University College Dublin. For years Coffey has directed the placing of lectureships and professorates. He has played a subtle political game in his University, and he acted up to the end as if he himself ran the entire clerical routine answering, mostly not answering, letters person-ally, talking at random when one wanted to discuss a subject with him, being purely arbitrary when it came to a decision. In spite of him there the National [University] has progressed. His work was in building up the institution, and his work was served when he had been less than ten years in office.

We were discussing fairies.[121] 'The people in one of the islands see strange things,' I said, 'horses galloping on the strand in the early morning and figures in which they believe. They never seem to think they are not human until afterwards and so are not frightened.'

'Phoebe and I both saw figures once,' said Mrs Keats, 'two figures in the sky of an evening. They were big figures and very plain.'

'They might be a magnified mirage,' said Rivers.

'And another time, in Ford Street, London, Phoebe said, "Look, Mummy," but I couldn't see anything. She had seen a man with a whip in his hand in the sky.'

Phoebe came in jumping with excitement. She had a basin of potatoes, which P.J. Mullen had produced. They each weighed about two pounds. 'They don't like them much here,' said Rivers, 'but that comes from putting on a lot of seaweed manure.'[122] I had never seen so many big ones. Phoebe wanted to send off one by post. Rivers wanted to bake one in the ashes.

As I walked along the shore I saw two men gathering seaweed. They were putting it up on the rounded heap of dried [sea]weed, built like a cock, with an under foundation of stones. Its height had increased since I came here. It is now close on eight feet high and is supported by props of wood at the sides. Further on, as I lay reading, a man driving sheep came my way. We chatted of the weather, fish, shortage of salt. 'There's plenty of salt over there,' he said pointing towards Galway.

'Now, don't deceive yourself,' I said, 'there's a great shortage of salt on the mainland. Indeed, I don't think people will be able to kill their pigs and that will be a terrible loss to them if they can't salt their bacon for the winter.'

Always they think in remote districts that towns and cities have plenty of food and that they are pretending to them that there is a shortage. The Church evidently is the only place where such an impression can be destroyed and where they might be made to face this reality of shortage.

'And what about light,' I asked, 'have you any?'

'A few bits of candle.'

'And what are you going to do for the winter?'

'I don't know,' he says, 'no one does.'

'But you could make oil from fish, couldn't you? The old people did.'

'Oh, yes, they did do the same,' he said as if he were speaking of another world well removed from him. He would make no effort to meet the situation. Necessity alone would force them to act, to act slowly and long behind time.

We discussed land. Land here is measured in terms of fourths. He has half a fourth in two [quarters]. A fourth is ... acres.[123] 'There's no land,' he says, 'save Mr Johnston's.'

'How did he get his land?'

'He got it in the bad times,' he said, 'when the people weren't able to pay the rent, but it never had much luck. Onaght[124] he got that way, and one night seven and twenty [of his] cattle were driven over the cliff.[125]

'But he hasn't Onaght now?'

'No, he hasn't, but he has more than he wants where he is.' Actually [Johnston] has the only continuous strips of good land on the island. The sands, from the little bay on the North/East here at Port Murvey, are said to have blown over this part of the rock and Johnstons have formed the basis for land.[126] 'Johnston,' O'Brien said, 'was offered land up the country in exchange for his land, but he refused to move.'[127]

'Couldn't he be moved whether he liked it or not,' I asked. [128]

'I don't think so,' said O'Brien. 'Anyhow the dividing up of Johnston's land would not effect any change here. The sea is their living, and this is not being made use of properly. They are not landsmen though land must become more important here as their fishing skill and courage dies out.'

'The cattle are good here anyhow,' he said. 'Once in Ballinasloe Fair the buyers would first come to O'Flaherty's cattle and would always buy them. They were fine powerful beasts.'

[Those] days that are gone. The usual story in Ireland, plenty of fish then, plenty of kelp, more sport and enjoyment, dancing and drinking, big fights, sore heads, great regattas in the mainland lasting all day, races on the strand, crowds, talk and excitement. All along this coast wrecks of smacks rotting quietly.[129] Nobody ever removes the wood. A memory of great events. Now with self-government and land of their own comes bitterness and dissatisfaction. At last they face responsibility and reality, and they don't like either.[130]

Pat Mullen and P.J. were discussing where they would shoot their nets. The discussion lasted at least half an hour. The girls reported it this evening.

'When I was on Bofin,' I said, 'I was ready to sail to Galway on Halloran's *Nobly*, a fifty-ton boat.[131] We came aboard, and Halloran talked of raising the anchor. 'What do you think, John?' I asked.

John looked at the sky and at the wind direction, then he looked into the sea thoughtfully. 'Maybe we should,' he said. 'The wind is easterly but I don't know.'

'What do you think, John?' asked the father.[132]

'Well, it might get better, and it might blow harder. The wind might shift, and there's Slyne Head.[133] Maybe we should go, but I don't know.'

'What do you think Pat?' he asked the second son. Pat thought slowly; he was the younger, and answered as doubtfully. Nobody was willing to accept responsibility. O'Halloran probably was trying to make the sons decide for I had heard before that he was a dangerous man, meaning that he would take a risk at sea. I couldn't see much of his daring then, but I had not much respect for sea then. I have more respect now and somehow less impatience about it.[134]

The conversation threaded itself in a ring of three. The triads of knowledge weaving a Celtic design in, out and through decision. I wanted to shout 'Well, I'll take the risk,' but I didn't. At the end of this sailing ping-pong, which must have lasted half an hour, it was decided not to go.

'I'd go,' said Halloran to me when he was asked again, 'but the boat is partly John's now.'

That's nearly impossible for the English to understand, that indecision.

Charlie Lamb arrived ... undersized, with a saffron beard, and a homespun hat of the fisherman type, and homespun clothes, with sandals.[135] Sandals are certainly not the footwear for this island. Boots are out of the question on the rocks as they get cut to pieces. Pampooties without doubt are the best footwear, then canvas shoes. Luckily, I bought a pair of new canvas shoes, which will last for a short time. The girls' shoes are now a patchwork quilt of holes. Lamb sat in the chimney corner and grunted. He is not very talkative at times ... The others threw darts, and after a time he went home with Johnston.

**Friday**

Fine morning wind from North East, slow blowing. Fish plentiful again today in the nets at the pier, but often P.J. Mullen and his crew get more fish than do the bigger currachs. I was to have been called this morning by P.J., and I woke up before dawn and talked to P.J. telling him I could not sleep and so would remain in bed. Afterwards I found that I had not been called as they were afraid there would not be room for a fourth [in the currach] in the choppy sea.

Everyone here is having jerseys made. There are a few people in Onaght who knit for Betty Rivers.[136] It is a long job this knitting two weeks or more, and they charge twenty-five shillings. Rivers when in London tried to put the sweaters on the London market. '"Do you mean to say," they said, "that you pay peasants twenty-five shillings?" They had been used to paying eight to ten shillings to Highlanders for their work.'

Sweaters are sold in Achill for thirty shillings, which is a big profit, certainly five shillings should be a good profit on an article which is already considered dear.

'I sent their patterns up to Dublin,' said Rivers, 'and they sent them to Donegal. Now that wasn't fair. Each woman has patterns of her own. But a good deal of patterns are said to have come from a man who knitted. He spent most of the winter in bed, and they say he invented many ideas.'[137]

It would be interesting to compare the designs with old Irish designs. The colours are grey, which is natural wool, white and indigo. Indigo takes longest here, and there is great secrecy about it.

'Actually, they use urine,' she said.

'But they use urine everywhere there are cottage weavers,' I said.

'There seems to be some good virtue in the urine in the month of August,' she said, 'because they say that is the best month to use indigo.'

The criss is of many colours, but they do not know how to blend their colours.[138] Last time I was in Aran I picked out a very fine criss from a woman, and I showed her how good her pattern was and how easy it would be to sell such a pattern to visitors with taste. But I don't expect she paid any attention to me. They could make a very fine combination of brown and white, but they use shop dyes and nets as the natural brown.[139]

They are very jealous of each other's sweaters. They each think their own is the best. They won't go to examine patterns in each other's houses, but if they see a sample in Miss Rivers', they jump on it eagerly and examine it thoroughly.

At lunch the question of violin repairs came up. There were two good repairers of violins in London, Mrs Keats said, and only two.

'Did they perform on the violin?' I asked.

'No, these men did not play.'

She was able to distinguish the tone of a violin when one was being selected by friends of hers. 'I remain in one room then someone plays a series of violins in another room then reverses their order, and I pick out the good one, and pick it out again in its order to make sure.' That would need a fine ear for music, I thought.

Very few, I find, have ever seen Russian films.[140] Rivers had seen one, but there must have been opportunities in London before she came here to see good films. Russia was then suspect, and the idea of a Russian film was expected to be propaganda and not art. Actually, the idea behind their films was propaganda, but they were skilfully directed so that aesthetic values predominated. I expect Russia made more friends through her films than through any other of her activities. She had seen some of René Clair's *Le Million,* that almost spontaneous experience of a French director and his absolute accuracy in his use of the ridiculous.[141] Also *La Kermesse Héroïque*, she had seen.[142]

It's hard to describe a picture accurately from memory, and yet when people talk of a book they seize on a character to discuss or the treatment of an incident.[143] She tried to tell the others of *La Kermesse Héroïque*. I tried to supplement but I don't know if we both were able to convey any idea of the droll character of the film, which made fun of its own history.

'It was not well received in Flanders,' she said, 'as one village evidently remembered some such incident.'

Mrs Keats did not seem to regard films as an art form. She must be lost indeed in Ireland as there is no studio patter, none of the acclaim that an artist meets with especially a singer who is more in the limelight and used to adulation. She has enough poise and sense of reality to dispense with flattery, but friendliness of people working in the same medium, she must miss.

No one plays cards here.[144] That is a good sign in a way, for cards are – to misquote Johnson – 'the last refuge of a scoundrel'.[145] They are an excuse for lack of good talk which comes from an interest in life. The majority of people won't talk because they are not accustomed to it and are afraid of betraying themselves, their gaps, but countrymen talk because they have no feeling of inferiority about their minds. To them talk is as natural as eating. Pat Mullen's talk is not very interesting, I find; perhaps it needs to be directed, but he is a natural storyteller. He can embroider and weave … This he neglects in his writing when the action ceases. Then he becomes pedantic … His words become painful then for the sense of talk has gone out of them. Actually his speech is interlaced with 'Goddamns' and 'bloody' and 'bastard'. In the book, that is *Hero Breed*, there are no curses.[146]

The strange thing about people who like to play cards to pass the time is that they are surprised when you do not play cards. They always expect you to conform to their pastimes, but they definitely resent you talking on subjects you feel about with others when they are present. They feel out of it, isolated and lonely.

Mrs Keats and I had been talking about Virginia Woolf.[147] *Between the Acts* I was reading. It had a beautiful sense of words, which fitted in place so easily that you could think they fell there naturally. In reality they must have meant as hard work as lines of poetry. There was an exquisite elusiveness about them. They went in and out like water lilies on a pond, always looking exactly right.

'I can't understand her suicide,' she said. 'A person like her should have such a richness in life that she could not go out that way.'

'Yes,' I said, 'it was a great shock to read of her death as one felt her work had yet to come a good deal more of it, too.'

'But she must have had an extraordinary nervous sensitivity. Everything must have amplified for her. I notice that ordinary, kind people are always very cruel to such sensitive people. They go out of their way to hurt them,' she said.

'Yes, they don't understand them. They think they are adopting a pose when they think as originally as they feel, and they want to reduce them to herd level of thought, feeling and action.'

Country people feel about tinkers as the average person thinks about the artist or about perceptive people.[148] The tinker moves across their line of life, moves in and out, through it, camping besides their feeling, eating close to them, but never of them and never sharing anything. They hate tinkers because they will not conform to their laws and customs. People have a contempt for them for tinkers do not care for their principle God-land. The tinker uses strange tools and has knowledge of horses that are magical almost. He is as full of wiles as a gombeen man or a shop-keeper, and yet they admire sharp practice and cunning and very much in one of themselves.[149]

This island has, so far as I know, produced three writers: Liam O'Flaherty, Pat Mullen and Barbara Mullen.[150] The islands have contributed to Synge[151] and Flaherty's *Man of Aran* movie, but I don't think anyone else has written of them.[152] Rivers was to write a book on Aran, but she probably would have to wait for publication until she went to live somewhere else.[153] Irish people may put up with a novel, but they don't like to be written about in a book as objectively as such a study would write of them. She could make an excellent book on the islands as she is sympathetic, sensitive, understanding and has a peculiar awareness of their moods and vagaries. Her liking for them would not cloak them from her, and it would not be a book of praise or flattery, as are books generally of travel in Ireland.

Barbara Mullen I don't know of. She lived in America, is now a very successful actress in London, has published records, how many I don't know, but there are three in the house, and has written *Life Is My Adventure*. How good her writing is I don't know. They could not write about Aran, I feel, but what would be of immense value would be a book by Liam O'Flaherty, about his growing up in Aran and his early days until he joined the British army. It would need to be written with some philosophic attachment, less of novel form, which would make a Russian grotesque of a non-fiction book. He said he would sometime do such a book, but I doubt that he will write it.[154]

After dinner I set out to walk to Kilronan to have a chat with the doctor. I met Charlie Lamb near Kilmurvey Pier. He was not sure what he was going to do. I had my notebook in my pocket and thought I might be able to do some writing as well as perhaps talk to the doctor, a vain hope generally as I don't meet people and write in the same afternoon. Lamb wanted to know where I was going, and I said for a walk and to Kilronan. He did not know if he could get a lift back, but came with me.

*Charles Lamb*, A Quaint Couple, *1930*.

Lamb speaks under and through his beard. He is hard to understand at times. He wears a soft green tie, the banner of artistic detachment. Most artists can wear colours as women can, but in this country Seán O'Sullivan,[155] Maurice MacGonigal,[156] in ties, Lamb, in ties, perhaps Harry Kernoff in ties, are the only sign-bearers of their profession.[157] Jack Yeats wears a black tie, a black hat and a cut-away coat.[158] Why it is called a cut away? I don't know for it is not cut away. That remark I wish to withdraw for Jack Yeats wears a double-breasted coat and not a cut away. He wears a heavy overcoat like a farmer's. Cecil Salkeld can wear a purple coat tie with aplomb.[159] The younger groups, the non-academy painters, usually go in for startling or painting colours in dress. Seán Keating wears a flat hat or none, with a beach jersey and a blue suit. Kernoff wears a black hat.

'Old Johnston was a great character,' said Lamb.[160] 'He was a bottle man and drank steadily, claret as far as I could gather. He was very kind to his neighbours.' Once when Lamb was staying there, he heard him sawing away each day at an oak beam that had come ashore.

'He was cutting out pieces for currachs, which he would later give to the fishermen. He had a feudal sense in his relationship to his neighbours but not as feudal as his predecessor, O'Flaherty.[161] The Johnstons were Protestants. They came from Clare and are related to Francis MacNamara, but they are Catholic now.'[162]

'Liam O'Flaherty was a great friend of his,' Lamb said. 'He used to come over and yarn with him, and he got many a story from him.'

'Liam married the wrong woman.'

'I know,' said Lamb.

'Yes, it was a bad start, I think,' I said, 'to run off with another man's wife for Liam had too much to fight against after that.'[163]

'If he had married an Irishwoman, he could have made a home for himself.'

'I don't know about that,' I said. 'It would perhaps have been hard for Liam to gather sufficient experience tied down to a child-producer.[164] He had to travel and explain himself and that made for unrest.'

'He tried to buy the old lighthouse once, but the government would not sell it to him.'

'I wonder if he could have settled down in Aran. It would have been better for him.'

'I know,' I said.

'I like his stories best,' said Lamb. 'I never liked his novels.'

Lamb had once gone on a trip for six months with a caravan from Carraroe to Achill. He had a horse and ambled along at his own pace.[165] That would be an ideal place to paint. He had met An Paorach in Newport when he had encamped on the Quay.[166]

'Power is a very odd fellow,' he said. 'Seán O'Sullivan and I were out in the Bay with him once in his boat. We decided that he was a frustrated boy scout, that he hadn't grown up in many ways, but we definitely liked him and his sense of the sea.' I suppose Lamb drank his pints of porter in every pub, but I don't know what kind of painting he was able to do on his trip. His talk has more or less to be dragged from him.

We met a man with two tea chests tied on to his ass, one on either side. It could hardly be tea I thought, but it's a light and easy way of carrying supplies. Lamb must have guessed what I was thinking of. 'He's a peddler,' he said, 'and he goes throughout the island.'

'They're decadent the types here,' said Lamb as we passed a number of isolated men. They were not outstanding like the fine men I had seen in currachs in the South Island, but then they were in their element, the sea, and in their natural place, the seat of a currach. I had seen a few fine-looking men near Kilmurvey, but on the whole the islanders were poor in physique. The young children look rosy and fat for they are fed on milk, then they go off some of them at 5 or 6, but some last until they are 10. Then they definitely fall away for they have not enough to eat. They look worse than slum children who are more poorly fed, but slum children have a quicker intelligence for their minds are early alert; here they become listless and apathetic.

Pat Mullen says there is too much inbreeding here and that the priest, by stopping amusements, has driven away their exuberance. 'One time the men here married Connemara women, but now the Connemara girls have bicycles. They have the bus to take them to Galway where they see clothes, and they have the movies. They wouldn't now marry an Aran man. Signs is on them.[167] There's a fine collection of Aran people in the lunatic asylum.'

Lamb looked at stones with a builder's eye. He builds himself, and his father was a builder. 'These stones,' he pointed to the well-trimmed stone wall without cement that borders the main road, 'are of little use. Do you see these seams? Well, you couldn't build with them. They'd split off in time. You'd have to search around for good stones.'

Aran is a builder's paradise. Helen would have been happy here.[168] She could design and plan very cheaply to her heart's content, and she could build a good cottage in no time. But there is no wood for the interior, and she would be as badly off as she now is. She has wood but no building stone within easy distance, no sand save at a distance also, but there is wood enough if she would risk the unseasoned material near the house.

Cecil Salkeld's name came across the conversation as I remembered the poem which he had sent to me which he had printed himself but which I had not acknowledged.

'Cecil is very odd,' said Lamb.

'He's a very nice fellow,' I said, 'and he has his own ways. We are too set in ours, to opt out by what we consider normality.'

'Cecil came down to stay with me for a while [in Connemara],' said Lamb, 'but he stayed in bed all day. I said "Cecil if you mow a bit of the lawn, I'll give you half a dozen bottles of stout." He mowed the lawn alright, but a year later I heard his talk of all the mowing he had once done in a day. He had then forgotten that it was in my place he had done his little bit of mowing.'

'Cecil doesn't need much of any experience to write an epic in his mind about it,' I said.

'Did he sail any of the boats when he was with you in Connemara?'

'No, he didn't go near a boat. He talked a great deal to me of a boat he once had on Lake Constance. He knew all the right terms for sailing.'

'I suppose he was on a trip in a few yachts and imagined the rest,' said Lamb.

Cecil had always talked to me about mountaineering as if he had climbed the Alps backwards, but he fell from his high mountaineering place when I found that he didn't know that a climber used nails in his boots.[169] Similarly his knowledge of ballistics lessened itself on my strict analysis to a fairly poor knowledge of musketry tactics.

'He had two mothers,' said Lamb. I knew what he meant: his mother and his wife.[170] The wife, German, has no charm; indeed, she looks like a sheep's head. She leaves the room a short time after I enter to talk with Blanaid or with Cecil. But the children are full of life, the baby and Barbara.[171]

'His mother brought him up in a very Bohemian way at first; then she tried to change and was as strict on the other side; this when he was about 14.' I had heard that he drank then and painted, I think.

Cecil is hopeless in one way. He can't keep an appointment, nor a set hour. He has no steady capacity for work now. He lives in hope of being able to get enough money from the Radio to buy drink, or to borrow money from people for drink. I have gone three days in succession to sit for a drawing but no Cecil.[172] He had been in bed. 'Cecil is not feeling very well today,' Mrs Salkeld would say or 'he isn't up yet; he worked late', whereas in truth Cecil had been out drinking the night before. Then, if Cecil would be roused, this at 4 o'clock in the evening he would come downstairs, put his hand to his throat and say 'my throat, it's bad this morning'. Never would either of them admit that it was drink. He drinks badly. He drinks to get drunk. He will mix bad port with whiskey or Burgundy with stout and rum.

There is often a scene in which he begins to contradict his mother in a petulant way. 'Now, mother, I did not say that,' or when she remarks, 'Cecil, of course, does nothing now.' He will say, 'Mother how can you say that, I have done a drawing recently.'

'Yes, but it's the first drawing for six months, and you're over a year overdue in the printing of poems. You know you are, Cecil.' He takes money out of her purse. 'Cecil did you see a shilling which I left on the mantelpiece last night?'

'No, mother, I did not.'

'Well, it's gone now, and I know you took it, Cecil. You went out and had a drink.'

'I did not take it, mother.'

O'Brien's pub was closed. We went to Daly's next door, a small cottage with beer barrels to sit on and stools.[173] A sharp-faced man with good delivery and a punch in his words was swiping hard at the Government.

'Why don't they do something for the islanders?' Once he told us of the harvest of herrings that went in schooners to America. There was then a curing station. Herrings were salted down in barrels, men with carts got a good wage, money was plentiful, and the islanders used the sea.

'You can't blame the Government for that,' I said, 'it was the American government put a tariff on herrings and mackerel.'

'They should do something to help us to deliver our fish,' he said. 'If we make a good catch we have to wait over a day before they can be delivered in Galway and there's almost another day before the catch reaches Dublin.'

'But all groups of fishermen in other countries make their own arrangements. Couldn't one of your hookers by turn, or a boat with an engine in it, collect fish from the fishing boats and bring the catch straight in to Galway.'

He seemed to resent my intrusion. 'The Government must do it. There's too much talk about Government help,' said Lamb, 'and too little about people doing their own part.'

'How did you salt the herring for the American market?' I asked.

'We put them in salt first, then emptied them into another barrel, washed them, put on more salt, added brine, and put them back again.'

'That seems to make them last longer,' I said. 'Why don't they do that when they salt them down themselves.'

'They don't bother,' he said. 'That kills their market island here. The Connemara man likes them salted, dried in the sun until they are yellow, then put back again in barrels.'

'Salted mackerel tastes to me like thin pieces of wood dipped in vinegar,' I said. 'They have the consistency of thin slivers of wood and the taste of mud vinegar.'

The complaining man said, 'I don't like the taste of them either.'

'Once,' I said, 'there was an inland market for fish. They were carted and sold in all small inland towns as far as Roscommon, and I'm sure there would be a market again for them as inland farmers would like them.'

'I believe there would be a market for them,' he said. And so we reached an impasse. There must be some curing station erected here, some ice for fish or a depot in Galway, but some one boat must collect fish from the other boats and steam back with their catches to the rail head. Murrisk trawlers in our bay need such a boat.

'But you don't fish on Saturdays, Sundays or holidays,' I said.[174] 'You can't expect to be able to meet the market if you are not willing to go out every day.'

'We do fish on Saturdays,' the complainer said.

'Yes, you lift nets, but you don't put down nets on Saturday night nor do you put down nets on Sunday night, and so for trawling purposes or for the market, you don't fish between Saturday morning and Monday evening.'

'That's right,' he said. 'We keep Sunday.'

'I don't think Spain or Portugal or Italy keep Sunday,' I said. 'Their livelihood comes first.'

The *Dun Aengus* was another source of complaint.[175]

'Why does she come on Sunday? We want her on Saturday,' he said. She puts Saturday in with Sunday to bring supplies to the island, but she should take the fish away on Saturday evening.'

'She's Government controlled,' I said. 'At least she receives a Government subsidy, and I suppose she tries to make some money by bringing over tourists on Sunday.'

'But she's so good to us,' said another man, 'Why can't she come the two days?'

---

'Shortage of coal,' I said. 'She has two tons a trip, and coal can't be spared.'

'There's plenty of coal,' he said.

'That's your mistake then,' I said, 'for coal is very scarce, and you'd soon find that out if you used coal yourself, but you don't, and so you'll never know.'

The men went out. Daly did not say anything for a while. He's from the mainland but has been twenty years or so in Aran. I stood up. On the wall was a composite picture of Killarney, done a good while ago judging by the architecture of the houses. In front a round tower, a cross, monastic ruins, houses recessed behind, and in the rear water and mountains. The houses looked eighteenth century. At the base was a key to the numbering of houses and monuments. It looked very nice indeed but was badly stained.

'A panoramical view of the Lakes of Killarney, County Kerry, Ireland, Exhibiting the Mountains, the Stag-Hunt on the Lake and its neighbouring scenery after views taken from Nature by H. Miller … published by Haskell & Allen, 61 Hanover Street, Boston.'

'That's well over a hundred years old,' said Daly. 'A man here offered me £50 for it. I have never seen another like it.'

'No, neither have I,' I said, 'but it's badly stained. That was a very good offer considering its condition. It should really be in a museum.'

'Twenty-five years ago early potatoes were tried here,' he said. 'An expert was brought over from Jersey to show the Aran people how to grow them. They were about the size of an egg, and they were packed and sent to the Dublin market.'

'And did they keep it up?' I asked.

'No, they did not,' he said. 'They dropped it then.' Here they always plant potatoes on a Friday. They won't them plant them on any other day: Aran Banners and Epicures. Epicures grow very big here.' They had tried Indian corn here too, himself or a relative, and it grew well. Indeed, anything would grow well here as there is great heat from the limestone walls even in winter and in hot summer there is much more heat here than on the mainland.

We walked down to the harbour. I tried to get the tonnage of the boats there from Lamb, but he knew neither their tonnage not their make. He couldn't distinguish between a *poochawn*, and a hooker[176] … There were four boats in at the pier. I went over to talk to a merry-faced man with a fine nose to find out the make and tonnage of his boat, but he spoke no English. He was about forty-five or fifty. That came as a shock, the non-speaking of English. Why it should be a shock I don't know, but it suddenly brings you up against a foreign language in your own country, the foreign language being the native language and your language being the foreign language. And you realize that there is another way of life close to you that you can barely plumb save you have a very good knowledge of their language and have lived amongst them.

Lamb never talks about painting. I have never heard him express an opinion about it. He seems to have no interest in its intellectual side. He has never spoken about a foreign painter, living or dead. Perhaps he looks upon his painting much as a plumber looks upon his plumbing, something to get done with as a job of work and then forget.

'This is the first year that there has been a real Irish Academy,' Lamb said.[177] 'Every other year the Academy pays at least £200 to bring over pictures from England. That money could go towards helping an art school or studios for pupils.'[178]

'Why do they bring over pictures from England?' I asked.

'A custom,' he said, 'of the RHA, evidently begun when Ireland had few painters and was a province, in the same way as London pictures are sent down to country shows in England.'

We discussed Dr O'Brien. Lamb is evidently afraid to knock at the door of the pub. In some ways he is afraid of O'Brien who certainly has a mind of his own and is very independent on his likes and dislikes.

'He is very odd, the doctor,' said Lamb.

'Don't you think you are odd yourself,' I said.

'No, I'm not a bit odd,' said Lamb.

'Well then that's evidently your form of oddness,' I said. 'You don't think you're odd, but probably everyone else thinks you are.'

The effect of the moon on lunatics, foolish people, women and plants. Here they plant in the growing moon.

We returned to Daly's as the doctor was still not at home. Lamb was discussing vegetables with much aplomb, a subject I can now carry on an easy conversation in. Lamb evidently looks after his own vegetables, and he must, from his talk, have a fairly good garden. There is a good lot of enmity between neighbours here, Daly said, but that may be because they are all inter-related.

'Do you see that gate opposite,' he said. It was a little red gate. 'Well one man put it up and was making two piers. The neighbour knocked down the pier on his own side because he said it was his land.'

Five men came in. They sat down with a *Dia dhibh*. After a while in a whisper one of them stood a round. For about five minutes there was not a word in the pub until I spoke to Lamb to break the silence. They drank their pint each, and then went out.

'Who are they?' I asked.

'They're Connemara men,' said Lamb. 'I know them by sight. That's their custom. They won't talk when there are strangers present.'

As we walked home Lamb must have been buoyed up by his large pints of Single X.[179] 'They're very good in Aran,' he said. 'In Connemara when you broach a barrel the pints are flat in a day or two, but here the pints are as good at the end of a week as they were the first day.[180] There must be something in the air where that improves their pints.' That knowledge must be a great consolation for a visitor, but it's not much good for me as I cannot drink porter or won't now. I wish I could for whiskey is a doubtful quality in most pubs, and it is still more of a doubtful quality now. I notice Viv Barry cannot drink much stout now, and Stan Barry not at all, so this drink must definitely be acid.[181]

As we talked of John J. O'Malley, as a type of man who might help to run a province, Lamb said, 'but he's very ignorant.[182] When I was there [in Westport] with my caravan I went in for a bag of oats for the horse. He asked me what work I carried on. "I am a painter," I said. "What painting firm in Dublin do you work for?" he asked.'

We discussed the state of the country in an ambling way. 'I'm tired of this blaming of the Government for everything that goes wrong. What is needed is more of an individual and united effort. They have kept us away from war anyhow.'

'Yes, and they get no credit for it,' I said.

'The people would soon know the difference if the Germans took over the country,' he said. 'They wouldn't like to be ordered about even if it were only for their own good. They don't take dictation, and they don't want it.'

'A good number of people wanted to see England getting a good trouncing,' I said, 'but that was at the beginning of the war; they didn't want to see her beaten. Now, I think, a good deal of people here want to see the Germans win.'

In writing this journey with Lamb I find it as flat as stale porter. He has definitely little colour in himself and his conversations with me do not seem to have any 'lift'. Anyone I have talked to here is more interesting than he is.

**Saturday**

Somehow we seem to discuss the people immoderately. Mrs Keats wants to understand about them. She is very decent, but she has a distinctly British outlook. She does not understand the historical background and is looking at the effects produced by a cause now largely removed. Her daughter, Phoebe, is impatient about lack of artistic sensibility and of interest in the arts. Mrs Keats wonders if character can be built up so that people can depend on themselves. She does not realize how little real detached education there is in this country.

We all seem to discuss our drawbacks endlessly. That is either because we are sensitive about them or because they are very real or because nothing is being done to face our own weaknesses and to try to change them. There has been a cooking class in the West. The instructress imported ovens or oil stoves and showed the girls how to make sweet cakes and sponge cakes. It was so unreal that the girls fell off, one by one, soon only a few were left. It happened three years ago.

'It is so absurd to approach such a serious problem, bad cookery, in such a stupid way,' Rivers said.

'Even in the towns I find that the technical schools do not teach them classes to cook on turf fires. A technique for turf cooking must be evolved if it is to be of any use to the country people,' I said.

'What do the people who work for you think of your visitors,' I asked.

'I don't know,' she said. 'I'm sure they think we are all quite mad. They talk in Irish always amongst themselves, and, I'm sure, can make a good game of it. They have secret names for everyone in the house,' she said, 'and for things also. So I was told by people who were there who spoke Irish.' I can imagine the fun they get out of it when they feel nobody knows what they are talking about.

We were talking about the selling of pictures in Dublin. ' ... is no use,' I said. 'He has no taste.'

'Exactly,' said Rivers, 'and I blame Contemporary Pictures a good deal.[183] They had a great chance, their frames were very good, their taste was good, but Longford drank[184] and Deirdre McDonagh drank also.[185] Pictures sent to be framed were stained by being left face down on liquid. Pictures were sent out to be framed, carried under the arm of tradesmen, without wrapping. Gradually they lost their trade. We need someone like Egan.[186] He had good taste, he had a fine room for exhibitions, and he sold good art, colours, and materials. Now what we need is someone like Vollard, a man who sold good colours, was interested in painting and hung his clients' pictures in his gallery.'[187]

---

'NOBODY'S BUSINESS'

'With the war on there seems little chance of that,' I said. 'It's nearly impossible to get good brushes and good colours.[188] Brushes used in Ireland are no use, and so the creative worker is penalized. It would look as if this Government did not want painters to work in Ireland, but that is not true; it is only part of that great unreflecting mentality that is working against the core of our endeavour here.'

'Things get so bad at times in the country,' I said, 'that I feel like putting up a notice, which would read as pure snobbery, "people with creative tendencies welcomed".'

'Then you would be flooded out with Eugene Judges,' said Phoebe.[189]

'A little of him goes a long way,' I said. 'The first time I met him I liked him a little. He sat down and talked our language for a while, but he had a way of seeming to be profound about nothing. The next time I met him was in Achill. He was dressed like a Scots Guardsman off duty.'

'No, certainly not a Guardsman,' said Phoebe in horror as if I were comparing Judge to some exquisite I had seen or known. He had spotless tan and brown shoes, impeccable creases in his trousers, a walking stick, which he leaned on from the hips and a habit of saying 'ha' and 'um' in the middle of and at the end of sentences. Also, he stayed in Freyer's and enjoyed it.[190] That was a bad sign in itself for Freyer can be an insufferable hole. 'I thought Judge intolerable, a kind of pseudo-Olympian, and I kept out of his way afterwards.'

'Well,' said Phoebe, her light eyes shining, 'when he began to tell me that he intended to be an influence so that the younger Irish artists could model on him I began to get tired.'

'Has he such a swelled head as that?' I said. 'He never mentioned his influence in the future to me.'

'And he would point to a spot of colour and explain it as good painting as if painting could be explained like that. He said also that he intended to become more explicit so that he would be more understandable to a younger generation and so, I suppose, have greater influence.'

'The trouble about painting in this country,' I said to Rivers, 'is that painters cannot see first, and that secondly, they don't speak your own language. They can't see for no one that I know of has really painted this country. They dab at it, feel sensuously in terms of paint, but they paint with their bodies. The quality of mind that goes into good French painting is lacking here. I suppose we haven't got that quality of mind.'

'It looks like that,' Rivers said. 'None of them have painted the country. It is very beautiful, but they paint superficially only.'

'I wonder will we ever develop that quality of mind that a real painter needs. The painters don't ever seem interested in ideas. Any foreign painter, whom I know, always talked well. He was always full of ideas and of good talk. Keating talks well and is always interesting about people, and Seán O'Sullivan is interesting, but there is a lack in all of them.'[191]

'What do you think of Keating?' asked Rivers.

'I don't like his painting. It leaves me cold,' I said.

'Well, what do you think of his drawings?'

'I've seen some I liked, but a great deal of them were bad.'

'He can draw well,' she said, 'very well, and he is interesting to talk to, but he's dead.'

'Seán O'Sullivan can draw, and he can draw well, but I feel he can't paint. Always he ends up with a kind of marmalade product, sticky and overpainted. You feel that if you drew a bit of the paint of the picture with your finger, it would trail afterwards like a gob of marmalade lifted with a spoon.'

'But Seán is sensitive and humble. All the others seem arrogant and tight.'

'Yes, I felt that about him,' said Rivers. 'He is feminine and self-doubting and that makes him attractive to women, whom he understands. But he has debased his talent, and he knows it. He is in a vicious circle. I personally think that he was flattered too much by some of the Anglo Irish whom he painted and as flattery is rare in creative work in Ireland, or over-appreciation absent from the very great majority of the native Irish who don't give a damn about painting, he was smitten with the … praise. That is the danger I expect.'

One should be judged and accept judgement from one's peers. I thought anything else is love, kindness or flattery.

'I expect something like that has happened,' Rivers said, 'for I have seen some damn good drawings of his.'

'He was down with me for a while,' I said, 'and I had to talk to him straight.'

'How did he like it?' she asked.

'He took it well,' I said, 'for he has a sense of humour and was interested in the way I told him off. One thing, he hasn't the usual inhibitions, but instead of making some good use of this for his work, he uses that freedom for promiscuous fornication and over much drink.'

'MacGonigal I don't know,' she said, 'but I know of. He's a queer little person.'

'I know him and like him,' I said, 'but not as a painter. He mixes a kind of nationalism with paint. Seán O'Sullivan says he has a fine feeling for paint, but I have seldom seen it. He does [not] know when to leave go of a canvas, nor does Seán O'Sullivan. He is very bitter about contemporary painting, as bitter as is Austin Clarke about contemporary poetry.[192] Seán resents non-academy painting mainly, I think, because it is done by the Anglo-Irish or by Imperialists.'

'Who is there left?' I asked. 'Norah McGuinness.[193] What do you think of her?'

'She has great facility in quick rapid work,' she said, 'but she doesn't seem to be able to organize in depth.'

'Is that why she can't use oils?' I asked.

'I don't know, but I feel that about her work, it is unorganized at times.'

'She has done some lovely gouache,' I said. 'I know that for I have one of them, but in her oils she becomes muddy and I don't know what happens in her portraits.'

'Her portrait of Sheila Richards was definitely bad,' she said.[194]

'Evie Hone I liked best,' said Rivers.[195] 'Do you know her?'

'Yes, I do. She is Godmother to the baby,' I said.[196]

'I spent an evening with her, and I felt that life is worth living. Her [stained] glass is beautiful, and she keeps on getting orders. She is happier and is working better now that she is a Catholic.'

'There was great hostility to her becoming a Catholic,' I said. 'Some of her friends talked to me as if she had a disease, and as I did not know of her conversion I was concerned for the state of her body. Later I found it was the state of her soul, they meant that for I have one of them, but in her oils she becomes muddy and I don't know what happens in her portraits.'

'That leaves Jack Yeats,' I said. 'He is the most profound to talk to. He definitely knows facts of creative work that are delightful to listen to. He doesn't often talk, but when he does there is a very fine quality to it. His mind is open to ideas of all kind.'

'I like him,' she said. 'He is very nice indeed, but I don't know where he is going. He has looked off from one manner to another, and he hasn't yet found himself.'

'I like some of his new work,' I said, 'very much.'

'Yes, so do I, but the still lives are the best things in it,' she said.

Here in this house you can sit down and talk, and if the talk is interesting you can forget about everything else, for it seems to help your other work. But there is a danger in talking too early in the morning. It uses up too much. Perhaps the best time to talk is after dinner so that the evening is free or in the night time late. It's hard to fix on proper times, but if you have done a good day's work you are tired as a rule, and it takes someone else's effort to lift you out of that lethargy. If you love to make your own effort always to lift conversation then you become a little worn out, or frustrated if you fail.

Last night the Northern Lights came streaming across the sky like searchlights moving across to and fro.[197] They were white, not exciting to me, but very exciting to the Keats who thrilled about them. They have a capacity for wonder, these girls, especially Phoebe.

'She has good emotions,' I said to her mother. 'What does she mean to do?'

'I don't know,' she said.

'She plays well on the violin, and she attends art school. She seems to be interested in painting,' I said, 'but is a little dispersed. I suppose she will find herself.'

'She is much more emotional now,' Mrs Keats said. 'When she was extremely self-conscious, a stage she is growing out of, she was more controlled in expression; now she is completely uncontrolled again. I remember the first play I went to with my brother. I was then twenty-one. There was a way out for two people in a room, and they were in danger, but they didn't know about it. I stood up and shouted, "get out, get out before it is too late". My brother was utterly ashamed, and I really spoiled the play.'

'I can well imagine what your brother felt,' I said.

'But what is the good of listening like a slug as if you had no emotions. Most audiences are like that.'

'If you saw cattle being sent out to the steamer from Inishmaan you would see emotion. Everyone, especially the women, seem to lose control of themselves. They scream and shout. The men are busy trying to throw the beasts and then haul them out by a rope behind their currachs. The men are knocked flat in the water, but they don't seem to mind it, and they don't get hurt; neither are they cruel to the animals. Sometimes a beast breaks away, the women shoo them with lifted petticoats and seem to stop them that way. Horses are the great danger for they might easily put a hoof up through a currach.'

'I'd like to see that,' she said.

'I suppose it replaces our idea of pure drama, for it is dramatic,' I said. 'The setting beside the sea, breakers coming in, currachs waiting in the water, and behind the women as an excited tempestuous chorus.'

*Elizabeth Rivers,* Loading Cattle for Galway from the Aran Islands

Anne Kelly has made up her mind to go tomorrow. She is full of irres-olution. 'I can't leave my father for so long,' she says.

'Is he sick,' I asked.

'No,' she said, 'but I know I should go back.' She twists and turns mentally, indecisive, for she wants to remain here where she is happy, but yet she wants to go home, and I know she will go home. 'I can come out again on Wednesday and stay for a week or so.' She is very anxious to go to America and will end up there. If she had any relative on the far side to vouch for her, it would simplify matters.

Phoebe was talking of rabbits on the shore as P.J. [Mullen] had intended to go to Inishmaan with a ferret and spend a month hunting rabbits there.

'Don't talk about rabbits here,' said P.J., 'for if the [men] hear you, they won't go out fishing.' It's unlucky according to him to talk about rabbits, foxes or hens.[198]

'What about the priest?' I said, as old Lavelle from Renvyle told me, it was unlucky to mention the priest when out in a boat. He didn't seem to think the priest meant anything to them.

'They would use the quay when rabbits are being brought on to a boat,' he said. Pat and P.J. had superstitions, but then they are banned people so far as the priest is concerned and free people in their own minds. [199]

'Anne [Kelly]', said Mrs Keats 'did a strange thing. She cut three buttons off the uniform of the dead airman who was found in the net.'[200] Tony went down along the shore that morning. I saw her coming back hurriedly, and I asked her what was wrong.

'She told me, "You know, Mummy," she said, "I don't understand death. It has no meaning for me." But think of the other girl so insensitive.'

Yet Anne is very sensitive. It is like a shy person in a room, they draw attention to themselves by some gaucherie, and the very thing they wish to avoid – attention by their state of mind and movements. 'She had night-mares for three nights in succession,' said Mrs Keats, and I don't wonder.

I was talking about Indians[201] in relation to children. 'They don't smack their children,' I said, 'and they never talk down to them.'

'How very sensible,' said Rivers.

'For them a child is an individual. I find that Cathal, who is now 5, can understand an explanation or a conversation.[202] I don't talk down to him. He doesn't like baby talk. He thinks I'm "a silly-billy", as he says if I pull his leg too much. And the Indians allow their children, from the age of 8 or so, to sit in at their councils. That gives them a sense of dignity. They learn to sit quiet and to listen to argument and exposition and to learn the wisdom of the elders. I suppose also it teaches the elders to steady them-selves in conversation and not to be rash, as it would look bad before the youngsters if they gave hasty advice or lost their tempers.'

'How very sound,' said Rivers, 'and do they come in silently to a room and sit down without saying a word?'

'Yes. They do.'

'Here, too, in Aran they do that. Children will come quietly in a room, sit down when you are talking.'

'I suppose I understand Indians so well because I understand a little of our own people. I hate to be asked questions or to have my photograph taken.[203] I want to stay quiet at times and not talk much and so do the people. Indians also know whether you are *simpatico* or not. You cannot be false to them ever in your mind.'

'That is absolutely true about the Aran people.' Rivers said. 'If you are sympathetic to them, they know it at once.'

With the Indians I did not want to know of their way of life too much. I deliberately shut off my interest so that they would not feel or resent my curiosity. I could feel with them. I know and share the common human emotions. I could not find what they were thinking of, but I found them jolly pleasant, full of fun, with a great sense of humour. They have a secret name for all whites, and they extract great fun from this secret and from their reserved feeling about whites. To them they smell, but they are polite about it. I always liked that thought because whites are so superior about other racial smells.

'I didn't know that,' said Mrs Keats. 'I know negroes smell, even if they bathe every day. And they don't like the colour of whites.'

'When you live close to Indians, their bronze-brown colour is lovely. Anything they put on their face or body, paint or clothes seems to take an added colour, for their bronze-red would already need five or six painter's colours to reach it.'

'And what is the attitude of Americans towards them?' asked Rivers.

'It is improving,' I said, 'as John Collier has to do, or had to do with Indian affairs, but in my time the children were compelled to go to Indian schools in Santa Fe, 70 miles away, where first they cut their hair – a deadly insult to an Indian – then they tried to make them Protestants, and lastly good Americans.[204] When they returned to their Pueblos at the end of some years' training, they were unfit for work in a Pueblo and had to begin over again. As an old chief said to me, "We have our Indian religion, and in our Pueblo we go to the Catholic Church if we like to, mostly the women go. In the white schools they try to make our boys and girls Protestants, and when they come back home it is very hard. It takes maybe five or six years to make them good Indians again, and sometimes we don't succeed."'

'How horrible,' said Rivers, 'with all their talk of freedom and democracy.'

'It was even worse in the Navajo country,' I said. 'If the Pueblo Indian children returned home every year, then there was a solemn thanksgiving, for the old people really never expected to see them again, but Navajo children are taken young and kept for five or six years.[205] They have forgotten their Indian names, and I suppose they have been given some kind of a substitute name at school. When they are finished at school, they are sent back to the reservation. They don't know who their people are and so you often see five or six of them hanging around a trader's house in the reservation, unclaimed.'

When we passed the house of Mr Moloney, the schoolteacher, I said, 'He is fond of trees and plants, that man.'

'He is,' said Pat Hernon, 'but he spends a lot of money on them. He even gets some of them from Dublin, and it's not much sense. It costs too much money.'

'Do you not like them?' I said. He was non-committal. The price of the shrubs had upset him. 'You'd probably drink the price of them in a few months, and you'd have no trees at the end of it all.'

'But the porter is good for me,' said Pat.


## Sunday

Everyone slept late to celebrate the Sabbath. I went to second Mass, Pat Hernon driving me on his horse and outside car. He is a quiet man, talk has to be pumped out of him, but he is staunch. 'He is a good friend,' Rivers said, 'and very straight.'

Once in Kilronan some nuns came off the boat, and Pat had them on his car.[206] The priest came past. 'Good day, Pat. I'm glad to see you are driving Christians now.'

Pat looked at him. 'Maybe,' he said.

For some reason we began to talk about Robert Flaherty. 'He was very kind,' said Pat, 'and we liked him. He was simple, but herself was more of a lady.[207] She used to work the camera too, but he used to lose his temper. It's no good in flying too high; it doesn't do any good.' Pat spoke of Flaherty's temper as if it were a kind of pride.

'It must have been hard on him,' I said. 'The light is very bad here. For a photographer you may have to wait weeks for the proper light, and then if everything isn't right the whole scene or the good day is a failure.[208] I don't know how Flaherty was able to stand it. I thought he was very sensitive and understanding. In other countries light conditions in the Arctic or in the South Seas, were easy to shoot in. He must have been in a terrible state of mental excitement when there was a really good light-day in Aran.'

Most of the people knelt behind the seats on the floor in the little chapel. There was only about ten people using seats whereas most of the

'NOBODY'S BUSINESS'

people could have fitted in. The priest's Irish was not good. He had been a curate in Africa and had come home for health reasons, but the people liked him, I think. He was not strict and kill-joy like the Parish Priest.

The doctor's door opened to my knock, and I sat on a barrel. 'I'm sorry you didn't get in the other day,' he said. 'I was out at the back.' Probably he didn't want to let me in or he didn't want to let Lamb in.

'Lamb,' he said, 'was in here the other day. "I'm very hungry," he said. "Well, if you are," I said to him, "drink a few pints of porter and that will ease your hunger." I felt I have enough to cook for myself without having to cook for Charlie Lamb.' He doesn't like him much I can see.

'He was always talking about Winston Churchill's niece to me. She had stayed at his place.'

'Do you really think he was impressed or did he trot out the name to see what people would say?'

'He was impressed,' he said. 'You know that book of Gogarty's where he tries to get his own back at Joyce?'[209]

'No, I haven't read it,' I said.

'There is a scene in a pub near Holles Street and there are two medics in it, Gogarty.[210] ... Now I know ... he was in Holles Street in my time and that often makes a book interesting.[211] You read it more carefully then for it seems more real to you.'

'Did you know Gogarty?' I asked.

'Yes, I met him once. I was in McKeown's Hotel in Leenane, and I was reading a book on psychology.[212] Gogarty asked me what I was reading, and he looked at the book. "I'll send you a really good book on psychology," he said. And right enough he sent me on a book from Fannings that cost thirty shillings. That was very nice of him, but I wasn't going to let him send me an expensive book like that, *be gor*. I wrote to Fannings and found that Gogarty had paid the bill. He then wrote to me and asked if I expected him to send me a Lady Aberdeen present, and he explained it later.[213] Lady Aberdeen, whenever she stayed in your house, sent on a watch from Dublin with an engraved "Presented by Lady Aberdeen". Then by the next post you got the bill from the watch-maker.' The doctor laughed. 'So that's an Aberdeen present.'

'You are fond of pictures?' I said.

'Yes,' said the doctor, 'I am, and I have a few good pictures, which I must show you. I remember a painter stayed in this house once when I was young, and do you know who it was? Holman Hunt.'[214]

'And did he paint anything of Aran,' I asked.

'Yes, there was the head of a boy which I saw somewhere. It may have been in a gallery in Liverpool.[215] The Pre-Raphaelites were interesting,' he said.

'At least they broke up a certain complacency,' I said. 'Ford Madox Ford has written a book of memoirs in which Holman Hunt is mentioned a good deal.'[216] Lamb's wife is somehow related to Holman Hunt or to some of the Old-Raphaelite crowd.[217] Possibly a great number of painters have stayed here from time to time. I wonder if anyone has ever thought of collecting the works painted about a locality and of putting them into a gallery as an exhibition.

I looked at newspaper cuttings of boats, all sailing, which he had glued on cardboard in the shop, a boat drawn on the back of a chocolate box by a niece of his and photographs of paintings of boats. There was one boat with a peculiar stern. 'That is a Connemara boat,' he said. 'They have sterns like that, and the people in her are gathering weed. They go out a few miles from shore and use a *clachean*.[218] It's a long pole about sixteen feet long with a piece of wood on the end of it. They keep twisting it round and round and then pull it in covered with red seaweed. The women work in the boats in Connemara.'

'Do you remember about Arkin's Castle? We were talking about a cannon ball. See, here it is.' He showed me a small cannon ball.

'If you weighed it,' I said, 'I might be able to find out from a book on gunnery what weight of gun fired it.' The ball weighed two pounds and eleven ounces.

'Lamb was annoyed the other evening,' said O'Brien. 'I was talking about people who had no hair on their bodies, and then I went on to talk about homosexuals. Lamb got annoyed. "Why don't you talk about literature," he said.'

'Do you remember the day we were on the Middle Island and couldn't find Faherty. I was over there yesterday on a case, and I found he thought you were a Local Government Board Inspector and that you had come to see about his leg. I had recommended him for a pension, which he got, and he was afraid you were going to check up on him. He was near the house all the time.'

'Who were Johnston's forebears?' I asked.

'There was an old lad, O'Flaherty, and he lived in a kind of feudal way. That would be well over 100 years ago. He kept two women, but he wasn't married to them; one was an O'Reilly, ... both from Connemara, and as he had no son, he adopted a boy who had a daughter who married a Johnston from Co. Clare, a Protestant.'

I went to the steamer for two women had been expected, and we were wondering in Kilmurvey what they might be like. Rivers does not take everyone. In fact, I'm sure my coming was unusual, and she is right, for the whole household could easily be upset by one person in our midst. Phyllis and Phoebe, all dressed up, were on the pier lying on top of it. They waited outside the gangway trying to pick out people who might be the visitors. At last Phoebe decided on two. 'Oh, there they are,' she said, 'regular Chelsea.' I could not pick them out nor could Pat Hernon, but at last Pat Mullen had them to himself. One of them had a rucksack which might contain painting materials. Anne Kelly's father was on board going home. He is a dummy and so is his wife, and so are all in his leather shop.[219] That was a dreadful fate for a young girl, for Anne; now that I understood her circumstances, [it] did look as if she were deaf also. She had the straining as if she was trying to understand. No wonder she wants to go to America, but maybe living with dummies is not so bad as we think. Yet it seems a dreadful fate, to condemn a young girl to live in a house where all are deaf and dumb.

When I returned to O'Brien's, Brian was there and Pat Hernon. He had a man in a suit, and I stood him and his friend a drink. When they left, I found out that he was a guard.[220] If I had known that I said, I would not have stood him a drink. I don't like guards. All my dislike of them since the civil war coming to my mind, even though that had been blotted out by their decency since the Local Defence Force began.[221]

'He's alright,' said the doctor.

'He is not,' said Brian softly so that the doctor would not hear. Brian had run poteen often into Aran. 'The last lot I had,' he said, 'was sold to the sergeant for he bought it from another man who bought it from me.' Brian seemed to have smuggled a lot of it in his time. His pledge has gone since …[222] I saw him drink six pints of porter whilst I was in the shop, and he made me drink some whiskey, which I was afraid of doing for I was very hungry.

Two women came in to see the doctor. The younger woman had a child, wearing a shawl around her waist and long clothes.[223] … She carried a baby and wore a thick shawl. The shawl looked very handsome. 'They cost £6 now,' she said.

'And do they last long,' I asked.

'Oh, they do last long, but we don't wear them often, save going to Mass or to Galway or when on a visit. They are very heavy.' She had been three years in England and had two children. She was from the South Island. There the fishing had been good also. That island has the best fishermen. They catch ling and cod as they are nearer to the banks. There is a good deal of Clare blood in them and that seems to have improved their physique. 'They work hard, the creatures,' she said when I spoke to her of the spring fishing.

When I arrived back the other two guests were installed. I had to walk for Brian was pursuing me. Pat Hernon had arranged with himself that he should drive me back to Kilmurvey. 'When are you going back,' he asked on the pier.

'I don't know,' I said, 'and anyhow I'd just as soon walk, but I'm going to the doctor's.' I thought he would not wait for the boat went early today, but he came up to the doctor's at about 4 then left the doctor's at 6.30, and I was persuading him to go home on his outside car. Brian was feeling friendly, wanted a few more drinks, and also wanted to get me a cup of tea when he knew I was hungry. Pat Hernon again met me and asked me when I was going home. 'Not yet,' I said.

I couldn't persuade Brian to go home and Pat who followed me up on his car wanted to drive me. Lamb saved the situation for he suddenly appeared on his bicycle. He wanted to stand Pat a drink. Between Brian, who would insist out of good nature, and Hernon, who wanted to drive me or who thought he should drive me, I was in a quandary. I walked on hoping to cover as much ground as possible. I was overtaken by a Quinn girl, a nurse home on leave from England, whom Brian had given a lift to the first day I came to the Island.

Rivers said to me during tea, 'I meant to tell you that Pat Mullen and Pat Hernon drive for this house, and Brian does not, so you can please yourself. There is some difficulty now because Brian drove you the first day you came.'

'I asked him to drive me,' I said, 'as I did not know anything about your drivers. Indeed, I had to walk a good deal of the way home, which I wanted to do anyhow to avoid Brian and Pat Hernon, as both of them wanted to drive me.'

'You did right,' she said, 'that was the best way out of that difficulty.'

The two new arrivals were at the far table with Phoebe and Phyllis. One was very small. She had goldenish hair, lines on her face, quite young and was married I soon learned. She was pert. The other was middle height to tall, wore a good homespun dress and had brown eyes, a kind of sorrowful face hers. All the others seem to be getting on very well. The tall girl addressed the small one as 'Smith', the tall one was known as Cynthia.[224]

**Monday**

Mont Saint-Michel came up as we discussed France. To me it had never been interesting.[225] My imagination had been built up about it. I had imagined the soft radiance of old stone sculpture, an ease that old building has, but Mont Saint-Michel was a disappointment save for sunset and the racing tide. Rivers had felt the same about it save that she had had a moon there to soften the buildings.

'It would be best to buy and to read Henry Adams on it,' I said.[226] Brittany seemed to be associated more with her nose than with her mind. Small towns where people threw their refuse out of doors and where the harbour tide swept it away later.

'Perhaps the memory of bad smells lasts longest,' she says, 'for I was then a child.'

Rivers has some fine bawneens with printed patterns on them. Someone, a friend of hers, stayed here and made a few of them.[227] 'No. They're not very difficult,' she said. Helen would perhaps like to try her hand at that.[228] They would [make] excellent hangings or drapery and would sell well, I should think. It would be an outlet for her and more creative than making curtains and hangings.

Smith is chirpy still. She has a pert abrupt way of speaking and of moving. 'They're strange in shops,' she said, 'the way they talk in front of you as if you weren't there. I went into a shop in Rathmines, and I could hear them discussing me, two men, as I stood in front of them out of the corner of their mouth.[229] It's disgusting.'

'It's certainly not an Irish habit that I know of.'

I hear Phoebe and Phyllis on the quay at Kilronan talking about a young child from the South Island as they stood beside her. 'She's enchanting. How divine.' 'She's simply exquisite, such good taste,' and so on as if the child or her mother had no existence apart from being a subject of their admiration. English people are more inclined to gush and to sentimentalize in public at full lung sound.

The brown-eyed lady, also married, Cynthia, is quieter and nicer. All now call each other by their Christian names: Jordan is James, Pat Mullen is Pat, his son, P.J. and B.R. is Betty Rivers. I am the only unnamed familiar for I am 'Mr'. However, I can survive that.

The girl who looks after the baby is Julie. She is a pretty looking girl from Gort na Gopple and is about 16.[230] 'Her father wouldn't let her leave the island,' said Rivers, 'and he's right. She's too good looking. She has been here two months and in that short time has learned English which she did not know before she came here. She is very quick and intelligent, and I am sure is capable of learning and of learning well, for nothing can be done with such girls when they are 20 or 21.'

I went to see two of the women who get work done for Rivers. One was Mrs MacDonagh, Patch Fada's wife who lived at [the] first bohereen beyond the schoolhouse.[231] The other was Naneen, Mrs Mullen of Onaght. The weather held fine, but the light was dull. The sea was calm, and the Connemara shore veiled in a mist. Mrs MacDonagh spoke English very well, a grey-haired very pleasant woman, but excited she seemed when she heard I wanted a jersey. She had no grey wool spun, and just now she was working on jerseys for the young ladies. 'Did they want them soon or were they going to leave in a hurry?'

She brought out a cap rounded and studded with bobbelins.[232] 'These bobbelins is very hard to make,' she said, 'and the indigo is difficult too. It takes a long time, and it's best in the hot weather.' Did I want bobbelins?

'No, I don't want bobbelins because the pattern was just as good without them.'

'Anyhow they're new,' she said. 'I don't know what they all want bobbelins for.' She called, 'Gerleen, Gerleen.'[233] 'She's a very good worker,' she said.

Rivers had told me about her. 'The girl has no dowry and looks meek,' she said, 'but when she gets talking to other girls she's lively.' 'Gerleen' came out. She had nondescript fair hair, a reddish loose dress and a beaten expression. She took down measurements from Patch Fada's wife: forty inches for chest, outside the elbow, inside the elbow, then the head of one of their tams which are warm in winter – thirty inches.[234] 'Why that's the same as the little girl. I must measure for you again.'

'Imagine if he knew, "Patch Fada",' said his wife, as if it were a secret name. To her husband, a fine man with a good eagle beak of a nose. 'He has Irish.'

'No. I have no Irish,' I said, 'but I understand a little.' They have the same sense of the secrecy of their names as they have on the West road.[235] There everyone laughs when I talk of 'William a Brick' or 'Jim Vrdóg'.[236]

'Oh, you know them well,' they'd say, as if it were a great secret.

Naneen was an old woman with grey hair.[237] She wore a black shawl and was winding wool. The kitchen was full of men so evidently a kind of parliament is held there in the evening. She showed me some crisses. None of them were of the right colour: one was homespun so I chose that one, but I had no money. 'I will bring you over some money in a few days' time,' I said. We chatted with the group for a while, but it was a forced talk. They made no effort to help me out, and when there was a silence I had to draw out words again to keep what little of talk there was going.

There is a new wall around the Seven Churches out of keeping with its ancient appearance.[238] The stones are broken on top so that the new limestone glints blue and shows up against the old grey of unbroken and rounded stones. It has not served much of a useful purpose for twenty sheep were quietly grazing inside. Nettles were thick, the place had a neglected look. The old cross with the Greek fret stood upright, two pieces of cross lay on top of a wall. Inside the best church someone had used both grass and chalk to outline early crosses and had left the ugly marks of handiwork behind. Whether this was an idle change or not I did not know, but some people mark this before they take photographs.

An old woman came up to me with a criss in her hand. '*Sé pscillyngi,*' she said, six shillings.[239]

'It is too small,' I said.

'*Sé scillinge,*' she said. I tried to remember the word for wool but couldn't. I asked her by pointing to the edge of the criss. She said it was homemade, the *crios* was, but certainly the wool was not. She wanted to give it to me, and said I could pay her another day, but I didn't want to take the criss with me for it was both too short and made from shop wool. Again she offered the criss and said I could pay her another day.

A tall ladder of a man was puttying under my window when I got back so I talked to him as I wrote. He had a hawk nose and a fine humorous mouth. 'Potatoes,' he said, 'up to date are the most of them we plant and some of them gets Banners too, but they aren't much good for eating.' Where he spoke of the Government, he referred to it as 'he'. He did not think much of the Government on account of what Pat Mullen had said to me, 'They talk about the Gaeltacht and then offer a price which is far below a living wage, and I wouldn't mind if they hadn't so much talk about trying to help the districts that spoke Irish.'

£4.10 a ton was the highest price for the best grade of kelp last year, then £2.10 for the lowest kind. It takes something like thirty tons of wrack to make a ton of kelp 'and there's great labour in that,' said Pat. They weren't satisfied with what the Inspector said about a price, besides when they send on a sample from here it may be two months before a reply comes back as to the value of that kelp, and if a man has to wait that length to find out whether it will pay him or not, he has lost the two months that he might have been getting ready for more wrack if his first sample paid him.

James Johnston then got in touch with a man he knew in Galway. 'He'd never had anything to do with seaweed or kelp before, but I said to him there's a good market here if you can offer £5.10 a ton for kelp irrespective of its merit.' When the Government man heard of that he went wild at the idea of the islanders selling to an outsider after all his trouble for he probably had made an outside contract himself and wanted to fulfil it. Anyhow the Inspector raged and abused, but the islanders got good money for once.

'What money would really pay you for a ton of kelp?' I asked Pat.

'About £9 or £10,' he said. As the tall one, with the humorous mouth, said, 'You may be working a week in bad weather, and you couldn't get much out of her.'

Johnston is selling kelp for manure just now. I don't know what he gets per ton, or how much he has sent away, but it is mixed with some phosphates from crushed rocks in Clare, as Judge Cummins's output is under contract. Nitrogen, phosphates and potash are the three important fertilizers. Now, the rods [of kelp] contain potash and seaweed contains nitrogen which disappears when the weed is burned. Potash can be done without, but nitrogen and phosphates cannot.

*Annie Hernon knitting close to a cottage hearth, 1952.*

'NOBODY'S BUSINESS'

Flax was once grown on this island, but I have not learned anything about it or what amount of it was grown. Hay I found drying, being placed on top of the walls instead of leaving it into small cracks. Oats or rye they lean against the wall in single sheaves.

Naneen seems to do most of the knitting as most of the knitters, mentioned by Patch Fada's wife, were Naneen's. 'It was Miss Power put me first on to the jerseys,' said Naneen.[240] 'Did you ever meet her?'

'Yes, I met her, and I bought one of her dolls,' I said.

'Did you now,' said Naneen, delighted. 'It was myself made all the clothes for them, but it didn't at all pay me, and since that I knit caps too.' She evidently began her new kind of rounded cap for Miss Power. If I had Helen's measurement I could send her one, but I don't want to take a guess at random for the caps should fit accurately.

'Was she excited,' asked Rivers, when I told her I had called on Patch Fada's Naneen.

'Indeed, she was,' I said.

'She was in the Show in Dublin,' said Rivers, 'and people all around talked as if she wasn't there and said her costume was a fake and wasn't worn at all.[241] That is because they never come here in winter. The costume is worn by all to keep out the cold. Naneen was very ashamed and wanted to come back home.'

**Tuesday**

As I was writing I was told there was a Fr Quinn outside to see me. He had met Anne Kelly who had referred him to me as having an interest in archaeology.

'I was looking for a *bollán*[242] this morning up at Teampall Mhic Dharaigh.[243] I wonder do you know anything about it as I can interpret it.'

'I did not know that a *bollán* needed interpretation.' Then he told me in a rush of words that he was searching for certain types of crosses, which followed papal orders as to the way in which a cross should be made at different times. He was able to interpret divisions into fifes ... . Then he went into the ancient way of dividing the host in pieces, five pieces, the priest eating the central portion so that quern stones could represent a host.[244] The bosses on stone and metal crosses had a symbolical meaning and a numbered symbolism.

'For instance the Cross of Tuam is ninth century for there they used a boss under and over the outstretched hands.'[245]

'I make it out from its sculpture to be of the twelfth century,' I said.

'Oh, that's a mistake,' he said, 'and MacAlister and others fall into that mistake.[246] It's really the ninth century.'

'So you don't believe in the development of sculpture. Are you interested in sculpture?' I asked.

'No, I'm not,' he said.

'Well then,' said I, 'we'll leave the matter rest.'

He had been to the out islands, *Cruach Na Cara*, Mason Island where he had photographed a cross with a Christ's head on it and to High Island where he had landed twice.[247] It's a pity that there cannot be some kind of coordination. He should take notes on sculpture. I would certainly take notes on symbolism if I knew what was needed.

'I saw Dr Coffey,' he said. 'I'm an old Royal man, and I wanted to write a paper for my MA, but they would not accept it.'[248]

'You find it hard to penetrate Coffey's head with anything he does not want. But didn't he give Henry Ford an honorary degree? Why don't you demand you get work done on symbolism.'

He has swallowed the *Stowe Gospel* whole, as far as I could see, and quotes large sections of it at ease.[249] He objected to Imperialists being in charge of Institutions. 'Take the National Library,' he said, 'there was a manuscript there, and there was a gap. I suggested the words missing, and Bert and MacAlister would not accept them, but a violet lamp came on and they used it on the worn places and right enough I was only one letter wrong. They congratulated me, but Bert said to me afterwards, "Are you going to publish your finding; if so [don't] do it for three years."'

'What did he mean by that?' I said.

'He is a scholar alright, but he kept source material of recent events unrecorded and has done nothing with 1847 and 1848 material, and it is only now that it is being catalogued. There was a professor to whom I lent my manuscript, and he said when he lectured he would acknowledge my findings but he didn't. It was published in the paper that I suggested certain things, and people would say that I was stealing his ideas, so I wrote a letter to the paper and contradicted the paper report.'

'The scholars, or pseudo-scholars, seem very thin-skinned to me,' I said.

'Why they aren't glad when someone discovers something in their field [I] don't know?'

'And so it's you who uses the chalk,' I said.[250] 'That's a nefarious habit.'

'It helps to bring out the photograph,' he said, 'besides, it's not faking.'

'It would be in sculpture,' I said. 'You left a stick of chalk behind you in the Seven Churches so I expect everyone will have a go at it now to imitate you.'

'Did you see what the Parish Priest did at Killeany?'

'Don't blame him,' he said. 'Charity, you know. He did his best. If all parish priests took an interest in archaeology, the people would have respect for remains.'

'I don't argue with you,' I said. 'He has cemented pieces of two different crosses together, all three pieces being in safe hands up to then. He has placed the cross where it can't be properly seen, and he has placed it inside a building instead of out in the open.'

'And the altar,' he said, 'did you see that?'

'I did,' I said. 'To me that was funny to have Arkin's Castle vomit up its unecclesiastical stone.'

'He meant well,' he said.

'That's a great book,' he said, '*Saints and Shrines of Aran Mór.*[251] Do you know it?'

'I do,' I said, 'but the RSAI has better information.'

'That's what I'm going on,' he said. I did not say anything, but I felt he could miss a deal of material that way. He is anxious not to be influenced by other people's conclusions, which is good, but he should very definitely know where all his material can be found. However, he has visited islands that are seldom visited. Ard Orlean for instance on which landing is not only difficult but risky.[252] Even Françoise Henry had not been on it.[253] He has been some years in Ireland but has not read her books.

'I met her once,' he said, 'and I explained my theory to her. She did not seem interested. I thought then she might be a friend of MacAlister in the National and did not want to encourage anyone to go against their opinions.'

'No. I think she would have an open mind. She is very careful and capable,' I said, 'and about the best of them all.'

Out of a clear sky he said as Mrs Keats came into the room, 'I don't want to boast, but I found a method of focusing antiaircraft guns quickly on a target. When they are aligned on the ground first they miss the target by a little. When you swing them up and sight and though that angle is small, it makes a great difference when you fire. And I have learned to use a new method when shooting,' he said. 'I hope you will pardon me for talking about such things being a priest, but I shoot a lot of rabbit. Do you see those beams there,' he said pointing to the roof. 'Well, if you call out any one of them, I will swing this pencil round as if it was a gun and I will be deadly accurate on it.' Phoebe selected a beam and he sighted on it.[254]

# 2

# *Inisheer, Aran Islands, August 1955*

Women.[1] [2] This place is a matriarchy says Seán Keating, but how does one recognize that aspect of it? The women stay indoors and the girls, he says, but when I go West there are a woman, a man and a boy working in a rye field. The man pulls the rye up by the roots, and when it has been stood for a while against the wall, it is then put in a kind of round sheaf. With them was a boy. Another day I saw two girls, a tall boy and a young boy, in a field working at the rye. The rye seed is kept until the following year and planted then. The crop is pulled up by hand out of a sandy soil. Indeed, here on the roads which are fairly level, the seeds of docks turn brown red showing at least that fields have been weeded.[3]

This absence of women is important enough. Only occasionally does one see a red skirt, that of an elderly woman, when the steamer comes in on Wednesday or Saturday.[4] Occasionally a few girls of about 15 or 17 sit on the strand but only when the boat is due. A few young girls normally wander about the strand, from 5 to 7 or 10, and an odd woman may bring down an ass for turf to the pier, but the bulk of women are absent save at Mass on Sunday.

*Seán Keating*, Two Girls waiting by harbour for hooker

Mass. Here there is a Mass at 8.30. We are called at 7.40, without hot water for my shaving. No fire is lighted for I can smell the oily smell of paraffin when I return due perhaps to be a burner being used. Some men sit around before Mass, but the women go in directly after waiting for twenty minutes for Mass to begin. The tiny seats are close together so that long legs must be swung to one side and kneeling is a kind of trapeze act for the kneeling form comes out more than half way cutting the shin bone which has to use it, not the roughened knee cap.[5] The shunting process is carried on from the outside. Nobody stands up for anybody else but shunts along from the outside. A seat holds six grown men, and as they kneel one notes their broad shoulders. On the right, young girls in front, 5 to 8, in bright dresses, young boys in grey homespun and white sweaters. The neck is not rolled but is buttoned, and on Sundays the trousers is worn long nearly to the ankle. Next comes visitor women and later boys in black sweaters or black wool blouses rolled back at the neck in a fold, behind the neck. [Men in] *braideen* waistcoat, bluish grey or grey blue over a blue sweater and trousers of *braideen* then heavy socks or pampooties.[6] The socks have a pattern of white at times on the toes and they are strongly built. On the left, women beginning near the altar with black shawls and then the grey brown shawl or the brown speckled shawl further down. Girls with long hair tied with ribbons. None of the girls, old or young, wear anything on their heads. The men at the end kneel on the floor or throw themselves down on their knees and elbows prostrate at times or squat during the sermon. The sermon takes about twenty minutes so that Mass lasts fifty minutes as a rule.

Nobody leaves before Mass is finished, then the right hand side comes out first then the women's side. Then men, mostly the young men, watch the crowd pass out, but on the second Sunday I noticed that the men from the two western villages went home as soon as Mass was finished. When Mass is finished, the priest goes over to the Middle Island where he says Mass. On Sunday the men, a group of them, gather on the rocks near the sea shore, and in good weather some boys, old and young, bathe from the rocks, but I do not know if any of them can swim.[7] The women do not come down on the shore on a Sunday, and I doubt if any of them fish.

Currachs. Currachs are kept some distance up in between a surround of upright stones forming up a rectangle. As there was no flush of fish this year, I did not see any real catch of mackerel, but one evening at 9, I counted nine boats about a half a mile from the shore. Usually each boat had three men, and the most aft man looked after the lines. In most boats there is no bailer, no sod of turf or tar for emergencies and often a leak through lack of thought. A piece of canvas stuck in with a piece of stick or a broken ... to keep it in place. The men are more careful about their boat landings when they fish as they lift it in out of the water, put it up on one side, a man gets in under near the bow and then the other two get under and plod upwards. But when the steamer comes in, boats are often pushed ashore ... and this can be severe on the tarred canvas, and they are usually put ashore with the stern inmost.

The [fishing] line we used had a spinner at one end, a piece of bone through which the line went, then another line further up and the weight before it. Then there was a hand grip beyond which the line did not go. One keeps it clear of the gunnel on high water for the proper turn of the spinner or the sudden pull of the mackerel. The spinner or bare hook used at first, then the mackerel skins.

I asked Coley about his bitumastic.[8] Could it be used on the canvas [for currachs]?[9] He did not know. It had never been used. It seems to me it would give colour and variety of colour, but it would not be as cheap. In all cases the strakes are not painted. In a few currachs green paint is used on the top strakes but not on the bottoms: nine [strakes] to a round. This means a deal of nails, copper nails, but boat nails for the oars. There is no method by which fish can be carried in [from the currach] save by holding on to their gills with a finger.

P.J. Mullen came in with a policeman in his white Cornish boat, said by him to cost £1,100. He has been fishing hard, doing without sleep as he has, I expect, to gut the fish. He is trying to collect lobsters regularly, but the last time he picked them up, they had been five weeks in the pots, and, he says, three to five dozen of them were dead. He would like to collect them weekly. Then Cormac and I had best put out a pot each, then the islanders, being jealous, will rush out with their pots so that you have a chance. Five shillings is now the price of a crayfish. I must say that it is good to see P.J. busy.

Turf Boats. Every day when the wind is East the turf boats come in.[10] The turf price is now £17.10, and at Kilronan it is £15.10, so they say here. Kilronan is eight miles away or nine but on the tack I expect the addition could be six or seven miles.[11] This year the turf has been well dried. The Connemara men buy a lorry of turf, put some of it by to make a boat from the accumulations, and then they pack the turf into the hold [of the turf boat], a small space in the centre and aft on top of the deck. Also, thirty donkey creels to a boat load.

*Maurice MacGonigal,* Unloading Turf, Kilmurvey Pier, Inishmore, *c.1954.*

When the turf boat is a mile away, a currach goes out to bargain, and the currach is held on by hand or tied while the bargaining goes on. The price is, I understand, the same in all cases, but the bargaining must go on. Turf is thrown up by hand, three men usually on the boat and one of the buyers. When the wind is too much North/East, the turf boat is afraid of the rocks, and it leaves full. There is another place, sandy ground, around the Eastern point at … and I have seen turf landed from a currach on the strand while the turf boat was at anchor.[12] About four turf boats can unload in a day, but the turf has then to be withdrawn to leave more room. It can be piled up against the wall near the woodside edge or asses and horses can carry it away. This is a time for the young children. Men or boys sit side saddle on the rump of their asses or horses, but when they come across this strand from the village … the boys do not sit up [on the asses], so as to spare their beasts. Thirty loads then means sixty journeys, each single double journey is one and a half miles to two miles, say two miles, thirty times two equals sixty miles. That would work out at thirty miles a day as it takes two days to bring home the turf. Also, in that time it has to be lifted up and then stacked at the other end. Simultaneously a trawler comes out from Connemara to pick up the dried sea rods which are shrivelled on the pier.[13] They are thrown down into the currach and piled up, then the currach takes ... the material to the trawler anchored about a half mile or so away out in front of the strand. It seems a waste of the islanders' time.

The steamer. No respect for the islanders is the usual term. When a coffin came out from Galway with the mother from the house to the South of us, the coffin was not landed until 5 o'clock. The *Dun Aengus* goes first to Kilronan, disembarks passengers and goods, then makes for the South Island where it remains about an hour. Then to the Middle Island where the pier is being built and where there should be at times a longer wait. This steamer calls twice each week; once in the winter on Wednesdays. When the steamer smoke appears around the corner of the Middle Island long point, people begin to move down. They sit on the sand and await the spectacle. Once there was a busy Wednesday ... as the Legion of Mary had invaded the Big Island, and five or six currachs brought in passengers. On the next day nine currachs were ready to jostle for position at the loading sides of the steamer. In rough weather it is difficult to get down into the currach, and in winter the steamer often fails to lower either passengers or material into the currachs. This Wednesday 17th [August] there was a big crowd on the strand of local people in groups of ages. A fine crowd of five girls with jet black hair. Near them two flaxen haired girls whom I had seen working at [the] rye; the visitors, separate or together; boys in groups also.

Currachs. All are three oared (six oars) here, but I notice the currach builder is making [a] four oared currach with thirty-eight holes for the cross lathes – but nine of the holes are in the bow. The stern is not tipped up but looks to be flat and up; only forward at the twenty-ninth hole [strake] does the prow use the canvas overlap outside, but how much it does overlap I could not gather, and it is very well tarred. I must go down again there to take further observations. The wood at the seat corners is pretty twisted and is all of one piece.

The delay in the steamer not coming first to the small islands is due, as Seán Keating says, to the Parish Priest, Fr [Thomas] Varley.[14] He is not popular but is also fond of money. Fr [Thomas] Killeen is revered here by everyone and missed. The Captain, from the steamer point of view, cannot leave Galway until 9 as if it left at 8 no breakfasts would be served in the town. On the steamer cups of tea, biscuits and bread and butter are sold. Also now a bar to one side served by a lad in clean whites from the Railway Hotel. When the time comes for the barman to close, he closes down without any preliminary notice. People have to wait in line for their tea. There is no other type of food. If one wants to go to the Middle Island, one may leave Galway at 9, arrive Kilronan in fine weather at 1.30, leave it at 2.30 or 3, arrive South Island at 4, leave at 5 or 5.15, arrive at Middle Island at 5.30, leave at 6.30, reach Kilronan at 7 or 7.15 and leave for the city at 9. Not a very agreeable prospect as regards food, but the smart young man who serves at the bar rings when the steamer is on the way in.

Hunting. Seán Keating who has been coming here for forty years told me about them. 'The first day I came here,' he said after tea, at about 8 pm, 'that I would go out shooting. O'Flaherties is about half a mile away,' he said. I went with him but the distance increased for he went as far as the other shore. His quest – rabbits, oystercatchers, curlews. 'Rabbits do not come out in the mist,' he said. The mist became thicker as he went to the South/West shore where three-ton boulders have been driven up by seas. On the way back we went up another path way which became almost thigh narrow. It was strong under foot. The broad wood had disappeared. Boulders at stray angles stuck up as we walked. He turned. 'We're on the wrong road,' he said. I was some distance behind in the mist. 'I'll go back again to the crossroads, and then I'll find the road while there's light,' but by this it was close to 10 o'clock. I, in the meantime, searched around for a cow shelter in case we would have to spend the night there, but at last he found the road and off we wandered.

The O'Flaherties. It was then that he told me about the O'Flaherties. Every kind of person came to the Big Island as an expert, and O'Flaherty was very impressed with experts as he was an uneducated man. He was very generous, and Pat Mullen was a kind of supervisor who, being anxious to look after his own interests, was unlikely to take too much of an interest in those who came in to make use of the O'Flaherties. [17]

Coley in the morning is brought out by me to diagnose the weather. If the wind is South or South/West then there may be rain, but the tide may tell if the wind is gusty. That all makes for rain as well as the high tides when the tide goes out. North and North/East are steady enough but were at times wild. South/West wind can be warm even in the winter. The Westerly wind these days, August 18/19, West, steady, does not make for rain. Keating looks for the clouds beneath for they are the rain bringers. So far Coley has been sure enough.

Crops. Potatoes are bad here, soft and veiny almost, while on the Big Island they were good and floury. Keating says they do not change the seed. Year after year the same seed. ... Coley tells me that an agreement with a man in the Big Island gives them fresh seed each year. This year, however, the onions have failed, and they were a new special kind of onion sent by the Agriculture man.[15] So we do not know why. So, Cormac and I suffer. Onions should grow well in sandy soil. This year there was a blight which they had not seen (even before) or for a long time. Carrots do not grow big here, nor do peas grow. I wonder then what does best in sandy soil.

Today I saw a little boy come up the road towards me as I was going back for tea. He scurried away back, and when I rounded the corner I saw him hiding in the distance with another boy. The children are very shy indeed. Often when I come to a girl of 9 or 10, she is too shy to whisper the reply in Irish. The grown boys are shy.

I have only once or twice seen a man smoke here, then a cigarette. They smoke a little in the pub. The women do not smoke, though the old women smoke. And so their wants are reduced. The young men drink pints in the pubs, Keating said, to show they are men for they make money building walls, making quarter acres, work on the roads, fishing, gathering sea rods at £4 a ton. That is easier work than the sea weed which needs to be turned.

Keating, the hunter, may bring back a curlew or a rabbit, or oyster-catcher. He sets off at 9 o'clock with his gun or 8.30. One evening he brought in three oystercatchers, beautiful slim birds with long reddish feet and a ring of red around their eyes. They run from rock to rock on the sea or keep out on points. He stalked this group by going out hidden on a shelf of rock and then when they saw him, they came back in, and he fired with No. 3. I often came across curlews myself and terns. In bad weather [other birds] come in diving near the shore.

The lobsters and crabs are fed regularly. Men gut the fish which they catch, clean them thoroughly, cut off the heads and throw them into the [holding] pots. These are circular as are the French pots. Stones [are] tied inside of them. Who taught them to make the circular pots?

Currachs. Nine [in the] East [village], two at Boat House, and twenty-one on the strand.

Horses. They are on the Commons, a sandy stretch, but they suffer from gravel.[16] To [eat or] pick the horse uses its lips first and nuzzles around the grass, but how their stomachs stand it is another matter. Today,

Sunday, I saw horses as I went over to the lake, one a very fine dapple grey. They went down to the lake, walked in amid the green slime and nuzzled the water.[17] They did not drink for long. There is now dried salt on the edge. A good number of birds, swallows, sea swifts and black tipped seagulls come here, and it seems water hens, but I could not be sure.

In the lake the women from the … [Castle] village[18] wash clothes, and the Dane catches eels.[19] I saw him at Mass the first Sunday, a nice-looking lad with long beard, full beard rather. He has a two-oared currach. He fishes in the lake for eels, and he keeps them alive there in a container. Recently he went to the mainland to see if he could dispose of his eels, but as he came back on the 20th [August] I do not yet know the result. He wanted to become a Catholic here years ago, but the priest, without instruction, could not receive him. His mother, a Lutheran, objected, but he came back again, received instruction, became a Catholic and now he lives here.

Fish. The people will not eat eels, but they will eat conger eels which are of two kinds, the black – in among the rocks – and the white, much larger further out, or vice versa. These are salted and are good to eat. The rock fish and gurnet have bones, but the bream is the fish which all eat and like. They catch another fish, blue-fish, a great big one which will bite on a turtle … but that is no good to eat. Eels lie quiet in the currach if you don't keep shifting your feet away from them, but they will get out of the currachs by their tails, and if they bite there is a small grip forward in their mouth which if cut gives them no grip. But if they bite, they close and keep the grip closed.

The fish taken by the trawler decays quickly or that taken in the net so that net mackerel or rock fish does not last as long as any of the line fish. Blood helps a fish to last even when it is salted. They have never eaten 'sea pig' or *muca mara* or porpoise though they ate it in Kerry.[20] Mackerel, a lump of, is the bait for eels.

Wells. There is at least one well with a pump, but the best well is down on the sea shore, but the water comes into it. There are no shelving tanks as on the Big Island where they have been for thirty years, but they would need them at the South and South/West end of the land.[21] They have wells, they say, in other spots on the island.

Here then, as they pay no rates, the Government supports them: £5 for each child, £ … for a certain depth of well, £60 for making an acre of ground. They have subsidy help, £490 this year for a bit of a sea wall near the Quay, payment for roads.

*Elizabeth Rivers,* Seaweed Harvest, Aran Islands

Kelp. Kelp they can pick for themselves, rather sea rods which they sell when dried at £4 a ton. It is collected when there is a surge or when a rough sea breaks off the stalks. This has now been happening in the West along the minor cliffs. Lads carry up the rods fling them up on high, spread them out for a few days on the rocks, then raise them on low built up lines of rock to dry when thrown across it. Then the ass can carry the burden, I expect. Here also were cocks of seaweed with stone walls around them drying away.[22] One big cock, blackish looking, thirteen yards in circumference and seven to eight feet high. Next is a pier to be built 120 feet out in the sea, twice as far out as the present pier. I expect that will allow them to land all their turf and permit a boat to come there at any tide, but I expect the *Dun Aengus* will not come there save on a fine day.

The last day was fine, and many people landed. I expect the small islands could take more visitors if the steamer came first to them. The steamer was not due to come first on the 20th [Saturday, August] but the low tide at Kilronan made it awkward. What tourists need is good tea with cakes on board, rashers and eggs, salads or most of all sandwiches for if one leaves at 9 am, one arrives in the Middle Island at 6 and in the

East Island at 4 pm. Then they [have] no new facilities in the Big Island for trippers. Anyhow the *Dun Aengus* is an old dangerous steamer which could be seriously injured if it grounded in a heavy sea. The woodwork is rotten as can be proved with a knife. Years ago, two perhaps, there was an account in the *Irish Press* of the new boat, but I understand that she has not yet been laid down.[23]

Fishing. Often there are ten or thirteen currachs out in front of the strand in the evening for mackerel, then again a few set off early in the morning for the Cliffs of Moher for rock fish. Morning and evening the currachs go out to the lobster pots. If a conger eel comes into the pots nothing else will come in, but it will not mind the lobster if it is inside. Cormac says that crawfish are found out towards the light house to the South. The day's sea work there varies. Three months with the turf boats which come often five or six a day, but their head wind is West or South/West, but they do not like the period of surge or the wind East and North, when the rise of sea sways the boats anchored at the pier.

The groups on the strand are interesting when the *Dun Aengus* comes in, especially when after a high tide the strand is sloped upwards sharply and keenly. Again, it is a question of age groups. A few men, a few grown boys, young lads together, young girls 16–18, 12–13, 6–8, grouping in line seated at the back to the West currachs. During low tides currachs are close enough to the sea, but these days they are high up. In winter higher still and then tied down by ropes firmly to keel there in position in from the winds.

It seems that winter is the working period, preparing land for rye and potatoes and the few vegetables, making land by bringing up sand either in one sack across an ass's back or in two small boxes carrying, I expect, two hundredth weight of sand, about 300 of them to an acre, says Coley, but the amount of seaweed to be placed on top is not so much.[24] I expect the walls are built this time of year. During the [First World] War there was fishing. Sean Conneely … I expect had the control of exporting fish. But then there were no trawlers on the outreach so that the fish were left at peace for a while. The Spanish trawlers seem to carry a good deal of wine, a bitter yellow wine, a red wine and sherry which they used to sell, but of course *sub rosa*.

The groups on the strand reminded me of Degas, his Lane picture in England, of the people against the strand.[25] Mrs Holbrook, on Inishmore, rather a Yank, who paints, made use of herself in a way by talking of painting in regard to the landscape. I asked her to take a photograph of the rock at the foot of the Castle. For over half a mile of ground they have ivy-coated walls on top, twelve to fifteen feet high, but the forms being somewhat rounded they stand out at intervals like a defensive base with towers. Further up about eighty feet or more, there is an area of grass or stone and standing back the cliff rock rises again in another series of fortifications, again rounded at intervals. This recession takes place at about 7.30 in the evening due to the slanting sunlight. Above, the Castle stands against a sky at night sometimes golden below shows on the rocks, to the South/East warm green, limpid green, softly glowing in the evening sun against the blue black hard stone, but for the most part the stone on the shore to the West is limestone, pitted grotted rocks with sharp torn caverns and then a further layer of hard rock on a slight cliff as one moves to the West. Now and then a granite boulder.

The best fields seem to gather around the lake in the hollow, where there is shelter from West winds. North/East winds and the lake itself with its four swans would be beautiful at the edges save for the green verge of slime, twenty to thirty feet out on the West and East side. One day as I lay to the South, I heard a kind of dipping noise as if there was a splashing, but I found it was due to seabirds dipping their beaks in the water. The pool itself is brackish and communicates with the sea.

Is there a rain measurement kept? Maybe at the lighthouse. Anyhow it would be interesting to know what the rainfall is as it seems to be less than on the mainland. Rain, I expect, passes over to strike the mountains, the Cliffs of Moher, and the stone fortress of Burren. I do not know what is the worst month here, but I expect February–March as the West is rough, stormy, and blowy. Yet the water, they say, is not bad here.

In a dense heat fog, not really a fog but denseness in the sky, and for a mile out to sea, heavy, slight even at times, then warm from a due East wind, the mackerel came in. Seventeen currachs out at sea. Coley came in with mackerel, but I took one out of the currach, and I brought it in for I was an hour late for tea.

A very strong smell of sea along the shore today. Keating's story of the German in Ireland talking to two policemen. He had bad English, but they persevered.

'Are you married,' asked one.

'Yes?'

'And are you long married?'

'Six years.'

'And have you any children?' he said.

*A young woman spinning, Aran Islands, c. 1952.*

'Not one.'

'Oh,' said the guard in disappointment.

'My wife,' he said, 'is what you call unbearable.'

'Well,' said one policeman to the other, 'what he means is she's impregnable.'

'Oh,' said the other policeman, 'that's not the right word. I know well what he means.'

'Now, wait a moment, he means she's inconceivable.'

Keating's other story [was] of the Limerick priest. He was an easy priest, evidently and his [pews] were always crowded. This night there were hardly any at the other [confessional] boxes, but his clientele stretched across the church. Then suddenly he put his hand on the door, stuck out his head of the box, looked at the crowd and shook his head, and as he turned to go back into his box, he said, 'and you say he's mad about you, that's what you tell me'.

The Spanish mackerel which they say they can't eat can be eaten and is or was accounted as worth 2/6 in London in 1904 so that goes for fish which is inedible.[26] I suppose also they think crab can't be eaten. They put it out for bait for their lobster pots, throw it on the sand and then, I expect, bring along bits of it in their currachs. I saw an elderly man, who Cormac well knows, on the strand today. He had a cat-fish. It looks to be of the shark family as does the dog-fish, but it has spots on it, light grey with spots. Its head was cut off and given to the lobster pot, but the remainder of it wriggled on the ground. It would wriggle for about another twenty-four hours, he told me.

Cormac and I went with Miss Gleeson and Mrs Holbrook to see one of the sewers who weaves jerseys. She has been having blue jerseys knitted blue bright, but the islanders wear a heavier and a darker wool as heavy on their two strand whites. The woman in this house hardly made any measurements, took them, I mean, although I asked how to take them, but she made a few perfunctory gestures. The island boys do not use the wool sweaters, and they use a more simple form, buttons at the top. This a very much lighter sweater than Cormac's which is indeed very heavy when compared to them. Here there were two children, a beautiful fair-haired girl of about 8–10 and a wonderful two-year-old boy.

Another day I went off with the same two ladies to see a Conneely girl, but I found she was the daughter of the old man who had lost an eye.

# 3

# Inisheer, Aran Islands, 10–29 August 1956

It was raining when we crossed the Shannon, and as we neared Athenry [Co. Galway]. We could see the ground deep in water in certain fields as if the rain had been pounding for days. Near Galway as we passed the last inthrust of sea, close to the railway station, the tide roared in in a sweep under the bridge as if it were a mill race. I supposed all of this land under sea near Galway would have been reclaimed by the Dutch in their country, but here, where we do not work the land we have, why make trouble with more land.

Galway, where we missed what few taxis there were as we were at the end of the train and came out also by the main entrance door, meant a walk in the rain. I brought my rucksack and a small parcel, a shoulder bag while Cormac had his heavy bag and my light brown case to carry down to the hotel.[1]

We had the same room as we had occupied last year, No 17, at the very top of the house; a good climb of four stairs up.[2] The outer door opened on to a small platform which gave a back view of Galway. Cormac and I had a double bed. 'I suppose you'll pull the [bed] clothes off me as usual,' he said. Evidently, I pull the clothes off him at night. The next single bed would have another occupant. Last year the young American who was at

Oxford stayed there when we returned from Inisheer.[3] He wanted to pay less for his bed than the ordinary, Mrs Ryan had told me. When I went downstairs, she said, 'Do you remember Mr [Selig], the American who was here with you last year. Well, he married Miss O'Hara, and he was here since. He married her on a Monday, sat for his exam on Tuesday, and then left for the States.' She was a good harpist, who made an impression at the last Edinburgh Festival and was doing alright, I understand, on Radio Éireann.

As we went out to eat it rained, and it had become heavier when we walked down town so that my corduroy trousers was very wet under my Sou'wester rain coat. One trouble about corduroys is they keep the wet for some time and are uncomfortable to wear unlike wool when wet.

### Saturday, 11 August 1956

By good luck the butcher was able to leave down our bags at the steamer. That saved us the shouldering of our luggage. Railway fare had again gone up as had meals on the train, two eggs, bread, and tea cost 4/3 which seemed unnecessary, and the steamer fare was now 27/6, an increase for the return of 2/6.

I did not put on my sweater, but I had my duffel coat, which indeed was needed. The weather became rougher as we passed out of Galway Bay. There is very inadequate shelter. On the lower deck waves which came in the ferry's course broke against the side and spattered over somewhat, but when the rain began the shelter on that deck could only protect about ten people. Above the people sheltered in the narrow passage between the life boats or in the cabin but a number were sick. They were as usual very inadequately clothed. Girls in light frocks, often without raincoats. What one needs is a sweater or heavy cardigan and a strong coat to help to break the wind. Sea air is usually cooler than the land air and on the return journey, if people go out for the day, they do not get in until 10 or 11 at night. By that time it is dark and cool.

A group of Dublin boys and girls on the top deck sat with their backs to the division boards from the hold, and sang songs in unison.[4] Four of the boys belonged to some city choir and that explained their range of voice, their orchestration, and their variety of songs. There should be, I think, a leaflet on board giving information about the Aran Islands for the travellers by boat. We arrived in Galway at 7.25 leaving Dublin at 3.25, and there is, I think, no way of getting an information leaflet at the hour we arrived in the city.

I saw Becker[5] on board staring hard at me, the usual beginning of the five-hand trick,[6] but I did not give his wife or himself an opportunity to memorize my face, but I stared hard at them, and they retreated.[7] Becker was down as a spy in the Second World War, working for German Intelligence. Yet he can come to Ireland, spot me and taunt me on an Irish steamer and pass me on to Irish people who reply to his hand movements.[8] A tall thin priest was very insistent with his hands and was able to point out to me many others of his kind.

This morning I found that I had forgotten my razor in my hurry. There was no shop open in Galway before I left, and when I landed at Kilronan, Cormac was unable to buy a razor, but before we left the pier Joyce, whom I knew, promised to send me back a razor on Tuesday by ferry as he thought he had an extra razor. Kilronan looked desolate enough in the rain. This is the first time we were unable to see Dr O'Brien as the captain had told us he would not delay long at the Quay.

When we left, the thin priest, who had been wandering around looking as if he intended to speak to me, finally came up. He did not introduce himself but said, 'I recognized you from the photograph on the paper about the film.'[9] I did not respond much to this gesture as I am tired of being spotted in my own country. But he talked on. He had read my book,[10] read the articles in *The Sunday Press*, and had been a Republican in the Civil War.[11] What was his name? Laughton, I think.[12] Two of his brothers were in the movement, and one had been in gaol in the Civil War. He had been at Rome in 1921 and had brought a report of the situation to Monsignor O'Hagan, whom he had great respect for.[13] He knew the General of the Carmelites and the people in Rome who were Republican, who then in the Civil War came together for comfort.[14] We discussed the times now and the spirit then. The youth organizations coming from farm work seemed to be the only form which had any strength. I told him about the Northerners who had sold out on the question not of the Treaty, but of the money which they would gain.[15]

We saw Coley Conneely, then Sean Conneely and his sons, but we were taken ashore by someone whom I do not know or whose boat I do not know.[16] We were brought up to O'Donnells, where we met the woman of the house, *bean a tighe*, which gives the English name.[17] Here, a few years ago we had a very good meal when we came over with Dr O'Brien and then later a meal with the nurse and with the nurse from the Middle Island.

Cormac and I have a double bed, a small table which holds a looking glass, a small table or support for a zinc basin, a chamber pot of metal. Three nails on the back of the door. A small hanging whiskey bottle with a feather duster in it for sprinkling the holy water, and a ledge under the window. At first glance one thinks this is an impossible situation. Where will I hang my clothes, where will I place my books, my toilet articles, my dirty clothes. But gaol has already solved many things in one's mind. Last year we had a bed each, a press for our clothes, but no small table, yet we managed through the use of our bags.[18]

We saw a few people whom we recognized from the last year and whom we shook hands with, but I do not know many of the men here to talk to. The lack of Irish is a bit of a void in a way for some of the older men speak English with difficulty, Willy Conneely of the one eye, for instance.[19]

In the O'Donnells' dining room there were photographs, one of a Royal Irish Constabulary man and a small one of an Irish Army officer in Free State uniform, so one of them must have joined the Staters.[20] There was no Volunteer Company that I knew of in Aran. Peadar O'Loughlin and I had no help here beyond talk when we came over in 1919.[21] We did not organize a company, and what good a company would have been I do not know. Yet it might have prevented talk and would have been of use if people had later to visit the island secretly. Two religious pictures and a religious calendar on which is a Murillo cover 'Church Art Calendar' for the Catholic Home. The cover is alright: Our Lady with a baby about 7 years old standing on her knee, and I do not know what the other pictures are like. A few enlargements of women's photographs, two small paintings, one of a man with a cap, another of a naval man.

Two girls who said they are Civil Servants and who had been wandering around through Clifden and the West before they came here.[22] They seemed to go from one private house to another in their travels. In London, they mention a private house they stayed at. One works in the Gaeltacht Guild Industry in Beggars Bush, the other is in the office where they print the warning notice when you do not pay your annuities and from which offices the annuity and [illegible] notices are sent out.

As with all Aran houses the breakfast begins well at first – rashers and eggs. I said to Mrs O'Donnell, when she apologized for not having 'shop-bread', that I would prefer cakes and that at home we once used whole wheat all the time.[23] For this one we had brown bread, a [bit] doughy. It fills you too much, a visitor later told me, as you eat too much of it.

## Sunday, 12 August 1956

Up for first Mass at 8.30. Fr [Tadhg] Moran has become fatter. He put the young lads out of the second pew and shoved them together into the first, crowding them. They wear their new sweaters on Sundays and their tweed trousers which come down well on them. The little girls sit in the front seats on the left, their hair tied up on top with a ribbon, even though today was wet. Sisters, then with knitted jackets, green and blue, home-knitted and hair to the neck, but no plaited hair as have the Inishmore girls of that age.[24] Women with the paisley shawl, brown and black shawls, and visitor women to the right. The men from the blue grey waistcoat of *braideen* to a grey black, thick, blue black sweater, trousers well pleated behind for the rump. I expect the boys of 16 are more attractive in a blue jacket with sleeves buttoned at the sides, right and left hips, and a grey trousers. The men's side have few prayer books, but the girls, Bridge and Teresa, said that the women used prayer books.[25] On our side, except for strangers, beads. The kneeling place is damned uncomfortable as you are not able to stand up straight for the gospel. As usual a sermon in Irish lasting fifteen minutes. All the girls went to Communion beginning with the smallest girl and then carrying on down on the left side while on the right the men joined in. Not many men went to Communion. As usual the younger men stand up against the wall outside the church while the strangers and women pass down. A wet day.

On the 15th there was once a round here of the wells and a visit by currach to St Brigid's well in Co. Clare, but that now is dying out or dead.[26] Last year a few people crossed to Co. Clare, but I do not know who will go over this year.

It is cold indoors in the large house, on the ground floor — three rooms to the right of the hall door, three to the left; six rooms upstairs — too many now as she has two boys at home and the two girls gone. There is a fireplace in the dining room and one in the front bedroom adjoining ours, but no fire lighter in either. In the evening time visitors come in, the two girls stay oft times in the kitchen, where sometimes there is heat, but not on this night that I went out. The two Civil Service girls were there with the youngest of the house who when asked to play took down a fiddle, tortured it strangely, then fooled with a mouth organ, so that I left the kitchen and went to bed to keep warm.

The windows of the bedroom face to the shop and from it one can see movement. The priest when he comes out in the morning, the crowds going to Mass and any little movement there is. Down to the sea on the right another vista of movement as men go down to put out their boats, or to bring up stuff to the shop. I have a lamp anyhow and when the weather gets cold through rain, I can get into bed to read, but I forgot to bring my Shakespeare which I meant to study in this kind of quiet insulation. The island is certainly a good place on which to read.

Teresa says that women supervisors are better than men. They evidently take more kindly to the monotonous work. 'It's no place for men,' she says, meaning that their brain is not occupied. According to her some of them read well. She reads and was reading a cut-down edition of *Moby-Dick*, which left out the rhetoric. I expected *Don Quixote* could reasonably well be cut down to eliminate some of the tedious adventures and stories, but in the end in such a book you have to accept the boredom as you have to do with people. When you live by yourself you are seldom troubled with banality which naturally we accept from people in our surrounding. Mother was accustomed to make use of it by repeating a line, 'very historic' she would say as she looked at a building.[27] She again repeated it a few times, and that repetition indeed covered her interest. Although in ordinary observation, she was astute enough and quite able. Kevin says she reads well, and he lends her books.[28] She is, indeed, cut off from me as she has a contact with America through Cathal, and she would write away of any information she had about Cormac.[29]

This is away from the Civil Service. They get about a month's holidays in the year. I expect that is ample. They are like the Army. No sense of responsibility about making work, risk the ups and downs of the world or the disasters that overtake people in business or in professions. In the end their minds get addled. If they do not read they become lazy and that burden of no real responsibility, they must carry into their lives. I could see the girls thought University graduates as people who think too much of themselves. That I do not know. The professions are isolated, and I do not know [that] the people look down on the Civil Service … from the school point of view that seems a post of honour, from the country point of view.

The nasal tone of their speech here. Mrs O'Donnell speaks nasally and others also whom I have heard here but not all. There is a good deal of elision as in any spoken language, but then I do not know what they read in Irish. It is out of the subsequent generation who, having been taught to read Irish, can show what they understand or appreciate

No work except at the pier, where they began to work this spring. It is to be enlarged until they can suit the steamer to land goods at the end. But it may take three years to finish.

## Monday, 13 August 1956

Wind more or less West. Alright if it does not swing South/West, but better if it goes to the North, where it will remain cold but steady. I went across to the South/East hoping to shelter from the breeze in the rocks, but when I found shelter there was little sun. There are two Danes now in the 'Dane's House'.[30] That reminds me of the 'Dane Hole' when we were children near Pat Ward's house at Rosmoney.[31] With one's back to the land/sea, this place suddenly becomes isolated. Shags were drying their wings on the rock and in the sea they seemed to be able to rouse themselves out of the water and to flap their oily wings for a while before they took another dive.

The lovely green water on the shore above the sandy bottom is very beautiful as it comes up on the shore in waves. Now and again the cliffs of Burren stood out well as sheer rock.[32] Along the coast southward as it was full tide, tufts of white showed as the sea broke against rising rock, but at some intervals sand appeared along the shore on one beach at least. Very few birds in the sea, shag and seagulls and an occasional kind of a wagtail whose tail is long and quivers.

Turf boats have now begun to come. This is the second [boat] although it is so late in the year. The hooker anchors off, turf flung into the currach, carried up by handfuls, thrown on the beach, and again thrown on the sand, and again brought up further out of reach of the tide. A wasteful process, but then nobody seems to have any other work to do here at present. No fishing, a few boats out, but no fish to eat. Bacon and cabbage for dinner, cabbage thick in the leaf, well sopped in the juice. Luckily I found to my wonderment that I did not get any indigestion from it.[33] The Civil Service girls did not like it, but being hungry, they ate it.

The cat was told to 'get out of that' in English.[34] Animals spoken to in English always. Where did this come from? The Cromwellians would probably be the first English settlers on the Big Island.[35] As around houses there is not adequate fencing, the dogs, especially at night, are prepared to yelp in chasing asses from around the house. They keep on yelping. The ass does not move usually or the dog attack, but if any animal moves, such as a cat, the dog goes for it at once, but if the cat faces the dog quietly the dog keeps quiet.

Flowers are a difficulty to grow here. Asses eat marigolds and roses but do not touch fuchsia, carnations, or geraniums. Also they eat privet. That is a difficulty which might be avoided as there are enough small fields into which a donkey can be pushed out of the way. The marigolds grow well as we found in Tomás's house where Cormac and I went in to call. It is one of the few thatched cottages on the island, and it has a lovely kitchen with an open hearth.


## Tuesday, 14 August 1956

The problem of breakfast. Cormac is up at 8.30. The girls next room sleep or they go to Mass. If they go to Mass it is 10 o'clock, and the breakfast does not come in until 10.45, and then it is 11 or 11.30 before I leave the house. As lunch is at 2.30 that leaves little time on a warm day in which to trap sun if there is wind.

Away to the South/East beyond the barrier of the last village … is the lake,[36] low enough below the road passing through the village and leading South.[37] Direction is hard enough here unless I remember that from Coley's house the Castle is South and the first valley before Black Head is East.[38] That then makes the last castle on the Cliffs of Moher due South. Save on a very calm day waves come into spray along the cliff.

In the sea East/South/East is a black buoy marking the rocks.[39] The lake below is green scum except to the South, but the noise of lapping water can be heard and on certain days, a battling noise to the East where women are washing clothes.

As I passed the Dane's house this morning I saw the young bearded Dane run lightly down towards the lake. When I was on top in my sun place, I saw him lift up waders from under a rock, go out into the water, pull up a box and examine it.[40] That was, I expect, his eel trap, but I did not see him take anything out of the box.

Today lunch was bacon and cabbage, yet no bad results, which shows that I am getting philosophical about food or that my mind is at ease.[41] Possibly worry is more responsible for indigestion than anything else. The morning was beautiful. I lay over the lake in my small plateau and the sun was so warm that I took down my trousers so that sun could get on to my hip bone at the back. When I got around the corner of the village Formna the wind from the West met me harshly. That indeed shows how isolated the lake area is from a westerly wind, but often a wind sweeps around the corner when it passes the eastern end of the island and blows right in from the North/East.

The Civil Service girls are preparing sadly to leave on Thursday. They both speak Irish well, both sensible although when at dinner when I said that foreign pictures[42] were prevented from coming in, the dark girl, Teresa, who has a slight black moustache, said, 'that's a good thing for Irish artists'.[43]

'No, as a writer, I protest against that view, for foreign pictures help to sell Irish pictures and if Irish paintings are not good enough one is glad to see Continental work or to see it bought. Do you wish to have English books and English translations of American books kept out of Ireland?'

There was no answer to this. Always we are hit culturally by the Civil Service for few of them give a damn about creative work although some of them may read well.

### Wednesday, 15 August 1956

Wet and cold. One dodges in and out or paces up and down the small dining room which is so damn cold in bad weather. Truly the kitchen is for Irish speakers. Islanders come in there at night and the talk is in Irish, so a non-Irish speaker becomes bored. I expect in a way you have no right to be here unless you speak Irish, yet above at Sean Conneely's a fire is lighted in the dining room in cold weather at evening time.

The really nicest thing on the island is the young ass foal, about a month old, in a small garden outside the house. It has a delicate head, large eyes, grey-black hair, and markings in black like its mother. It nibbles grass, lunges at her teats, but if she does not want it sucking, she kicks up her left leg and lunges upwards with it. A few times I saw her bring her tail sharply across its nose. Now and again it bucks around vaulting upwards in an amusing series of jumps for its legs are nearly as long but not as ungainly as a horse colt's. The mother has inturned hooves which look ugly enough as I suppose horses do not wear shoes on this island. I saw a mule, a small mule, bring up five loads of turf in two creels with a bag of turf across on top of the creels.[44] He or it seemed to be the liveliest worker on the island.

The German girl has a nice voice. He who is rather undersized jumps up and down stairs at a rush, types away above or has someone, especially Mrs O'Donnell's brother, to read out or correct some of the other men's stories. For this he is rewarded with a cigar, which he smokes quickly as if it were a cigarette. Dr Becker is a doctor at Bonn University, and what he teaches there I do not know. He shoots his camera all around him when the people assemble for the incoming of the steamer. This week there was a steamer on Tuesday, Wednesday, Thursday and also one to come on Saturday.[45] Keating does not like Dr Becker, but then Keating does not like anyone I know of. He is a confirmed misogynist and disturbing in his pessimism.

A deal of rain today, and my back aches with the rheumatism or whatever it has inside of it in the bones. Dr Becker has been coming here for years, and I expect he now has a good collection of material, but I am sure he could have obtained a deal of his materials from Delargy.[46] The old seanachie gave material to the BBC for a broadcast, but they paid him and then he expected to be paid afterwards.[47] In a way that is unfair. BBC with its money, on Irish soil, should give only what they are advised to give by Radio Éireann or by the Irish Folklore Commission.

Women here never go out in currachs except when they are going to the steamer. As a result they are sea sick, a number of them, when they travel on the steamer. One of the drawbacks in this island is that there are no boats for visitors. The currach, even when it journeys to and from the steamer, has tar scattered on the inside, and if you sit on the bottom you catch tar on your clothes. As there are no sailing boats, no one can have the pleasure of sailing for enjoyment. No rowing, no sailing, practically no dancing. The music is made by strangers. A boy Seán ... came here on Wednesday. He plays the melodeon, Dr Becker plays a violin, and last year it was the strangers who played or sang. Even young O'Donnell from the kitchen cannot whistle a tune properly.

### Thursday, 16 August 1956

Last year I was told the young lads threw stones when people were dancing and sing[ing]. Now, what age they were I do not know, but I think the dance was broken up. Why the older men do not go for them I do not know, but evidently no one keeps them in control, and as they are hidden perhaps few know who they are. Also, I was told that when the girls went for some training in the school in the night time, stones were thrown at the windows, and when a dance was held in a house not far from this, stones were thrown at the windows. That makes dancing difficult, and it is hard on the girls. No one can sympathize really with the youth if some of the boys deliberately try to make a dance difficult to run.

We have been watching the sky for rain and the horizon for the steamer. There is an excursion to Knock and the Civil Service girls for that reason can make use of the steamer.[48] I watched the coast with my field glasses, and when it rained I got in under a slab of rock which has a wide surface underneath with pitted holes full of water, so my sojourn was unpleasant. The steamer did not arrive until about 4. Last night a dance began about 11 in the house. Sean ... and two fiddlers played away, sometimes the girls sang, but the girls were strangers. None of the island girls came, or maybe they were not invited. Another island mystery.

Tea was given outside in the dining room, and I could hear a drunken old man flounder around, but the dance kept on until 4. Teresa had the man, I called the 'mickey-dazzler,' from up beside Sean Conneely's. He is married so Teresa said in a kind of disgust. Cormac remained out there until 12 o'clock. He said it was 'scorching', and he enjoyed it very much. They stamped their feet to the music. The dancing was altogether sets, which is after all the usual country dance.

We waved goodbye to the two girls, and through my glasses I watched them on board as the steamer moved quickly away. It is always difficult to say how many visitors there are on the island; Sean Conneely has seven now, here Mrs O'Donnell's five, Coley Conneely six — eighteen in three houses, so I expect there must be twenty-five at least.

Cement is placed on an ass's back. That means two hundredweight at a time. It is a great wonder the paper covering does not break as it is lifted up from the sand in a man's arms. I saw cement dust come out of a few, but I did not see a broken sack. ... With any ingenuity here, they could derive a float on which to carry cement, such as is used by the pier authorities. The black Achill boat could bring in cement, but the men would be up to their nipples I am sure in the water.

Even here there is a division. Little girls sit by themselves, little boys [sit] by themselves, bigger girls in a group, then young girls, but very few elderly women unless there are friends coming off the boat, or there us a return of Marian pilgrims from Knock. The island men sit together also, or talk, the younger of them, to the visitors.

Seán Keating was anxious about the steamers' anchors. 'Were both of them down?' he asked. 'No, one,' I replied. 'If the wind goes North we will be alright,' he said, meaning that it would be dry. Seán belongs to the *Fáinne,* but he says *Fáinne* speakers now – by lack of practice – lose their tongue whether they leave off the *Fáinne* as a result I do not know, but they decline from their original numbers.[49]

On Wednesday three hairy-looking men had landed from the steamer. One of them rushing up shouting across the strand to Dr Becker who had taught German in Dublin. I suppose that is how he managed to spread his propaganda. The other seemed equally dirty in dull and light khaki. One had a beard and was quieter. Here in a way you are a kind of a hero if you shout in Irish and shake hands with the populace, but I don't know. Being primitive they sum you up quickly I expect. I do not know if they have nicknames on the islands, but in this respect they are probably like the mainland people. One thing I notice strongly as compared with the first time I came to this island, the mainland is no longer Éire, now they are dependent on it.[50] Visitors and excursionists come, and it is part of them because of the Dole because of the money for [speaking] Irish.[51]

### Friday and Saturday, 17/18 August 1956

Wet in the morning. Worked inside in my duffle [coat]. On Wednesday I had a fire for the first time, but it did not last long. The girls blew away at it, but it was old turf, not much of it at that, and it took nearly an hour to light, but then it crumbled out again.

I worked on 1920, but my booklet begins in March.[52] Only on a wet day can I work, but without a fire that is uncomfortable, and the cheery fire is not going to be given to me here.

At dinner a girl from the Post Office [came] with a telegram, but I did not send her out the money, but I said I would pay at the Post Office when my dinner was finished, 4/2 to pay because it had been relayed from Dublin. I sent it across to Cormac who read it also. That explains why Helen wanted to have Cormac at Greenwich so that he could be present at her divorce-wedding.[53] Rather a rotten trick to involve a Catholic in, but then she wants her will to work its will at no matter what cost to other people. Evidently it also shows that Cormac would never have had come back to Ireland. The Post Office has a very fine kitchen, the old kitchen I should think. In O'Donnell's and in Conneely's the kitchen is very small indeed even though they had a dance there the other night. The Post Office would be fine for a dance as would Tomasheen's house which is yet thatched. Below is an old well and behind it two waterlogged fields. The pump seems to have been smashed.

It looked as if it might rain. I moved over towards the school for I can always get inside through the gate to the small shelter facing East where the boys have a few boards to sit on. But when I got down to the shore I found a rock under which I crouched when the rain came. A few shags stood out on a rock awkwardly moving with their flat-footed waddle or jump when they move. There were about twenty of them in the water, diving at intervals so there must be fish around this shore. An absence of birds and of bird song. Few larks, few blackbirds, faint pipings, but few airleens near this shore, out to the South/West. Only a rush of starlings sweeping over you or chattering from the tops of houses in the evening time and to the West, jackdaws on rocks. You miss the bold worm. There are few seagulls down near the strand. That is no loss where there are heaps of them, but their voices are pleasant in an open land and remote such as this when they are a few together. More shags than gulls to the North.

A problem, this of Helen.[54] Would she have settled down? I doubt it very much. I noticed that when she became attached to the Theatre Group, she talked too much, especially at table when there were guests.[55] That rush of talk might be alright to her when she was with 'simple' country people who delight to hear of travel, but I was bored, and as a result talked less. I expect it developed because she was the source of money. She would then be listened to by better and more devious talkers and so gained an ascendancy. After some years, she felt she was the moving part of a cooperative and would seldom listen when I thought a problem out. Again, when she was back in 1955, she talked practically all the time on the journey to Dublin until my head was in a whirl.[56] When one does not talk much, save of necessity, then a gush of talk all the time is strange and one stands outside to judge. The English say we talk too much only because they cannot talk, save … creative workers, and they are unjust. Talk can be creative and some people think best when they talk.

The question of men and leaving the house work to women came up often enough with the Civil Service girls. They asked about … when men did the outdoor work and the women the house work as well as the supply work of carrying water, turf, vegetables for pigs, etc. They noticed Cormac who has been trained to carry and to serve. They admired the Germans who worked hard.

'But the Irish are trained to be lazy,' I said.

'How come?' said one Civil Service girl.

'When young, they do not help. They do not clean shoes, make beds, carry out plates from the table, wash up, dry, clean their baths, put out rubbish, sweep floors, fetch things from the ship, they don't work, sew or carry. And now they take the bus when they should walk. Also, they are taught to be lazy by long holidays, especially when they are at College. Three and a quarter months' holidays in the year.[57] In the school at about 9.30 whereas in Germany and France, they would be at school by 7 o'clock. So, they are trained to be lazy until they leave the primary school. Also, their parents help them at their exercises which is a form of cheating and of danger to the pupils.[58] Then the waste of time learning Irish which they no longer use when they leave school. They don't read in Irish and so do not produce writers of their demand for reading in Irish. (I have never been translated into Irish.[59] Why, I wonder?) Nor have the good writers such as O'Connor, O'Faolain. Therefore, a lazy people. The essence of this island is [il] dolce far niente.'[60]

Nobody works save the men at the pier. The sand is not pushed back. That is a Government business, and I do not know what land improvement goes on from year to year. In Inishmaan I wonder if the sea edge is planted with best and sand-restricting grasses to protect the made-land to the North.

No Irish for a 'swan' here and for other birds. There is Irish for 'swan' but there are only two on the lake with a young one. I saw a seagull glide towards the young swan. Quickly the parents hissed strongly with their beaks out to protect the young one which the gull came down many times in a dive but stopped there. No songs, no dances.

When I mentioned the priest in connection with dancing, Sean Conneely said that dances were cooked up by the lads themselves, and that they would destroy any hope. That leaves discipline to the teacher or the priest. There should be a council on the island of two young and of old men to discuss island affairs, and to make decisions.[61] Now it is the Parish Priest who gets things done. That is bad socially as the people will not develop socially.

There is a factory here which occasionally employs a few people.[62] I suppose they make socks, but I do not know how the distribution is made. Most people, I expect, judge the island as strangers by its peace, absence of papers, and certain simplicities, and this serves to make it a holiday centre, but not a place to live in.

Mrs O'Donnell does not approve of my washing in hot water every morning. However, she has now become accustomed to it. Breakfast: eggs two for me, one for Cormac, hard-boiled … Then a few times, a rasher and a sausage … Tea: a hard-boiled egg. Dinner: potatoes and butter, very good ideas.Cormac pounds the potatoes and digs into them. A sweet,[63] always the same custard and jelly, followed by a gateau, jam roll and tea.[64] The jam roll is monotonous, indeed sticky and sweet. In the evening, jam [on bread]. I do not know whether it is raspberry or strawberry, but it has a sweet taste, and I make use of it. Once we had a piece of lettuce.

It is strange that this part of the island, which keeps strangers, does not know how to keep them except at Coley's and Sean's (Conneely's). No attempt to grow onions, scallions, lettuce or keep cress for salads. Eggs – fried, hard boiled eggs – boiled hard, and meat … boiled … With all Mrs O'Donnell is a very nice woman, and as she is a widow, we respect her and are willing to help her by removing our plates. Here Dr Jim O'Brien always stayed for a few days when he had to wait over for patients. He couldn't afford to get married, he told her. Poor Jim, he has such a miserable life. No wife, no woman housekeeper.[65] Everything smothered in dust and the shop like an abandoned drinking den. Empty bottles, empty boxes. I think he usually has one bottle of brandy or a bottle of whiskey, and he keeps searching around for eggs when we came in for tea. Old bills, old advertisements, twenty years old. A gallant man for he is a good doctor, good to his patients and fearless. No wild sea ever keeps him from coming over with his oarsmen whenever he is urgently wanted.

I talked to Mrs O'Donnell about Coley, 'the micky dazzler', I call him. Somehow I never liked him. He approached me the first day I landed here three years ago and told me he had a good house to stay in. 'Why didn't he go home,' said Mrs O'Donnell. He was here until it was 2 o'clock. It was hard, I thought, on Teresa, as if he weren't here, she would have had a young islandman, maybe, to dance with.

Here, you would need to know sheltering places when the rain comes. The schoolhouse, but it is damn cold in the play shed. A few rocks here and there which give you a back for the wind, and slightly raised stones which give you cover. I suppose if you searched around you could find real cover, and then remember it for another year. Cormac and the islanders just crawl under a currach — that is indeed the best shelter especially if there are a few other currachs nearby to act as a wind break. The bow is raised more highly when the currach is placed upside down on the stones and under this you can read as I found when one day when I had to remain there for an hour or so as I waited for the steamer.

## Sunday, 19 August 1956

The usual call at 8.20, up and out, 8.30. Then we went outside. Keating was outside the wall when I arrived, and we saw Fr [Tadgh] Moran come out, walk up and down, look at the men, look at us who looked at him, and then we went back. I suppose that is part of the discipline if the seats are empty. The women outnumber the men at first Mass, and there are not very young children brought to it. Keating was in front of me, and I saw he had room enough, but suddenly another heavy man flopped on his knees, pushed hard on the man on his right who then pushed on Keating who looked up suddenly to find why the pressure but the pushing continued and Seán had to put up with it. Breakfast was then over by about 10 or 10.15, and I had time to get out early. Over above the lake I saw two men put a boat in the water, and when it was in the lake, I saw that the Dane and two men were in it. He remained in the prow and evidently his eel lines were in against the edge of the stone surrounding as the currach moved in five or six times on the way around the lake, but whether he picked up eels or not I do not know. The last time the steamer came I saw wood in bags which he received. Later I heard that he smoked eels. The two of them live together, but how they support themselves I do not know.

Currachs out after dinner but not many, as they do not go out to fish on a Sunday. Later in the evening I was told by Sean Brady that the boys of the house had brought him over to Inishmaan and that they packed into the pubs where they drank. The people there did not salute him, he said, but maybe they were shyer. It was a pity neither Cormac nor myself knew that they intended to go over to the Middle Island. Sean Brady says he read somewhere they were of a different race. I remember that there are a few red-headed girls there, though I haven't seen any of that colour for about twenty years here. I remember from the doctor that the women have a narrower pelvis and have more difficulty in giving birth, but I don't think the doctor even lost a maternity case there. The women, the young married women, I thought were very beautiful when I went there with the doctor, in what year was it — 1941 or 1942. Then I went around as a 'doctor' with him.

I talked to a red-faced man who seemed to be sunburnt, but he was an elderly islander, and I did not know his name. His grandmother, Fitzgerald, came from Clare and formerly they went every Friday to Lisdoonvarna landing at Liscannor, where they borrowed an ass and cart to bring up their fish to the Spaw [sic.], as they say. The Tans he spoke of with great awe.[66] There was a RIC sergeant who had once been in Kilronan, and he told the

Aran men never to answer back to the Tans, but let then have their say.[67] If they were angered they would not spare anyone, the sergeant said, but when the bridges were broken down, the Tans could not journey as well.

Maurteen O'Donnell one night here told me that a Volunteer Company was started here, escaped by the fear of their action.[68] 'Oh, they were badly wanted I know,' he answered. Now, nobody would be allowed to leave their brigade even when in action in the Tan War.[69] You stood your ground, and you kept in your area whether you liked it or not. I remember reading the *Doheny* ... book. Instead of being tragic, it made me laugh, but it really showed what the Volunteers had to put up with, what intelligence the RIC had, and how much people talked, and how little the so-called revolutionaries knew of good houses in adjoining districts where they could stay unknown to landlord's agents or RIC.

In the evening time a few grown girls came out to walk over the strand or out by the rocks beyond the boat house, but not many of them. Here at night there was singing and beating time with their feet by men from the Castle village, but the songs were discordant when Willie sang in English. He had a terrible voice and is completely reckless about what he does with it. He stretches a line like a bowman and then he shortens the next line.

There they were hundreds of foreigners there, French and English and Americans. They put out sixty fathoms of rope and let down a net which had a light rope, but a heavy rope would have been better, as when it drags on the ground, it drives the fish into the narrowing of the net.[70] In an hour or two they could catch fish, plaice, and it was plaice the Spa wanted for the Friday.[71] They'd get good sale for fish there then, but now he thinks there are not many at the Spa, but that plaice would be caught when the net is now dropped. Once he, who is the lobster fisher, caught a lobster a fathom between the clams and four stone in weight, the biggest he ever saw.[72] He sold it to Schofield who held the lobsters along the shore in Galway Bay. There is a spawning place out to the South of the Inisheer, and it's there the lobsters spawn in that ground. They last here until close to December. He seems to have the best luck as a lobster man. The weaver now for the past month has gone crazy about lobsters, so says Willie Conneely, and he will do no weaving until September, but he hasn't caught more than thirty lobsters in that interval. He weaves for the men and tailors, but the women do their own clothes.

That was a mistake. The oldish man is not the lobster fisher as he is a fatter man. I met him later on, and he promised to keep me a good lobster for next Friday.

Formerly Aran men bought bunnies in Clare at Ennistymon, fattened them and brought them back to sell them there.[73] Once Liscannor[74] was a prosperous place as they had great flags there which they used for roofing.[75] Boats came from England, filled up with flags and went away to England. That gave good employment, but it was before the First World War. Then it died away.

### Monday, 20 August 1955

My water, the tea water, came in first, and when I had shaved I brought it out to the kitchen as I was then clean and ready for my breakfast.

On the fine days, I wanted to get out to the South/East over the lake as that is the best place to avoid the Northerly, Easterly or the South-West wind. This time I went up to the right of the road from the labyrinth of walls which was first led across by a stile. This is easily built by putting long flat stones right across the wall and then by building on the top of them. A fine-looking young bullock wanted to make friends with me but disturbed my reading so much that I had to drive him away. There must have been five fields here interrelated by gaps, and several of them had a cross slat as in an old door; above that the wall next higher up. Soon I was warm, but the sun as usual was sufficient when it was strong, and there is little desire to read. Just bask and take the sun as it comes and wander back slowly to lunch at 2.30. A lunch of bulky mutton boiled maybe from yesterday's leftovers. That is a pity as island mutton can be delicious as I remember from Kilmurvey. But then you're here. Dinner here makes *Kabloona* more interesting.[76]

In the evening I went up the higher road to the West and got into a field near to a young heifer who wanted to be patted. They are often separated, the cattle, and that makes them friendlier to anyone who comes into their fields; no attempt here, as in the Big Island, to create watersheds, cemented, for water. There was a fairly good wind blowing. I could see the turf boats sailing away at intervals. Today there were four of them, and that gave an air of shipping to the beach. Once also they brought turf to North Clare, but now lorries bring them turf as there is no bog in the Burren. At one time that means poteen also. Here long ago poteen was made and a man came from Connemara to make it.

Cormac had gone away out with the lobsterman who also caught twenty pollock, but he didn't give Cormac a fish. They went around as far as Piper Rock, and Cormac rowed a good deal of the way as the lobsterman's second helper was ill today. Someone died from Formna and the villagers slowly go across to the funeral, a woman's. The grave headstones [are] written on in English.

Dr Becker moves out and in when I arrive at the door without speaking. But today, as I heard him bundle down the stairs speedily, I stood in the way so that he had to say, 'Excuse me'. Then I stood aside for him. He cooks some kind of pie, a meat pie in the night time in the kitchen, adds things to it and then brings it upstairs. The Civil Service girls often waited at the fire hoping to have a taste of it, but they never got any. 'Just like the Germans,' they said. They had learned by foreign travel. No one is so free of food, drink or cigarettes as the Irish. Germans and, I think, the French when in company do my offer cigarettes or a drink. The Spaniards as I know say 'buen proveda' and place their food as a gesture as if offering it, but they do not give any of it to you. 'Su casa' as if a gift but an ornamental keeping. I suppose the poverty, or former poverty, of the Irish makes them generous and kindly in their use of food. That remark on food led then to a discussion on cooking. Spain had impressed the girls although I do not think they drink or smoke, but they like the use of rice, of fish and of the satisfying dishes they had received. And they found in Spain that people knew who the Irish were. Even at the frontier they were passed by without [their] boxes being opened because they had Irish passports. I think Italy knows of Ireland also, but Germany addresses letters to Gaeltacht branch of the Tweed Industry at Beggar's Bush 'Dublin, Ireland'.

Dr Becker types away [in his room] above and then gets Maurteen O'Donnell to correct the Irish as taken down from other men.[77] Maurteen O'Donnell said something to me about charts the other night as if there were many upstairs.

I expect I have been reading more than I did last year. Two rather interesting books on war, one a diary from Italy of the byeways of war; the other an escape in France and Spain. An extremely badly written book on Madagascar, which should have been a joy to write about. It seems the French were subsequently excessively cruel there. A fine book on Joan of Arc by Sackville-West.[78] She quotes her authorities all the time. Today when I had finished with it, I must have dropped it on the way in, for I had noted all the things I wanted to refer to again; but as it is a Penguin I may be able to come across it again. Sackville-West has no religion, but she believes in things of the spirit. Poor Joan had a villainous time of it, persevering to the end against Christ and the Fifth Column and the English.

### Tuesday, 21 August 1956

How wonderful grey is as a camouflage material. I have been looking across the lake trying to locate a hammer sound, but I could not the other day. Now I find it as I noticed a black jersey moving above the rocks when a man was breaking up rock. Even now on the lake from a grey sky in certain lights, or against shore backgrounds the young swan cannot be distinguished as it is to one side of its parents, but they stand out clearly, and from certain light they shine. Perhaps they induce attack from their high lights, or rather in this neighbourhood ward off attacks. Outside the Finnis Rocks, it being two hours on the return tide, have waves rolling about 200 yards to the north of the Buoy.[79] Perhaps it is here the rocks are, and a vessel keeps outside of them. From Hags Head upwards the cliffs are recessed in shale which makes their form stand out.[80] In the morning sun, they are a deep blue in which no form can be seen from the beginning of Moher to the end.

This is almost a warmer day than yesterday, but there is a hard wind blowing in from the sea from the South East. I had to get into a field well below, in a hollow guarded by a give way. There I was able to expose my behind to the sun hoping it would work on the bad part of acetabulum, but even as I did a lad came along quietly and looked over the wall as he passed.[81] The boys here are as shy as the girls, I think. Patrick, in our house, hardly answers me. Perhaps he knows little English. Last night when I was observing the full moon, which began on Sunday, I said, 'Good night,' as he passed in, and he said, 'It is.'[82] Cormac says the answer is '*Tá*.'[83] You don't repeat the rest.

Dinner. Another lunch of thick slabs of mutton. However, there is a sweet now, peaches instead of jelly, a gateau which cost I think 1/2 for a jam roll which is anything but really pleasant to eat, and tea.[84] Cormac takes four cups sometimes. Some meals [were] from tin cans: salmon on a Friday, corned beef on another day, and mutton. The fish pollock is very bony, hard to extract the bones and difficult to eat as a result, but the potatoes are good, and there is always butter to use on these when mashed.

Afterwards I wandered out, but I saw a boat, with a small reddish sail, drop anchor. It was from Conneelys of Kilmurvey, I was told.[85] We gathered down to watch the inthrust of about fourteen people or more. They brought food with them and a few took it ashore. I did not know any of them. Later I went out to the West, but I got into a field where there was a sheep. The sheep turned out to be a ram judging from its enormous testicles and its unclipped fleece. He was very friendly, and he lay down close to me. For about an hour the sun was intense, the warmest I had yet met with this year so again I tried to warm my behind.

My watch, which in Dublin strays on ahead, is now no more than fifteen minutes fast off the priest's time, although today by his time it was twenty minutes in advance. Cormac brought along his clock which he adjusts from mine, but Mrs O'Donnell's clock is somewhat variable, but I find that she is ready for dinner when I return at 2.30. She uses an oil stove all summer, the fire but seldom. 'I don't use much turf in the year,' she tells me. Yet the small room to the front of our room has a fireplace and could be a warm room, I am sure, if there were turf and coal, and if that chimney draws properly. It is again extraordinary how the double-storey house stands out in non-conformity: O'Donnell's, Coley Conneely's, and Sean Conneely of the shop's.[86] Yet the only houses with fires are [in] the thatched houses.[87] The [flowers] were coloured red and yellow ... and today the reds flaunted bravely against the grey walls. Carnations are beautiful against grey and the golden yellow ... is brilliant also.

As I was warm from the sun I went up to Sean [Conneely']s for a bottle of stout, but I found the shop crowded with the recent visitors. Two men were close to the bar, and they were being gay in their insipid banality. What tripe they talked in their repetitious nonsense which has no humour. Evidently it had been fortified by glasses and pints in Inish Maán as it transpired they had been drinking in Flaherty's.

A Swede, a woman came in also, and at last Mrs Conneely, but when I answered her Irish in English she said, 'I'm surprised at you speaking English.' 'You shouldn't be,' I said, 'for I write in English, and it takes me all my time to learn it properly.' A woman who was sick, or had been sick on the boat, was given a brandy and I advised her to bring some over on the boat with her. The wind from the North had now increased in strength, and it was running hard, not so good indeed, for those who had to return. Many of the women were dressed in new dungarees, but their figures would best have suited skirts. Trousers on the fat are not too pleasant as they are mostly too tight. My banality said to his wife, who had been sick, 'It's the best thing that could happen for you'll feel the better after it, now that it's over.' Why one should feel the better of sick-sickness I do not know. To feel better because it is over is correct, but to believe that sea sickness is good for you is a rather fatuous view, which I have heard often enough. The poor island women must dread going in the boat as they suffer a good deal from sea sickness, and maybe the younger girls also. When you never see them in a boat except they are going out to the steamer or on a visit to one of the other islands or to relatives in Clare, it is difficult for them to get accustomed to the sea as a journey way.

When I called in to Willie C[onneely] I had to talk about his wife's infirmities. She is weak in the legs from the knees down, and the doctor did not tell her what was wrong with her. They kept her in hospital for a few weeks and then sent her back. Also she had the unemployment pension, 18/-, but now for the past few weeks she hasn't received it. Now she wishes to get a pension on account of her legs. Evidently she cannot use them much. I think she was tubercular, but maybe she is not. The other daughter, now in hospital, was tubercular, and her absence is a loss as she is an accomplished knitter and I think so is her younger sister. Three boys in the family. I am expected to prepare the description of her legs which would suit her to obtain the pension for ill health. I promised to ask the doctor about her if and when I see him on the next Wednesday, but Joyce also had something to do with pensions. They are a nice family. The old man gets the blind pension 29/0 per week, and that is now all the money coming in since the daughter is in hospital.

When we discussed claiming and the influence of the clerical, both parents became voluble. The priest always gives the credential when you wish to leave the island, and you have to go to him whether you like him or whether he likes you or not. The father said he wanted one of the boys to go to the technical school in Kilronan, but when the priest asked the father why the boy didn't go, the father said he didn't know. 'Tell him to come to me,' says the priest. So, the boy went, but said he didn't want to go. Fr [Thomas] Varley, then Parish Priest, had a row with the captain [of the steamer]. He wanted him to deliver the post in the Big Island first or to come to the Big Island before he went to the other islands. Anyhow, the captain stood out against him and said if he wanted to run the steamer, he could do so, but so long as he was captain he carried out his own orders. Either Fr Moran or the previous priest knocked down a lad with a blow. It seems three of the lads tackled three women and kissed them, and they complained to the priest. He sent up for young Donoghue from the Post

Office, and when he came down to meet him in front of Sean Conneely's, the priest hit him on the face and knocked him down. The boy got up, and he ran away, but that was the wrong boy; he had done no harm.

The size of eels is like the stories of the size of fish by non-professional fishermen. The black eel is very big, as broad as a foot in diameter judging by his hands as he described them and good to eat, better than the white eels which travel along the shores of the island. A big hook, and a gaff always needed when they are being brought in to the boat. They could sell them but it seems that it is now not worth the time they spend at it, the salting, the curing, the packing in a box.

When I sat in Willie Conneely's and talked of eating horse, they looked – the mother, father, sister, and brother – at me in surprise. 'God save us,' was the look on their faces. In Paris I said there are horse shops throughout, some have a silver horse head outside, and in the Blasket Islands, they eat seals. 'Did they ever eat seals here.'

'Oh, no.'

'Or dolphins?'

'No.'

'Well, they are good to eat, I am told.'

My story was like the tale at Murrisk [Co Mayo] when I talked to Ryan about the trawler and the work of the men. 'The French are dirty eaters,' he said. 'They put every kind of fish into a saucepan and they make soup of it.' 'Do you never make fish soup?' 'Oh, No,' as if soup were something wrong to eat as soup. 'Oh, they're dirty eaters, and they eat crabs.' 'Why crabs are fine to eat. And when you go to sea, what do you eat?' 'We eat bacon and eggs.'

Willie's grandfather was a fine currach builder. Now, they don't build as well in the round gap inside; they don't finish them as well and it's not such a good job. His grandmother was a Joyce. When he was growing up he was taught school by a Kerryman, O'Donoghue, and he taught him in English. He was a good teacher he said.

The flowers I passed I recalled about there being more of them last year than when we have. Well there weren't any ten years ago; that is a great improvement, indeed, for they make the gardens beautiful. Then, salt – 1/6 a cwt, flower – 2/6, tobacco – 0/2 per ounce, a pint – 0/2 so that money had multiplied by six in this respect.

'Did the old people take snuff, or did the women smoke?'

It has been wet these days, cold and wet. Last night I could hear Liam at his melodeon and then the German joined in with his fiddle, but he played the fiddle too fast as an accompaniment, and after a while I notice that the mouth organ stopped. Willie Conneely was bawling a song out of time, running one line into another as was his custom. Sean Brady, I was told, who 'has his name in the paper often' and works on the Radio, is going today. He had his leg broken by a bicycle. Mrs O'Donnell told me 'the creature, he has been coming here for the past five years,' she said.

The steamer was expected early today, but it did not pass out until 2.15, and, I suppose, was not into Killronan until 2.30 or after. Four tons of turf are to be landed in Inishmaan, and there's cement, seventeen tons for the pier. But the day is rough, wild and wet. The steamer showed up at 4.30. I got in under a currach to get out of the rain, and as I got in I found Cormac underneath. It's a good place in which to land yourself when the day is wet, and it was suitable enough for me to read *Don Quixote*. I have finished *Kabloona*, a wonderful book, very little of which I remembered since I read it in 1941, except this that it was a fine book and that it explained the Eskimos and their way of life well. I am reading *Don Quixote* fast now, but it seems in town I have no real time.

The reading of newspapers in the [National] Library ruins my back, gives me no ease, and turns me out as if I were an overworked drag horse.[88] That is why the island is a peace effort and a relaxation. With good grub ... it would be easy for me to feel happy here even on a wet day. Yet by this, all these objections have been waived as against the peace and freedom of the island and its restfulness. The wet days are the worst as they are cold inside, and it is impossible for me to sit down outside until the sun has warmed the rocks, otherwise my back will get worse while I am here.

Tonight, there was a fire for me, but the fire went out for me when I sat down at it. I tried paper and paraffin, then I nearly gave it up intending to get into bed, but she came in. 'What did you spill?'

'Paraffin,' I said. 'I shook it on top.'

'Why didn't you come out for some? There's a case of it outside' I'm used to turf, but I could not light this turf. It's too big unbroken not enough sticks, and I intended to go to bed. She made up some sticks, sprinkled oil on top, broke up a few sods and soon the fire was blazing. 'Maybe it was how you were telling me to make up a better fire,' she said. 'How would you know if I went to bed?'

'The only way to make a fire is to make a good fire.' Finally, it burned cheerily, and I remained up until 1 o'clock, which by island times is very late for me. *Kabloona* keeps me going as it could be applied somewhat to the island people.

The rain drops were big today and cold. 'It's like the winter rain,' a man said to me. 'It's big, the drops.' Here the old people were taught in English, and the young are taught Irish and English.[89] 'The Irish isn't much good if you want a job,' they say. The English isn't much good either if you want a job. It takes more than English at times to get a job, but it is true enough, they need the English for emigration. The girls go to Galway to domestic service to learn English, and as soon as they learn it they're off to England. Formerly they always went to America.

This island – Inisheer – could develop it seems in land and in visitors. For land they need hard work, the shifting of sand and seaweed from the shore and also the breaking up of stones to level down the gaps between the stones to a level land basis. It's hard work, but it's fair work enough for these men. For visitors they currently need something in the rooms to hang clothes on, hot water in the mornings to wash with, a fire in the room and decent food. Also a lavatory which works, a flush system. But in their own way, they don't worry. The kitchen here is more for visitors than for anyone else as far as I can see. You are supposed to be an Irish speaker and to share their talk, and if you can't, then you might as well stay out from them.

### Thursday, 23 August 1956

Hot again. Washdays are Monday and Friday, I think. Over at the lake they wash one day against the North side of the lake and other days on the West side. There is fine shelter here for all winds save East and South/East and at times South. Cormac said, 'You're up late today.' It was 10 when he came in with the water. 'But it's you who keep me late in bed. You get up at 8.30, go out, come back in at 10, bring me in a kettle, and then the breakfast is ready in a quarter of an hour. When you come in at 10.20 if you want to help me to get up, bring in the kettle at 9.30, and then I'll be ready for breakfast at 10.45.'

Last night I heard Mrs O'Donnell and the boys at the Rosary. Patrick O'Donnell wears corduroy tops because he is at the technical school, and at Kilronan he does not wear his island clothes. He began a decade, and his mother hurries with the Holy Mary, but when his mother says a decade, she begins the next Hail Mary by the time he has reached *Naomh Muire*, and it goes on all through with a wonderful rush.[90]

The moon has been moving further East each night, and the weather is supposed to get better as it goes East, but the bright red star, which arose the first night when the moon was over the Castle, to the East, I have not since seen. Sean Conneely's has a strange confessional inside the door.[91] Here the girls and children shyly ensconce themselves while they wait for Sean to come along to them. He deals with them very kindly, and I think he must be kindly by nature. The filling out of a pint from the jug is a lengthy matter, much wiping off of the foam before the creamy top comes on.

A talk with the lobsterman. He gets £2 a dozen for the lobsters which he considers a good price. Once the Bretons fished in close along the shores for lobsters, but now they cannot.[92] However, they left their pots. Sometimes he says boats do not come because they think from the clouds over the islands there is bad weather there just as we think by looking at the mainland when it is cloudy that the weather is bad. In certain winds the boats cannot come this way. If it blows from the East, and if it blows hard, North, West, and South/West, it is difficult to take the turf ashore in the currachs.


## Friday, 24 August 1956

A bad morning again, but when I went up with Cormac to the Castle, I found I could get in through the door which he thought was locked. Three rooms on the floor are dark because windows have been covered in and the ceiling smashed in the centre room. Above three rooms, good strong walls. When I came out although the wind blew all around there was sun on the South/East wall. Yet rain fell all around the other walls but the height of one wall gave us shelter. We read *Don Quixote* at the passage when Sancho Panza became the governor of an Island. They were cruel to Sancho, I thought, and the Duke and Duchess cruel to Don Quixote. The really mean thing they did to Sancho was they did not give him food. They knew he loved his food, and if they had any kindness while they were enjoying him make a fool of himself, they might at least have offered in compensation for the pleasure he gave them – food. Also, they battered him cruelly in the night attack and that also was uncalled for.

Looking at the Castle while I write the evening light [at] 7.20 strikes along the five or six outthrusts of buttresses, green with ivy and grass which leads the eye upwards for 100 feet or more. All the exterior seems a part of the fortification as if deliberately built up, some of it rounded and shaped almost as if turrets, were set in the stone as if the whole place were a properly set series of defences. The Castle above had a second wall in circumference as you can see by the blocks of brownish stone in position, but on top the nearest wall is no more than four feet high on top inside but from twelve to fourteen feet below on the outside. The basis of the small elevation is stone. There were a few carved gargoyles which have a human face on them. I saw the church in which Cormac has been digging. There is a head at the base of the original door on the South side as you face South/ East. On the other side, there is no head. No other ornament there except the decimated figure on the altar cut in slate. This is not old.

I was watching the horses as they cropped away on the commonage and the asses beyond the old burial ground where there are only a few blades of grass and many weeds, sheep and a goat. They are always cropping at the small bits of grass which spring up thus reducing their binding strength, and making it easier for the sand to give way. Sean Connelly of the shop says there are ninety-seven acres of commonage. If anything were to be done it would have to be enclosed and all animals kept off it for at least three years. Then after that something could be done about division of the land. Some seven years ago or more, bogs were offered on the mainland but only ten people were willing to accept the land. It would mean that families would have to move on to that land in May, cut turf, sell some of it, and pay their living expenses on the mainland. But it had to be passed by because people were not willing to accept of it.

### Saturday, 25 August 1956

Steamer leaves [Galway] at 8 today so I expect it will be here early. I wrote letters to Jean and Kevin and two others.[93] Then I went to the Post Office to post them, and later I went up the hill to get out of the wind, the hill behind the Post Office. At last I found shelter from the tearing North wind, which is indeed our security here. I lay down, and I read *Don Quixote*. Suddenly I got up at what was 1.20 and when I looked down the steamer was below. There was a big crowd below.

Seán Keating was going away, and I know he is sad when he leaves so he was more taciturn than usual. He had a defeated tinge to him, maybe because he has not made more a success of himself as an artist, somewhat because he has to accept a job other than painting to enable him to live. But he is too hostile in himself to help his students, I would say, although he knows, and everyone on the island knows him, he visits no house, and he speaks to very few people.

Boys continued to excite Coley's dog by throwing sand and stones in the air. He bit at the sand, sniffed at the stones, gulped pieces of seaweed, but he yelped in a shrill way which was piercing. I cursed him, but the boys enjoyed it as an unthinking sport. The yelping of a dog may have been music to them. Their voices are shrill, but naturally not as shrill as the girls. There is a great deal of nasal talk which sounds horrible to me.

*Seán Keating,* Self-portrait

The people here: the man who wears the hat, Keating and wife, he a schoolteacher who rents a house from relatives in the Castle Village.[94] Tracey, grey hair, attractive wife, three children, lives in the station as does the Engineer and his wife.[95] The old man lives alone on the strand. 'He hasn't a hen,' as Mrs O'Donnell says, 'nothing.' He came back here twenty years ago, his wife died, and he is now alone, his children in America. He is very lonely, poor man, especially in the winter. Mrs O'Donnell dreads the winter, as the old do, I expect. The cold, the long nights, they do not look forward to. They have no sense of beauty, no intellectual recompense, and talk, I expect, does not last forever. Here the dry battery has not been succeeded by another so that the wireless does not work.[96] That means weather signs have not been given out to this house and so they are ignorant of weather until they ask the neighbours. We went up for lunch, but when we came back the steamer was there yet waiting. A deal of cement had to be unloaded today. But I did not wait.

I went up the small valley at the back of the graveyard. The sand is pushing up slowly, and there I found a seat which gave me shelter and allowed me to remain on until I trapped the last of the sun over the rise of stone. As I came down I talked to a man, who was painting with coal tar the Finnis Buoy. He lives in the Castle village, and he talked of Clare. He had worked there. There was a story about Doon where an officer and some Tans had been killed. They went up to the nearest house as the bridge had been broken down, took out an island man who was working for a farmer and threw him, I thought he said, from one to another. Maybe he meant on to the ground. He was in hospital for a long time afterwards, but they dragged him slowly. This man had a strange attitude about the Tan War. He did not take part in it, but he was Republican, but he evidently felt no desire to participate. Some Clare men had been here on the run, but when I questioned him, they were men who had been in America for some time. [He had] no real knowledge of the other events on the mainland, but he believed in de Valera as an honest man.

## Sunday, 26 August 1956

Up at 8.20. The Mass call by tap on door. Windows were open in the chapel, but I had not put on my coat. A few men shunted into the seats, but about the Epistle time, Cormac said, 'I'm not feeling well.' He slumped down in his seat, and two of the boys helped to carry him out.[97] He did not get sick, but he remained outside the door. So, did I, and I was able to admire the beauty of the sea and the Clare coast as I stood at the door and during the sermon where men once smoked their pipes outside the door. Not many pennies are put in the box which is to one side of the entry.[98] They pay oats-money at stations twice a year, one in a different village, 2/6 each = 5/o and about £60 at Christmas.[99] That's a good offering, Mrs O'Donnell said.

Some good clover fields to the West of the lake, and there was one field East of the lake, which I thought had clover specially planted in it and maybe it had. It was so rich in red clover, but there's not much of the white clover.

That remark I made about flowers for the past ten years is not correct. They are here longer. Only the very old women were accustomed to smoke pipes. And garlic, they didn't like, Mrs O'Donnell said, when I told her it was good for cooking.

In the fields plenty of Lucullian breed, but now they are pulling out docks by the root and thistles, but already the thistles have seeded and the docks have dropped in seed.[100] It would be hard to persuade anyone here to change a custom on the use of food. I tried to explain about shelter to Coley's sister. But she still keeps her [flowers] in the open, so you say at last what's the use. No flower can grow save the wall is higher than its height and to the West, South/West and North, you need a high wall with a little cement in it, and a gate leading in to the garden so as to keep out the donkeys.

The girl in our house is ... She was a cook rather [than] the cooking instructress who remained here for a year to teach cookery to the girls. The pans are so bulky that it is difficult to cook with them, but at least I helped to introduce oil stoves to the island. She was given a stove herself as an ad[vertisement] by some company, and all I needed was oil. Often there wasn't oil for the school or for the house lamps as the steamer could not come out some weeks here. But why isn't the oil ordered for the school in a drum? Everything, of course, has to be landed here, but once they had their own boats, they could then serve themselves. They get £500 for building a house, and they have to report everything.[101] It takes £600 to build. Aran is not the worst place.

In Dublin when Helen talked about a new sauce, girls would say what could we want that for? There must be the desire to eat strange things, and the will to change diets in terms of interest. There is lettuce on the island, she said. It grows wild in Maurteen's (O'Donnell's) at the back, and the priest's housekeeper hunts for it. 'I could tell Mrs O'Donnell that you like it,' she said, 'and she'd get it for you.' But I would have needed to have brought oil and vinegar mixed.

She can teach them to make buns, but I did not notice any scrambled eggs or pancakes here. Once there was soup, a mass of flour it seemed to me, and the bones were given, I expect, to the dog, but no soup from them. In winter, they eat mutton [in] some houses, but then certain houses never eat meat, potatoes, and they don't kill their pigs here either. Certainly, they could grow rye and fatten a pig for the killing. Firm meat, no fat, but it would be too expensive, I expect. Did she deal with shell fish and fish soups. Salted fish: she grimaced when she spoke of, as it was tasteless. Yet they were accustomed to that once, and it must have been almost pleasant for them. The only taste they had there was for salt for greasy bacon which has a strong taste, and for hard-boiled eggs. I would like to get a schedule of the course. On wet nights her feet were coarsened with driving sand, and she was thoroughly wetted as she came and went across to the school. Was there even a fire there? Is her course based on the material available around them, onion potato soup, omelettes, egg flips, sweet cakes, rye bread, brown bread, fish soups, shell fish and sea weeds?[102] Who knows?

But when I asked was the water harsh? She did not wear a coat from spring onwards. She was browned at her spring holidays, and she had no cold this year nor for the following year. Last year, being a beautiful year, she often went to dances near the school and very often, as the sea was calmer in summer, crossed to Inishmaan, so there is life on the islands. And there were a few weddings when all work ceased. They danced, the men drank from a ¼ barrel, and the old men of 70 who were very nimble were delighted to be asked out for a dance. Yet in between she was despondent about having done any good. The sewing class was of great use as the young girls learned to sew and to knit.

In the evening time as I went to the West, I saw currachs going over to Inishmaan, but then the rain came as I watched dung beetles go up and down human dung, wandering back and forward through the grass. The best light here is the western light which changes the coasts and the island scenery to a kind of radiant gentleness, inducing form.

There were some young girls from Inishmaan over. One of them in a red petticoat and another, a red-haired attractive girl. They were waiting, I could see, for one of their number for he came along, a little tight, and they hurried him along to the boat, but the other boy was quite sober. The trouble about poteen from Connemara is that when it affects them, they drop their oars, which may work free from the [gunnel] or if they fall they fall on the side of the boat and it is upturned, then or if the sea is rough the other rower cannot hold it into the wind.

I met Willie Conneely in the evening at 9. When I asked him out for a drink, he said, 'I'll go back and tell my wife or she'll be worried.' Then we walked around to the pub. We saw a seal. Willie wanted to throw a stone at it. 'Leave him alone,' I said. 'Conneely's are seal people, and they should not be concerned with ill-treating seals.'[103]

We sat in the pub, but he's not much of a talker in English and he talks to questions as if his interior rhythm was disturbed, which I am sure it must be my English. The young fellows are different. The old story. The lobsterman said that the boy who was training for the boat could not go up for a can for him, or be inclined to go on a message.[104] 'They'd tell me more to do it myself.' At the shop Sean [Conneely] says they give [money] to the children at message time for sweets.[105] 'In my time if you got a penny you were lucky.'

The young lad, Anthony, came in to [Sean] Connelly's with two other lads. One of them could sing well, one of the group said. And the songs began in Irish. Anthony held his hand in a grip, swung it up and down, and waved it in a kind of a circle. He had a good voice. Then Willie Conneely began to sing. I did not know what language it was, but it was English. A series of sea songs taught him long ago by the Kerry schoolteacher about sailor lads and girls bereaved when they went to sea and were drownded [sic]. The others knew the verses as he halted every now and then having forgotten them. 'The priest would know if we were here beyond 12,' he said, 'and he'd say a word about it the next day.' 'Who'd tell him?' 'I don't know, but someone would carry the word.'

The lobsterman and the foreman, Buckley from Kilmichael, came in, and the lobsterman had enough of drink, I could see, for though I took one from him, he didn't take one from me. The others drank pints. I draw bottles and Powers whiskey neat; a strong whiskey it was. At about 11 one of Willie's sons, the youngest, came in with a cross face and told him he was wanted home. And in the end, he went at 11.30, first seeing me to my house.

## Monday, 27 August 1956

Cormac said he came in at 10 for me to say that there was a dance up at the school, and he wanted to go, but couldn't go without my permission. Mrs O'Donnell is very lonely at times, I expect. The old live their lives on their daughters as sons have little to do in a house except in winter and then perhaps they wander. The men have no games. I do not know even if they play cards. The women have the delights of gossip for they know everything. Today ... boat, the wooden boat drifted and nearly touched the rocks to the South/East of the strand. That was a matter for excitement and the telling and retelling of the news.

As the Dane was at his door, Cormac and I called in today. He showed us his room which he had built himself and his dyed materials. He buys his blues in France – indigo. He cannot buy them in Ireland, and he uses lichen for critter, yellow from onion skins.[106] Evidently, he means to carry on the dyeing ... and weaving of tapestry, which he showed us. He has, I think, been asked to weave for Buckfast or whatever, the new Benedictine abbey in the South of England, is called.[107] He hopes to be able to do more tapestry, but would like to spend time on it. Now he intends to get a commercial loom so that he can weave heavy *braideen* and dye it with indigo. The dye does not run on the body as does the shop dyes now employed, fading and running. They run, as Bridge Conneely, Willie's sister, says, on the wash. He tried to get a few of the village boys to weave, but he couldn't persuade them.[108] They weren't weavers, and they could not. He began to paint when he came to Dublin. He evidently went in to see pictures on drawings, and he criticized them then he found they were belonging to Seán Keating with whom he had been discussing the works in front of him, but they happened to be Keating's.

He showed me his method of melting wax with paint on the fire, and the result, very good. It is a nice mixture, and when clear on the paper, it does not rub off. He is preparing an exhibition for America. Funny, he says he has no money, yet he goes to Holland and Denmark went last year, he gets his dye ... direct from France, and he talks of a flat in Dublin. So, there must be money.

He had an exhibition last year, and what I saw in his wax which comes, I think, pure from Belgium, was sea rocks under water and above on top of the waves, but I would need to see more of his work to judge it.[109] They don't make crisses like the old crisses now he says. Now he can sell as many as he is able to make of the criss, but he is disappointed that he cannot get boys to be interested in the weaving. In fine wool good dyes and an artist who has feeling and a sense of form there is always a future when he goes into a craft. He reads well, I saw Herodotus on the table, Manur's life of … in French. 'That's a good book,' he said. 'I have read it five times already, and some of the paintings reproduced are in Denmark. Denmark is too material. Everything there is excellent. Cigars used to be o/7, now 1 /2, and they are much better than the Dutch cigars. But I was willing to leave it because it was too material.'

The sense of beauty keeps his life enriched, one can see here in his isolation, but his work of course keeps him going and that is, except tapestry weaving, a trade which leaves his mind as it does with a woman sewing free to wander.

Of the islanders, he likes them well. They are honoured when you call in to the house to visit them. What impressed him most was their sense of story. They can tell stories and amuse themselves. That we cannot do nor can other peoples. But I can see the Slavs and the Russians and the Greeks can entertain themselves. But I know it is a great attraction, this power of speech. In America, the people cannot make up stories for their own children, or for themselves, and that drawback makes them somewhat tongue-tied. The Dane did not know about the sculpture on the mainland, early Irish sculpture, for he did not know of the Clare monument, and, indeed, I may doubt that he has seen any of Irish sculpture. But he is understanding and kind. His friend, a Dane with a beard, has a two-oared currach, and he fishes eels and mackerel. Last year he caught a good deal of mackerel, and he sold a deal of them, Conneely Willy says, but when we talked about the Dane, he says he gives his letters when they are going away to the captain. 'That means,' says Cormac, 'that he does not want them to go through the post office.' 'No, he doesn't want people to see the address.' People here are secretive enough. Why shouldn't the Dane protect himself from pryers and gleaners?

We saw pictures of his exhibition. Siobhan McKenna, he is very fond of.[110] He saw *Saint Joan*.[111] One picture in the Irish pictorial showed McKenna and her [Helen], who helped McKenna with money to go to nursery.[112]

'But you owe me money, then why don't you pay me what is due instead of giving it to an outsider and clearing your honour if you think you have honour.'[113] However, there was no use in talking to the likes of her [Helen] about honour, I am afraid. Always I think of her husband, a long lump of flesh like a DMP man.[114] He is nice but dull. And I do not know, but that maybe she likes many an Irish actress [who] is as dull as cold mutton, or now this island's cooked mutton.

'Why do you Irish always ask if a girl is beautiful,' says a French girl at an American international exhibition ... 'Because maybe they do not understand intelligence, or are fearful of it in a woman.' There is a strange sense of beauty here felt for man and woman. It may be a survival from heroic times. The sense of beauty gone, only land, sea and the body [are] left to them.

'Books can be dangerous enough,' said the Dane.

'I don't know,' I said 'personally, yes, but for you and ignorant people.' Then he ceased to speak as the young man came into the house and went upstairs. There was a sleeping sack in the corner, but no pictures on the wall below. Sample of the *crios* he makes, but no painting that I can now remember. 'That's a different book, *The Idiot* by Dostoyevsky, and a dangerous book,' he says. 'I don't know, but it's an upsetting book for the uninstructed mind. That young man read it.' The young man I feel sorry for as he is too much driven inwards. Both of them go to Mass and to Holy Communion each morning. That itself relates them to the island, but I would not know how secure an anchor it is.

We two, who had overstayed our visit, then wandered away with a goodbye to the Siamese cat with its wonderful blue eyes. It is having kittens, he said, and it was friendly with Cormac and myself, which is unusual enough with Siamese.[115] 'It was very shy at first and would run upstairs when people came in here.'

I remember what Mrs Conneely Willie said about [the Dane] eating seal. They were shocked at it. He spoke about the seal chops himself. It must be a difficult island for him to understand, indeed. Who does understand it, that is a foreigner? We went along down by the lake to search for garlic. What of it I brought back last year lasted in the drawer in Sussex Road until now.[116] Some of it, while the fresh garlic the shop sold garlic decays after one has bought it a month. How does one preserve garlic, maybe by putting it in olive oil, I think. I did that at one time when I put olives in a bottle. We picked the garlic which grows on the roadside and in three fields. The best garlic is in the first field near the sea, but it also grows down at the lighthouse, Cormac tells me. I suppose it was once eaten on the island, but now they talk of it with disgust.[117] Strong tea, strong bacon, strong cabbage, strong salt fish, and I expect at one time strong salt and some butter, but no strong smell of garlic. Many people, I think, buy the shop bread rather than make [oven bread] ... or potato cake. I saw the girl, 'the cook', walking with the priest and a young man, and she was holding his fingertips. Island news says that he is a relation of the priest's.

As I came back rain began close to the buoy, but when I was at the door it was heavier. Afterwards when we had finished our meal, a girl walked in and said 'Hello, Mr O'Malley,' and 'Hello Cormac.' I thought she was Liam Redmond's daughter somehow or how could she have known Cormac.[118]

Later, it began to rain and hail, heavy white hail rattled off the window of my room. Then came thunder. Sudden enough and cold in August. For an hour or more heavy clouds had been moving over the land on the Galway side, but I thought as the Connemara people might think, that heavy clouds over Aran need not be a bad sign, but before I went into the house the clouds had piled up out to sea. The North wind would anyhow make the wind cold. In the meantime, the girl and a man had come into the room. He was talking about marrying, but she was certain that she would not like any man over 26, but he persisted in a half humorous way, a faltering way but he kept on. There was nothing left for me to do except to remain quiet inside and read my Jacquetta Hawkes book on *A Land*.[119] It is a good book written very much like the book on the sea written by an American.[120] The same deft use of words, the same hard lump of scientific material in both and adequate and very pleasant manner without any sentimentality or softness.

It is strange to think of a daughter of Redmond, being the handler of her money and the drainer of her reputation, meeting the two of us on this island and of being able to report to Helen that we are here.[121] Anyhow, her talk through him cannot harm Cormac for I suppose her remarriage[122] may mean that she will relinquish the 'Quest for Cormac'.[123]

The Dane sent me down Graham Greene's book on Mexico.[124] I had spoken of Mexico to him, and I expect he thought that a book on Mexico would interest me. He left word with Cormac that I could leave the book behind in case I had already read it.

Later in the evening I went across to the teacher's house.[125] I found him in the garden where he was planting strawberries, strawberries from Inishmore. 'You'll have to build your wall higher,' I said, 'for strawberries do not like wind.' … He would have to heighten his West wall, but he is somewhat protected from that wind by the ground outside. The deadliest wind is the East, which may last for a month at a time. Normally it is dry, but that is no advantage to its sharpness.

I don't see why a man would not be proud to build a good garden here. Maurteen O'Donnell showed us from the outside his brother's enclosed garden. It was well built. His wife died sometime after Mrs O'Donnell's husband, and then he left the place for a while. Now he is in Mayo, where he built a house for relatives of his.[126]

# AFTERWORD

# *Luke Gibbons*

Commenting on the privacy of diaries, Susan Sontag suggests that words are seldom conveyed to paper for the sole benefit of the writer: 'Superficial to understand the journal as just a receptacle for one's private secret thoughts – like a confidante who is deaf, dumb, and illiterate.'[1] Diaries rather are best conceived as imaginary dialogues, things one would like to say if one got a hearing, thoughts looking for secret sharers in the future, if not in the here and now.

This is very much in the spirit of the labels 'Nobody's Business' that Ernie O'Malley attached to two of his diaries in the present publication. Like his revolutionary activities, O'Malley's writing is quintessentially modern in that it is constantly directed towards the future, what was coming next, or what could be better. The diaries recording his Aran experiences thus represent not only escapes in space – away from his home in Burrishoole Lodge or his last residence at Mespil House, Dublin – but also in time, from a present weighed down by the conformity of post-Revolutionary Ireland, and the cultural torpor of centuries of colonial rule.[2]

Though the diary is a genre devoted to introspection, O'Malley's Aran journals are not exercises in interiority, still less retreats into the self. What Yeats writes of Synge's use of dialect could well be applied to O'Malley: that only through writing 'could he escape self-expression, see all that he did from without'.[3] This helps to explain what might be referred to as 'the gap principle' outlined in the diaries, one of the distinctive traits evinced in O'Malley's dealings with others, or in his attitudes towards art and the environment. Looking at the loose but artfully constructed stone walls of Aran, O'Malley notes that instead of gates, gaps are created to open up spaces rather than close them down: 'The gap principle is always used here [in walls] away from houses. Stones are piled up to fill a gap, torn down when a beast passes through, then built up again. The fields are too small for gates, and there is not enough wood to use for a gate-fence.' If the romantic seeks fusion with a community, an organic connection with a sense of place, the modernist reverts to the 'pathos of distance' (in Nietzsche's phrase) but with an awareness that gaps, acknowledgments of difference, create their own affective ties. The outsider need not be an outcast: distance can lend its own enchantment to the view.

It is striking that the figure of the tramp or tinker – at once inside and outside their respective communities – is presented repeatedly as capturing the precarious position of the artist in the work of J.M. Synge, Jack B. Yeats, Louis le Brocquy and O'Malley himself.[4] This was not due only to roving and impecunious lifestyles: the tinker also displayed expertise and skill in practising a craft and, closer to the avant-garde sensibility, possessed secret language and codes not readily accessible to strangers. In this O'Malley was reminded of his contacts with Native American communities in New Mexico: 'I suppose I understand Indians so well because I understand a little of our own people .... With the Indians I did not want to know of their way of life too much. I deliberately shut off my interest so that they would not feel or resent my curiosity. I could feel with them. I know and share the common human emotions ... They have a secret name for all whites, and they extract great fun from this secret and from their reserved feeling about whites.'

Unlike J.M. Synge, Patrick Pearse and similar visitors to Aran, O'Malley was hampered by his lack of Irish in interacting with the local people: 'And you realize that there is another way of life close to you that you can barely plumb save you have a very good knowledge of their language and have lived amongst them.' But his diffidence on the islands cannot be put down to language alone. For one thing, Aran Islanders such as Pat Mullen tended to laugh at the Irish they heard on the radio: '"He can't speak Irish. His voice goes up and down." The people here can't understand Irish on the wireless.' Had he a mastery of official Irish, O'Malley would still be at one remove from his surroundings, an aloofness he had already experienced as a revolutionary organizer in the countryside during the Irish struggle for Independence. Though 'representing' the people in whose name he was fighting, O'Malley had no illusions that the names of the ideals he was pursuing were on everyone's lips, whether 'the Republic' or 'self-determination' itself.

Yet he had a keen eye for the material conditions of coming to consciousness, not least the importance of placing *forms* of self-respect and self-expression at the disposal of the people. He takes issue with the new modes of 'suburban' architecture lording it over the vernacular forms of the islanders, particularly the kind of two-storeyed houses occupied by the priest, doctor and teacher: 'Their houses show their authority. They [do not] centre the lives of the people in their building. "That is easy talk," my conscience says. "Do you want priests to pull down their fine two-storeyed houses and build a cabin?" "No, I don't, but when they have to build a convent, chapel or house, they should build it as the country man does if they live in the country. There is no use in crying 'back to the land' if people of intelligence build suburban houses in the heart of the country, equip these houses with suburban taste, and then expect to stop the retreat to the city."' O'Malley admired the capacity of Native Americans, though living in destitution, to incorporate their visual forms into modern architectural styles (helped by the indigenous turn in American modernism pioneered by friends of O'Malley's such as Paul Strand, Edward Weston and Georgia O'Keeffe) and his attraction to the dynamic work of Diego Rivera, David Siqueiros and particularly José Clemente Orozco in Mexico lay not only in their advanced political sentiments, but in their experiments in vernacular modernism.

O'Malley looked to modernism because it sought to recast rather than reproduce existing realities. When a conversation with Mrs Keats, who had inherited a farm in Boyle, Co. Roscommon, and her daughter Phoebe, gets around to farm animals, the exchange seems to prefigure Orwell's *Animal Farm*: '"Hens refuse to recognize change," I said. "They're conservative." Then they both spoke badly of hens with real relish. I could see that they had made misery in Mrs Keats's life and in Phoebe's. They are an incalculable force, hens, the most annoying of all farm creatures.'

Much of the diaries can be read as O'Malley's thoughts on the need for change among islanders as they faced the gradual encroachments of modernity on their lives. So far from being cut off from the outside world, as the romantic myth of Aran would have it, the impact of emigration, visits of French and Spanish fishermen, the increased dependence on the steamer *Dun Aengus's* excursions from Galway, the introduction of paraffin oil, radio, and other commodities, the awareness of the Second World War and, above all, the pressing need for new modes of employment and income, all bear witness to the juxtaposition of old and new on the western seaboard.

The diaries continually feature schemes for bringing about improvements in fisheries (techniques, markets), textiles (especially the distinctive crafts of knitting and weaving), kelp-gathering, horticulture, animal husbandry and so on, but O'Malley looks back on his first-hand experiences of the Pueblo and Navajo peoples in New Mexico to recall the destructive potential of a one-way 'civilizing' process. The forced modernizing of Indians by incarcerating young Pueblo or Navajo in boarding 'schools of correction', and decking them out in western garb, is a case in point, depriving indigenous peoples of their most elementary ways of life. Robert Flaherty's documentary film *Man of Aran* (1934) is praised for being the first not only to register the native voice in cinema but also to cast indigenous peoples in leading roles.

The aesthetic, to O'Malley, consists in the capacity to look twice at what is taken for granted, attending to other ways of seeing latent in *form*. This is not solely the preserve of artists but is also to be found in everyday life, or those areas that have not been stifled by adversity, domination and habit. 'In Ireland,' he writes in his essay on Jack B. Yeats, 'the visual sense is not strongly developed in terms of creative painting, but there is a fine feeling for colour, well expressed in small towns where white-wash is mixed with paint powder to give house fronts a fascinating texture of tender pastel shades.'[5] On Aran, this sensibility is to be found in the intricacy of stone walls and currach design but also in patterns in knitting and weaving that found their way into garments marketed at home and abroad through the enterprise of the painter Elizabeth Rivers, and Muriel Gahan in Dublin. 'Each woman has patterns of their own .... It would be interesting to compare the designs with old Irish designs. The colours are grey, which is natural wool, white and indigo. Indigo takes longest here, and there is great secrecy about it.' For this reason, the sending of patterns to Donegal, not to mention the availability of cheaper products from the Scottish Highlands, was not welcomed: 'They are very jealous of each other's sweaters. They each think their own is the best. They won't go to examine patterns in each other's houses, but if they see a sample in Miss Rivers', they jump on it eagerly and examine it thoroughly.'

O'Malley is careful to point out that the mood of acquiescence in the countryside is not to be glossed over but 'needs great understanding, sympathy and thought. It's the very well-educated and the deeply taught or the untaught creative worker who can understand [the rural] people. They are really difficult to understand. One must be educated to them. The Irish approach is to consider that "we come from there, and, of course, we understand them." That is completely wrong.' Rather than a mystical communion, it is intellect and the creative imagination that fathom the silences and renew the potential of the people: 'We are not detached enough even to see them, not alone understand them. There's a wisdom of the heart for your own family, but I doubt that there's a wisdom of the heart for your own nation, when your mind is not stocked and thoroughly equipped. The Irish have a definite facility, but their drawback is that they think they know things and that most of them are experts.'

This anti-intellectualism goes against the grain of the old Gaelic order, but the difficulty is that the great visual achievements lie firmly in the past: 'Was it conquest brought this suspicion [of ideas]? At one time the Irish were open to every idea, and when their best work in manuscript and metal work was being done, they were able to keep abreast of every foreign idiom in their work and to absorb or to change it. Conquest shut them off from the outside world.' Looking almost in despair at the treatment of Aran's rich heritage of ruins and antiquities, O'Malley noticed that a local priest had cemented three fragments of two different crosses to preserve a monument, a kind of modern 'restoration' the island could well do without. The Church's philistinism O'Malley puts down to the Penal Laws and the break-up of the old Gaelic order: cultural nationalism invented continuity where the modernist saw fragmentation and rupture: 'In Ireland there has been a complete break in artistic tradition. You can't expect to compel a people to do without churches and their decoration for over 200 years, do without rich vestments, ritual, choirs and sing the richness of ceremonial in their church and state, and expect people and clergy not to suffer for it.'

In 1919 O'Malley had landed on Inisheer to organize (unsuccessfully) a Volunteer unit to bring resistance to the islands: 'There was no Volunteer Company that I knew of in Aran. Peadar O'Loughlin and I had no help here beyond talk when we came over in 1919. We did not organize a company, and what good a company would have been I do not know. Yet it might have prevented talk and would have been of use if people had later to visit the island secretly.' Thoughts of life on the run, and in captivity, during the Anglo-Irish and Civil Wars are never far from the surface but in keeping with involuntary memory, are usually prompted by chance, external encounters. He meets a priest on Inisheer in 1955 who recognizes him from his articles in *The Sunday Press* (incorporated subsequently into the book *Raids and Rallies* [1982]), but his initial desire to turn away alters when he is informed that the priest – 'What was his name, *Laughton*, I think'– had not only taken the Republican side in the Civil War, during which one of his brothers was imprisoned, but also brought reports to Monsignor John O'Hagan in Rome, whom O'Malley had met in Dublin in 1922 and refused to entertain his 'peace' entreaties, but later befriended in Rome. Cramped with his son Cormac into a small room with few creature comforts, his feelings of discomfort are again tempered by war memories: 'At first glance one thinks this is an impossible situation. Where will I hang my clothes, where will I place my books, my toilet articles, my dirty clothes. But gaol has already solved many things in one's mind.'

The returns to Aran in subsequent decades might be seen as a continuation of his revolutionary mindset, with the emphasis shifting from military to cultural and artistic concerns, spurred on in this case to ensure that Cormac would learn Irish in a safe and secure environment. The same precision is evident in scanning the landscape for movement, the eye for detail, the incisiveness in summing up a character: 'The windows of the bedroom face to the shop and from it one can see movement. The priest when he comes out in the morning, the crowds going to Mass and any little movement there is. Down to the sea on the right another vista of movement as men go down to put out their boats, or to bring up stuff to the shop.' At one point, O'Malley notices that Teresa, a young civil servant visiting the island, is 'reading a cut down edition of *Moby-Dick*, which left out the rhetoric' but in many ways the diaries resemble Melville's original novel, with its endless digressions on nautical history, sailing lore and fishing know-how. Though *Moby-Dick* amounts at times (with 'rhetoric' included) to almost a handbook for whaling, the excessive realism does not rule out a profound underlying intelligence, preoccupied with a whole different set of themes bearing on political, racial and religious matters.

In a similar fashion, though there is no focus on the self, or any kind of soul-searching, in the present diaries, there is no doubt of a personality shaping the style. Descriptions are often striking for their accuracy but they are not 'objective', for all the air of impersonality: they testify to the presence of an acute and attentive observer (if not quite in the shadows, as in Synge's case). On a visit to Inishmaan with the local doctor, Jim O'Brien, O'Malley partakes of the hospitality of a local businesswoman, Moya Flaherty, and notes amusingly the abundance of religious statues and iconography in the house: '"I must count them," I said. "I have never seen the like of this."' They constituted a record in his (admittedly limited) experience of piety, but the parting shot at the end could apply to the role of objects more generally – artefacts, architecture, antiquities, the natural environment – in his own negotiations of inner life: 'I suppose they [religious objects] could be symbolic of your inner state of piety, but they need not be.' At one point, O'Malley seems to bemoan the mate-riality of his surroundings, noting: 'Here in [Elizabeth] Rivers' [house] there is simplicity, the absence of things. Nothing to get in your way or set up a barrage between you and thought.' In truth, however, things, like language, helped him to clear a space for a kind of writing that at once sets him apart from, and yet a part of, his people.

Discussing the classic Blasket Islands memoirs, Tomás Ó Criomhtháin's *An tOileánach* (*The Islandman*) (1929), Muiris Ó Súilleabháin's *Fiche Bliain ag Fás* (*Twenty Years A-Growing*) (1933) and Peig Sayers' *Peig* (1936), Máirín Nic Eoin notes that they were written out of oral cultures, 'which traditionally eschewed the autobiographical': 'The result ... is lacking the psychological impact of much modern prose literature, and [these works are] of interest more for their ethnographic and social content.'[6] This leads Nic Eoin to borrow the term 'autoethnography' from contemporary accounts of life-writing to capture the outlook of the islanders: 'While these accounts may be autobiographical, their authors are usually motivated less by a need to present the self and more by a desire to represent accurately the social experience of [their] cultural group.' O'Malley, unlike native Aran Islanders such as Pat Mullen (*Man of Aran* [1934]) and Tom O'Flaherty (*Aranmen All* [1934]) – the latter whom he surprisingly fails to mention) – was not a member of the commu-nity he was describing, and thus his diaries could not be described as autoethnography, in the strict sense. Yet, in marked contrast to Synge, Pearse and authors of contemporary journals such as his friend Elizabeth Rivers (*Stranger in Aran* [1946]) and Ethel Mannin (*Connemara Journal*, illustrated by Rivers [1947]), O'Malley was born in the west of Ireland, returned to live there and, moreover, had distinguished himself in the fight for Irish Independence.

His assiduous collecting of folklore, recording of endangered lifeways and, indeed, determination to make a living in the west, may be seen as attempts to come closer to a population whose ambivalent loyalties often eluded him during the frequent harrowing ordeals of the Anglo-Irish and Civil Wars. In this sense, Máire Cruise O'Brien's words about Tomás

O'Criomhtháin may also extend to the Aran diaries: '... the objective record is so involved with the personality of the author that, on setting down the book, you feel you've come to know the man'.[7] The astringent tone of many observations and character judgments no doubt precluded their earlier publication (O'Malley had lost a court case for libel in 1937 following the publication of *On Another Man's Wound*), but just as it is said of Jack B. Yeats in one of the conversations in the diaries that he 'hasn't yet found himself' in paint', so O'Malley's writing can be conceived as still trying to find his way in words: 'Often it [writing] doesn't seem of the least importance save as a symbol to get oneself back to what one wants, to write again, but I expect if I could keep writing for a few weeks, I might break myself into something worthwhile. Otherwise I am only fooling myself as I could easily be cut in the opening.'

# NOTES

## Preface

1 The title 'Nobody's Business' was written on two of the 1941 diary notebooks.

2 Ernie O'Malley, *On Another Man's Wound* (Cork 2013, originally 1936).

3 This house had been owned by Owen O'Malley, whose two sons, Austin and Joseph (Jack) had joined the French forces after their landing at Killala in 1798. Thus this house, though not related to my father's Malley family, at least had emotional ties to an earlier Irish revolutionary era.

4 Robert Flaherty (1884–1951) was an American documentary and ethnographic film-maker, well known for *Nanook of the North* (1922), *Moana* (1926) and *Man of Aran* (1934); the latter was the first ever talking documentary film. He moved to Ireland and lived on Inishmore with his wife and family to make his film during 1932–33. He built a small studio in Kilmurvey, which later became known as the Man of Aran Cottage. To finish the film he brought the cast over from Aran to London to record the dialogue. While they were there he made a second film, his first synch-sound production and the first Irish-language talkie, *Oidche Sheanchais.*

5 Kilmurvey House was run by Mrs Bridget Johnston (*née* Coyne of Galway), recent widow of James Johnston. Fellow guests that summer included the American Ambassador to Ireland William Howard Taft IV, William Boggs, Margaret D'Arcy (Russell) and others.

## Introduction

1 Ernie O'Malley, 'Renaissance', *La France Libre* (Dec 1946–Jan 1947), in Cormac K.H. O'Malley and Nicholas Allen (eds.), *Broken Landscapes: Selected Letters of Ernie O'Malley, 1924–1957* (Dublin 2011), pp. 206–12.

2 Mary Cosgrove, 'Ernie O'Malley: Art and Modernism in Ireland', *Eire–Ireland,* 40:3 & 4 (2005), pp. 85–102; O'Malley and Allen, *Broken Landscapes,* pp. 403–06; Róisín Kennedy, 'Flamboyant, Gothic, Romanesque': Art and Revolution

in the mind of Ernie O'Malley' in Cormac K.H. O'Malley (ed.), *Modern Ireland and Revolution: Ernie O'Malley in Context* (Dublin 2016), pp. 17–27.

3 This is discussed in one of the 1956 diaries when one of the young civil servants staying with O'Malley suggested that this was a good thing as it would encourage the sale of work by Irish artists.

4 See for example Donald Akensen, *A Mirror to Kathleen's Face. Education in Independent Ireland 1922–60* (New York 2012, first published Montreal and Kingston 1975).

5 This is encapsulated in the foundation of An Tur Gloine, the stained-glass cooperative by Sarah Purser (1903–44); the decoration of St Brendan's Cathedral, Loughrea, Co. Galway (1902–40) and the design and decoration of the Honan Chapel, University College Cork (1915–17).

6 The Church was to play a leading role in the modernists' side in the controversy over the rejection of Georges Rouault's *Christ and the Soldier* at the Dublin Municipal Gallery of Modern Art in 1942. See Róisín Kennedy, *Art and the Nation State. The Reception of Modern Art in Ireland* (forthcoming).

7 Dermod O'Brien, 'The Churches' neglect of Irish Art', *Commentary*, 1, no. 5 (March–April 1942), pp. 1–2, 5.

8 Sighle Bhreathnach-Lynch, 'Landscape, Space and Gender: Their Role in the Construction of Female Identity in Newly Independent Ireland', in *Ireland's Art. Ireland's History* (Omaha 2007), pp. 73–84; Catherine Nash, 'Re-mapping and re-naming: New Cartographies of Identity, Gender and Landscape in Ireland', *Feminist Review*, 44 (1993), pp. 39–57.

9 Basil Rákóczi visited Inishmore twice in 1942 and held an exhibition of *Watercolours of the Aran Islands* in Dublin in December of that year. S.B. Kennedy, *The White Stag Group* (Dublin 2005), pp. 26–29.

10 S.B. Kennedy, *Elizabeth Rivers 1903–64: A Retrospective View* (Dublin 1989), p. 14.

11 Kennedy, *The White Stag Group*, p. 45.

12 Tim Robinson, *Stones of Aran. Pilgrimage* (Mullingar 1986), pp. 224–25.

13 *Elizabeth Rivers, Memorial Exhibition* (Dublin 1966), pp. 13–14.

14 Lucy Carrington Wertheim, *Adventure in Art* (London 1947), pp. 47–8.

15 James Matthews, *Voices. A Life of Frank O'Connor* (Dublin 1983), p. 194.

16 HSK *Irish Independent*, 28 April 1942, p. 2.

17 Matthews, *Voices. A Life of Frank O'Connor*, p. 194.

18 M.J. MacM, *Irish Press*, 1946.

19 'Drawings and Dolls', *Irish Press*, 12 May 1936, p. 4. (At the end of *Stranger in Aran*, a ghost story of Dara's is retold.)

20 Geraldine Mitchell, *Deeds not Words. The Life and Work of Muriel Gahan* (Dublin 1997), p. 81.

21 Men's jumpers were usually made of undyed grey wool or in a dark indigo blue.

22 Quoted in Mitchell, *Deeds not Words*, p. 77.

23 In a series of interviews that he undertook in 1945 of leading Irish painters, O'Malley notes whether or not they have other sources of income and security. See Cosgrove, 'Ernie O'Malley: Art and Modernism', pp. 100–01.

24 C.R. Vyvyan, *On Timeless Shores. Journeys in Ireland* (London 1957), p. 133; quoted in Mitchell, *Deeds not Words*, p. 88.

25 They are now in the premises of the Irish Countrywomen's Association at An Grianán in Co. Louth.

26 Robinson, *Stones of Aran. Pilgrimage*, p. 223.

27 Note from Patcheen Flaherty of Corough, Kilronan, Inis Mór, to Elizabeth Rivers, 18 December 1960, Elizabeth Rivers Papers, National Library of Ireland, MS 44,670/9.

28 Cormac O'Malley and Anne Dolan (eds), *'No Surrender Here': The Civil War Papers of Ernie O'Malley, 1922–1924* (Dublin 2007), p. xlvii.

29 Letter of O'Malley to Jean McGrail, 6 September 1955, reprinted in *Broken Landscapes*, p. 349.

30 Rivers also blames the demise of the Contemporary Picture Galleries partly on drink.

31 Robert Greacen, *Brief Encounters. Literary Dublin and Belfast in the 1940s* (Dublin 1991), pp. 23–4.

32 S.B. Kennedy, 'An Incisive Aesthetic', *Irish Arts Review*, 21, no. 2 (summer 2004), pp. 90–95.

33 Ernie O'Malley Papers, Box 20, Folder 19, Archives of Irish America #060, New York University Library.

34 Cosgrove, 'Ernie O'Malley: Art and Modernism in Ireland', p. 102.

35 David Hone, 'Charles Lamb', *Charles Lamb RHA 1893–1964. A Memorial Exhibition at the Municipal Gallery of Modern Art, Dublin,* 1–27 April 1969, unpaginated.

36 'Charles Lamb 1893–1964. A Memoir by Arthur Power', *Charles Lamb RHA 1893–1964, A memorial exhibition at the Municipal Gallery of Modern Art, Dublin,* 1–27 April 1969, unpaginated.

37 Todd Andrews, *Dublin Made Me*, quoted in Padraic O'Farrell, *The Ernie O'Malley Story* (Dublin and Cork 1983), p.108.

38 O'Farrell, *The Ernie O'Malley Story*, p. 112.

39 John Turpin, *A School of Art in Dublin Since the Eighteenth Century. A History of the National College of Art and Design* (Dublin 1995), p. 320.

40 Éimear O'Connor, *Seán Keating. Art, Politics and Building the Irish Nation* (Dublin 2013), p. 155.

41 Letter of O'Malley to John V. Kelleher, 7 April 1948, reprinted in *Broken Landscapes*, p. 263.

42 Mainie Jellett, 'RHA and Youth', *Commentary*, May, 1942, p. 5.

43 O'Connor, *Seán Keating. Art. Politics and Building the Irish Nation*, pp. 147–51.

44 Seán Keating, 'A Talk on Art', broadcast 27 March 1931, in Éimear O'Connor (ed.), *Seán Keating in Context* (Dublin 2009), pp. 78–80.

45 Seán Keating, 'Culture and Cant', undated, in O'Connor, *Seán Keating in Context*, pp. 154–5.

46 Letter of Margaret Clarke to Elizabeth Rivers, undated, after 1958, Elizabeth Rivers Papers, National Library of Ireland. MS 44,670/8.

## 1: Inishmore, Aran Islands, September–October 1941

1 O'Malley refers to Inishmore, or *Inis Mór* in Irish, and on occasion to Aran Mor in these diaries; the name Inishmore is used consistently here. Throughout these diaries he also refers to the North or Big Island (Inishmore), the Middle Island (Inishmaan) and the Small or South Island (Inisheer). This 1941 diary is written in at least five notebooks, of which the first and fifth have not been found, but the other three are in the Ernie O'Malley Papers, Archives of Irish America (AIA060), New York University Library, Box 10, Folders 7A/B/C. They were written in late September or October 1941. O'Malley wrote 'Nobody's Business' on the cover of the notebooks.

2 The Keats family, who were also staying at the Man of Aran Cottage with Elizabeth Rivers, consisted of Tony Keats, a retired British army career officer who had been stationed in India and held prisoner in Turkey, his wife, Mrs Keats, who had been a singer in London and inherited land in Boyle, Co. Roscommon, their two grown daughters, Phoebe and Phyllis, and their youngest child, Tony.

3 Roisin Walsh (c.1890–1949), Chief Dublin City Librarian in Pearse Street, was the daughter of James Walsh, a Tyrone hedge-school teacher who had vacated his home in 1918 when threatened with firebombing. The family moved to Dublin. Roisin, who was working in Belfast, was dismissed after 1920 when she refused to take their Oath of Allegiance, and she too moved to Dublin where she joined the library system. She was active in Saor Éire. She was the unexpected guest who arrived at O'Malley's home, Burrishoole Lodge, Newport, Co. Mayo, and triggered his escape to Aran. Helen O'Malley had designed the interior painting for the Pearse Street Library for Walsh and had become a good friend.

4 The bombing probably referred to the German Blitz bombing of London in September 1940.

5 Elizabeth Rivers (1903–64), born in England, educated at Goldsmith's College and the Royal College of Art, London and at the Académie Lhote and Gino Severini's École de Fresque in Paris. She visited Inishmore in 1934, returning the following year when she rented Robert Flaherty's Man of Aran Cottage just near the quay in Kilmurvey, and remaining there until 1943. She moved to London to participate in the auxiliary fire service. At the end of the war she returned to Inishmore and published her account of life there, *Stranger in Aran*, in 1946. She lived in Dublin, with periods in London and Israel, from 1946 to 1955 when she assisted Evie Hone in her stained-glass work. Her last one-woman show was at the Dawson Gallery in 1960. Rivers was an important illustrator and printmaker and was involved in the foundation of the Graphic Studio in Dublin in 1960. O'Malley refers to her by various names, but herein she is referred to as Rivers. She also published under the name of Elizabeth Joyce.

6 Galway Bay.

7 Julian Huxley (1887–1975), English evolutionary biologist and brother of Aldous Huxley.

8 Aldous Huxley (1894–1963), English novelist, *Brave New World*, published in 1932.

9 O'Malley had lived in Mexico in 1931 and was well read on Mexican life, art and its Indian cultures. He wrote 'mexsitoes' but probably intended to write

'mestizos' meaning people of mixed blood or 'mixed people'.

10  Dorothy Brett (1883–1977), the Honourable but known to her friends as 'Brett', had been the amanuensis for D.H. Lawrence in England and moved to Taos, New Mexico with the Lawrences at the invitation of Mabel Dodge Luhan in 1923, but when the Lawrences left in 1924, Brett stayed on. O'Malley met her when he lived in Taos in 1929–1932 and house-sat for her on occasion.

11  Wrack and kelp are forms of seaweed, which were harvested by islanders and burnt to produce a form of fertilizer. This production was an important part of the economy of the west coast. In the nineteenth and early twentieth centuries its distribution provided islanders and poor coastal dwellers with an income. The burnt residue was also used in the beauty industry and in the making of iodine and nylons.

12  Matthew Arnold (1822–85), English poet and critic. In 1857 Arnold was elected Professor of Poetry at Oxford. He is more widely known as a literary critic and commentator on cultural issues. His books include *Essays in Criticism* (1865), *Culture and Anarchy* (1869), *Discourses on America* (1885) and *Essays in Criticism, Second Series*, (1888). O'Malley refers to Arnold's influential *On the Study of Celtic Literature* (1967) in which the characteristics of Anglo-Saxon literature and Celtic literature are compared. The study stressed the 'sentiment' of the Celt. The book led to the establishment of a Chair of Celtic at Oxford in 1877.

13  Pat Mullen (1883–1976) was born on Inishmore, son of John Mullen and one of eleven children. He emigrated to Boston in about 1905, and became involved in labour and social issues. He married Bridget McDonough from Connemara, and they had seven children. Mullen was a member of the James Connolly Socialist Club and knew James Larkin in Boston. He returned to Inishmore in 1921. He later worked as assistant director on location for Robert Flaherty in the making of *Man of Aran*, 1932–33 and recruited cast members and appeared in film as a basking-shark hunter. His book *Man of Aran*, an account of the making of the film, was published in 1934. He later published *Hero Breed* (1936), *Irish Tales* (1938) and *Come Another Day* (1940). He emigrated to Anglesey, Wales in the early 1950s, returning to spend his summers on Inishmore. [Lawrence William White, 'Patrick Mullen', *Dictionary of Irish Biography*, 6, RIA, 2009, pp. 762–64.]

14  James Johnston (1884–1953), son of Patrick O'Flaherty Johnston and Lily Johnston, lived in Kilmurvey House, Kilmurvey, and had seven siblings. He was the largest landowner on Inishmore and often had difficulties with his neighbours and tenants. He married a much younger Bridget Coyne of Galway in the 1940s but they had no children. After he died in 1953 she married Sonny Hernon of Kilmurvey and their daughter, Tresca Hernon Joyce, still lives there.

15  Darts might have been played prior to 1932. Robert Joseph Flaherty (1884–1951), American film director who made *Nanook of the North* in 1924, made *Man of Aran* while living on Inishmore for two years, 1932–33. It was the first talking documentary film.

16  10 pm evening news on Radio Éireann, which was the Dublin-based national radio broadcasting station.

17  Reference to the BBC or British Broadcasting Corporation, the British government-run radio station's nightly news.

18 Ernest Hemingway (1899–1961) published this novel in 1940. Robert Jordan, the principal character, is involved in the International Brigade supporting the Spanish Republic in the Spanish Civil War. O'Malley also supported the Republican side in the struggle and spoke in their defence in November 1936 in Dublin. See *Broken Landscapes*, p. 129. Hemingway had read the American edition of O'Malley's memoir, *Army Without Banners,* after its publication there in 1937.

19 Ireland's Censorship (of Publications) Board (1929) banned many distinguished novels and indeed their listing of banned books could be seen in part as a guide to modern literature.

20 *Fiesta*, published in 1926, was based on Hemingway's experiences in Spain in 1925, which is when O'Malley had been there.

21 A principal character in the novel.

22 It is interesting that O'Malley recognized this characteristic of Hemingway's writing as O'Malley had himself maintained a relatively impartial attitude towards his subjects in his own memoirs.

23 O'Malley probably used 'bicyclist' as a term referring to Hemingway's sympathy for Republicans who often used bicycles.

24 P.J. Mullen (1917–83) was a fisherman, amongst other things, on Inishmore, married Bridie Hernon, and their sons, Paddy and Michael Mullen, lived on Inishmore.

25 A boatman and carpenter who lived at Acres, near O'Malley's home in Newport, Co. Mayo.

26 A pilot and fisherman who lived on Islandmore, in Clew Bay, Co. Mayo. O'Malley used to sail out to Islandmore and stay there and go sailing and fishing with him.

27 Midges would refer to midgies or small flies, which were quite common on Aran.

28 Dr John ('Jim') O'Brien (1883–1970) was the local doctor who lived in Kilronan. His mother, Margaret Hernon from Kilmurvey, married a Connemara man, John O'Brien, who settled into his wife's family home and became a farmer and publican. They had three daughters, Marianne, Delia and Alice, and two sons. Jim (Seamus) attended Blackrock College, completed his medical degree at the Royal College of Surgeons in Ireland in 1909 and returned to Kilronan in about 1923. He eventually took over the practice of the Dr Michael O'Brien (born 1849) of Killeany who had come to Aran in 1905 from Clare. Jim O'Brien was still in Aran in 1954–56 when O'Malley returned for the months of August. His sister, Marianne, married Martin O'Flaherty in 1903 and lived in Kilronan. Another sister went to the US, returned to care for their mother and married Ned Bannon. After her mother's death she lived in Kilronan. Dr Michael O'Brien's son, Conor (1895–1964), was a classmate of Liam O'Flaherty's, attended Blackrock College, left UCD in 1915 to join the 7th Leinsters Regiment and remained in the British army for thirty years.

29 O'Malley had found previously in Co. Mayo that if his wife accompanied him on a visit to local storytellers the tenor of the conversation and the social interaction changed significantly, and so when collecting folktales around Clew Bay in the evenings of the winter of 1940 he went alone.

30 Kilmurvey pier, just below the Man of Aran Cottage.

31 Mr Moloney. There were four schools on Inishmore in 1941. The Kilronan school principal was Patrick Hehir (a native Irish speaker from Clare who married Delia O'Flaherty, who was an assistant teacher there with Mrs Ann McHale); the Killeany school principal was James Donnellan, with his assistant Delia Mullin of Kilronan; the Oatquarter (*Scoil Cheathrar Álainn*) school principal was Mr Moloney, with his assistant Margaret O'Flaherty; and the Onaght (*Scoil Naomh Padraig*) school principal was Donie Flanagan, with his assistant Mrs Flanagan (his mother).

32 Moloney's school at Oatquarter was on the Kilronan-Kilmurvey road near Kilmurvey.

33 Delia O'Flaherty married Patrick Hehir, and they lived near Kilronan.

34 O'Malley's reference to an 'unisland' house might refer to his own view that this relatively new two-storey house was not similar to the other more traditional island cottages and thus 'unisland'.

35 O'Malley refers to the old thatched cottage here without allowing for the fact that some cottage owners might wish to build a more modern house. It can be argued that since the landlord often had a two-storey house, it was important for the doctor, priest and schoolteacher to have a two-storey house to show a certain status in the community not to mention modernity, which they could afford. It is also said that the priest's house had to be grand enough to host his bishop comfortably on his occasional visit.

36 In his diaries O'Malley often wrote dialogues with his conscience, for example, in New Mexico in 1929. See AIA060, Box 42, Folder 34, p. 71.

37 Dr Jim O'Brien ran a pub next to his own two-storey home. Pampooties are typical Aran slippers for men and women made out of cowhide. Men wore them to go in and out of the ocean water to get into their currachs as the leather dries quickly.

38 Killeany, just south of Kilronan.

39 O'Malley had been a medical student and thus could talk to Dr O'Brien almost as a fellow doctor.

40 Molly Gill Egan ran a small boutique store in her home on the Quay in Westport.

41 Sir Martin Frobisher (1535–94) was Vice Admiral of Drake's West Indies expedition in 1585.

42 Sir Francis Drake (1545–96) was an English sea captain, explorer and pirate and familiar with the Elizabethan court.

43 This could have been a reference to the visit of Christopher Columbus to Galway before setting sail for the New Indies, but that was in the fifteenth century.

44 Sir Richard Bingham (1528–99), English military and naval leader, was president in 1584.

45 Possibly a reference to the O'Flaherty Clan of Connemara into whom Grace O'Malley had first been married in the mid sixteenth century.

46 John Masefield (1878–1967), poet, novelist and dramatist, was a close friend of W.B. Yeats and his brother, Jack B. Yeats, whom he met in 1902. He introduced Jack to J.M. Synge in 1905. Jack and Masefield shared a passion for the sea and for tales of piracy and buccaneers. He wrote *Philip, the King and Other Poems*, published in 1912.

47  *Sir Julian Staff Corbett*, published in 1916.

48  A coastal port town in Co. Clare.

49  Arkin's Castle was built by Cromwellian soldiers in the mid seventeenth century from the stones of four churches, located near Killeany Bay on Inishmore, and was garrisoned until the end of the eighteenth century.

50  Possibly the Irish Land Commission [Board], the successor to the Congested Districts Board or CDB in 1922.

51  The cemetery at St Enda's Chapel in Killeany.

52  Bent is a strong grass that could grow in sand. Marram grass is used there today.

53  A scalp or *scailp* is a gap, cleft or fissure in the platform of rock formations, and in this case it led down to the ocean.

54  A loy or *láí* is used to cut turf though in some parts it is called a slane or *sleán*. The murder by William O'Malley of his father in Connemara in 1873 (see TG4's 2007 documentary *Blood and Ink: the Legendary Running of the Máillach*) and the attempted murder by James Lynchehaun of Agnes McDonnell in Achill in 1894 (see the 1993 film *Love and Rage*) were the stories on which J.M. Synge based his principal character, Christy Mahon, in his 1907 play, *Playboy of the Western World*.

55  Purportedly he was principally kept in Gregory's Cave.

56  Possibly the Land Commission [Board].

57  O'Malley refers here to the Fianna Fáil government who at that time during the Emergency were jailing members of the IRA, some of whom were their former comrades.

58  A greeting meaning 'God be with you'.

59  Tea would have been strictly rationed during the Emergency war years.

60  A hundredweight or 'cwt' equals 112 pounds or over fifty kilos.

61  A stone is 14 pounds or 6.35 kilos, which represents an enormous mark-up in prices.

62  Rufous meaning reddish brown.

63  Suck refers to breastfeeding a baby.

64  Petticoats were often worn by boys up through the late 1940s. Having boys wear petticoats related to a common superstition that the fairies were less likely to steal a girl than a boy.

65  O'Malley was mistaken here as the play was actually translated into Irish by Connemara actor Tomas Ó Flaithearta. He might have been thinking of MacDara Ó Fatharta (MacDara Faherty) from Inishmaan, who was an actor in the Taibhdhearc (the Irish language theatre in Galway).

66  This is a condition where a boy has watery fluids around his testicles causing swelling of the scrotum.

67  *Bán* means white in Irish. Perhaps O'Malley is referring to a white-looking eel.

68  The nurse, Molly, married Mr Darcy, the schoolteacher on Inishmaan.

69  Building a house to look to the west was uncommon. There was a belief that the 'good people', the fairies, walked to the west side of a house, thus people would not extend their house to the west so as not to interfere with their path. There is a saying: 'Only someone stronger than God would build to the west of a house.'

70  Reducing the height of the walls reduced the exposure to the west wind.

71 Skied meaning skipped on the water surface.

72 A factor was an intermediary or buyer who would resell the kelp residue.

73 This hotel, then owned by the MacDonagh family, was located on Gorumna Island, off Lettermore Island, Co. Galway.

74 Poteen or *poitín* is illicit whiskey made from various grains, such as wheat, or potatoes.

75 A flail is used to thresh the seed out of the rye or wheat stalk.

76 Fr O'Malley was the parish priest for Inisheer and Inishmaan and later moved to Kylemore Abbey, Co. Galway.

77 O'Malley included 'could not' here, but given the context of this sentence the 'not' after 'could' has been deleted.

78 A Benedictine order of nuns ran a girls' school at Kylemore Abbey on the Leenane-Clifden road.

79 *Astragalus danicus* is a purple milk-vetch perennial herb, which grows on lime-stone and calcareous soil such as in Aran or the Burren.

80 Charles E. Nelson, *Wild Plants of the Burren and the Aran Islands* (Cork 2008), p. 160.

81 The graveyard at St Enda's Chapel, Killeany.

82 A hooker is a wooden boat made in Connemara that carried turf out to the islands, among other things, but in this case the turf had not been sold, and the boat left still fully loaded.

83 For more on O'Malley's visit to Inisheer in 1919 when trying to organize the Irish Volunteers there, see *On Another Man's Wound* (Cork 2013), p. 134.

84 Department of Agriculture pamphlets of which O'Malley obtained many to learn about diverse aspects of farming, animal husbandry, beekeeping, vegetables and others.

85 Kilmeena is a village near Newport on the Clew Bay side of the Westport road.

86 O'Malley refers again to his own preferences for a thatched cottage environment – more like the Man of Aran Cottage perhaps – rather than a two-storey house, like those he had always lived in, but he is ambivalent here as clearly he wants or needs more than a mere cottage for himself and his family to live in.

87 Louis MacNeice (1907–63), a Belfast-born poet, friend of O'Malley. His book was published in 1941.

88 Rainer Maria Rilke (1875–1926), Czech-born poet who moved to Switzerland; much of his poetry was written in French. O'Malley had translated some of his poems into English.

89 Fr Jack Hanlon (1913–68) was ordained at Maynooth in 1939. He had taken private lessons in art with Mainie Jellett, exhibiting at the RHA from 1934. In 1936 he was awarded the Taylor Prize and attended the academy of André Lhote in Paris. In 1943 he was one of the founders of the Irish Exhibition of Living Art. In the 1950s and 1960s he undertook a number of commissions for the Catholic Church, including the design of mass vestments for Pope Pius XII in 1957 and panels for the Church of the Holy Rosary, Limerick in 1958. He is best known for his watercolour paintings, exhibiting with the Watercolour Society of Ireland from 1940.

90 Máire Scully or Máire Ni Scolaí was born in Mayo and died in 1985. She moved to Galway where she pursued singing in Irish and acting and did many

broadcasts early on for Radio Éireann. She married Professor Liam Ó Buachalla (1899–1970), a professor of economics at NUI Galway, a TD first in 1939 and later Chairman of the Irish Seanad for twenty years.

91  Foley might have been Allan James Foley (1837–99), an Irish-born early international classical singer who also sang popular ballads and knew Count John McCormack. Mrs Keats might have heard of him and his records in her London musical circle.

92  The 'sins' probably included the Fianna Fáil government position on neutrality during the Emergency and thus not joining with the British empire in its continental and worldwide war efforts. O'Malley writes in 1946 explaining Irish neutrality in his article 'Renaissance' in *La France Libre*, XIII:74, in *Broken Landscapes*, p. 406.

93  Douglas Hyde (1860–1949) was the first president of Ireland under the new 1937 de Valera constitution.

94  Mrs Kiernan was Delia Murphy of Co. Mayo who married Thomas J. Kiernan, former director of programming at Radio Éireann in 1939 and later a diplomat, including postings in the Holy See, Germany, Australia and the United States.

95  There were twenty shillings in one pound.

96  O'Malley mistakenly referred to 'Dun Angus' instead of its correct name, Dun Aengus or *Dún Aonghasa*, which is a prehistoric hillfort dating from about 1000 BC perched on a 300-foot cliff edge facing the Atlantic near Kilmurvey House in Kilmurvey.

97  New milk probably refers to milk taken from a cow and fed immediately to a calf.

98  The RSA or The Royal Society of Antiquaries of Ireland was founded in 1849 as the Kilkenny Archaeological Society. O'Malley has joined the RSAI in 1935 when he returned from America and must have read an article in the *RSAI Journal* on Dun Aengus.

99  Mikhail Yuryevich Lermontov (1814–41), a Russian aristocrat writer, poet and painter who served in the military.

100  Probably *The Elephant Boy*, made in 1937.

101  Paul Strand (1890–1978), American photographer and film-maker. O'Malley had met Strand in Taos, New Mexico in the spring of 1932 just before O'Malley moved to New York and they stayed in touch over the years. O'Malley's letters to Strand are included in *Broken Landscapes*.

102  Paul Strand's film *Redes* was made in Mexico in 1937 and financed by the Mexican government.

103  Barracked meaning heckled, an old form of English.

104  An outside car is a sidecar or jaunting car where one sits on the outside not inside as in a trap.

105  Helen O'Malley was at that time proposing to build modern farm buildings to house the first tubercular-tested herd west of the Shannon as well as a dairy, cow shed, calf shed, pig shed, turf sheds, potato shed and studio.

106  A ranker is an enlisted man but could also refer to a soldier who becomes an officer though socially might be considered still to be a soldier.

107  Richard St Barbe Baker, *Men of the Trees*, published in 1931. He was the founder in 1922 in Kenya of the international organization called Men of the Trees.

108 Willie Walsh was the closest neighbour to O'Malley's home at Burrishoole Lodge. Pat Clarke was a farm hand at Burrishoole who lived nearby.

109 Sallies were used to make baskets and lobster pots among other things.

110 Arranged marriages were common in Aran, and throughout the West of Ireland, up into the mid twentieth century but more usual among farmers, shopkeepers or commercial families. It was a way to make sure that the land or business would stay in the family and accrete with new lands being brought in as dowry from the women marrying into the family. Elizabeth Rivers refers to this aspect of Aran culture in her book, *Stranger in Aran* (Dublin 1946) p. 36.

111 Another local story O'Malley knew was about Nora Kelly of Islandmore who married Pat Quinn of Inniscuttle, both in Clew Bay. Nora used to say that she went into Newport one fair day to see the 'shape' of Pat Quinn, whom she understood she was to marry, and she liked what she saw, and they lived happily ever afterwards.

112 The Irish language was used during the Korean War by Americans who were trained in Irish.

113 O'Malley mistook wheat for rye here. Thatchers used rye as it is could grow readily on the poor Aran land.

114 Eggs were typically boiled or fried.

115 Murrisk is a small village on the south shore of Clew Bay, three miles west of Westport and overlooked by Croagh Patrick.

116 Winkles or periwinkles are small shellfish. One needs to pry out the small fish. They are common on the west coast.

117 Queen Elizabeth I of England (1533–1603) ascended to the throne in 1558.

118 Bon Secours Mother and Baby Home, Tuam, Co. Galway, was in operation 1925 to 1961. It has recently been in the news in connection with queries about the deaths of children there.

119 O'Malley's view of the soldiers who became officers in the Irish Free State National Army.

120 Denis J. Coffey (1865–1940), President of UCD from 1903 to 1940. Coffey was president during all three of O'Malley's efforts at medical school and his son, Donough, was part of O'Malley's Dramatic Society in 1927–28 at UCD.

121 There are many stories about fairies on Aran and throughout the west coast, and O'Malley had written up folktales on fairies, among other subjects, around Clew Bay in the winter of 1940. These tales are lodged with the National Folklore Commission at UCD and the Archives of Irish America, NYUL AIA060, Box 15, Folder 18.

122 To cultivate crops seaweed is placed around the stems to help fertilize them.

123 A 'fourth' refers to a specific area of land.

124 Onaght is a townland at the western end of Inishmore, and is also called the Seven Churches.

125 Johnston's cattle were intentionally drowned, which is reminiscent in part of John B. Keane's 1965 novel, *The Field*, which in 1990 was made into a film by Jim Sheridan, where cattle are driven over a cliff in a local dispute.

126 Port Murvey is the small harbour close to Kilmurvey on Inishmore.

127 'Up the country' refers to the mainland, perhaps land offered by the Congested Districts Board or, after 1922, by the Irish Land Commission.

128 O'Malley is suggesting that the Irish Land Commission could seize Johnston's lands and redistribute them to his neighbours who could make an application for them.

129 A 'smack' is a small fishing boat.

130 O'Malley is commenting as to how the Irish farmers have not striven to improve their lot as had been expected after the achievement of the dominion status that came with the creation of the Irish Free State in 1922.

131 Bofin being Inishbofin. John Halloran, a fisherman there, had two sons, John and Pat, both also fishermen.

132 The father, John, is referring to his son, John.

133 Most western point in Co. Galway, and it has a lighthouse.

134 O'Malley had been sailing, often by himself, in Clew Bay for three years and had become quite an experienced sailor.

135 Charles Lamb (1893–1964), Portadown-born artist who studied at Belfast College of Art and Metropolitan School of Art, Dublin (1919–23). He first visited Carraroe, Co. Galway in 1921 and settled there with his family in 1935. He ran a summer school for painters from his home. He was a regular exhibitor at the Society of Dublin Painters, a modernist exhibition society, in the 1920s and 1930s. He also painted in Brittany in 1926–27. According to S.B. Kennedy (*Irish Art and Modernism*, 1991, p. 31) Lamb's work, which centred on depictions of the West, declined in quality in the 1930s. He was elected a member of the RHA in 1938. He died in Carraroe suddenly in December 1964. A highly regarded painter, there was a retrospective exhibition of his work at the Hugh Lane Municipal Gallery of Modern Art in Dublin in 1969.

136 Rivers was involved in commissioning and sending knitwear from Inishmore to Muriel Gahan's Country Shop at 23 St Stephen's Green, Dublin. This provided an important income to the women on the island as well as encouraging the continued development of the craft.

137 According to Geraldine Mitchell in *Deeds not Words. The Life and Work of Muriel Gahan* (Dublin 1997), p. 87, this explanation was given to Rivers when she first came to Inishmore in 1934. Interesting that a craft associated with women should be attributed to male genius! The traditional Aran jumper was not known before the beginning of the twentieth century. It made its appearance after the Congested Districts Board introduced deep-sea fishing into the islands and its design appears to have been influenced by the complex stitching found on Scottish fishermen's jumpers.

138 The criss or *crios* was made of wool as a waistband and used by men to hold up their trousers.

139 Tourists had been buying crisses from families on the Aran Islands for many years. Muriel Gahan had been selling them in the Country Shop in Dublin since 1931.

140 O'Malley had seen many Russian films while in New York during 1932–35 and had met the Russian film-maker Sergei Eisenstein and his cinematographer Eduard Tisse while they were filming in Mexico in 1931.

141 René Clair (1898–1981), French film director, made *Le Million* in 1931.

142 *La Kermesse Héroïque* was made in 1935 by Jacques Feyder and René Clair was associated with *Le Million*.

143 Picture here means a film or movie.

144 Visiting mission priests regularly condemned card-playing, which was actually quite common, but probably played privately, and thus O'Malley failed to observe any card-playing, a pastime he did not like.

145 Samuel Johnson actually wrote 'patriotism is the last refuge of a scoundrel' in 1775.

146 *Hero Breed* by Pat Mullen was published in 1936, and *Irish Tales* in 1938.

147 Virginia Woolf (1882–1941). Her last novel, *Between the Acts*, was published in June 1941, shortly after she committed suicide in March.

148 O'Malley had an interest in tinkers and their traditions. He mentioned tinkers in his New Mexican diaries, and he knew of them in his Clew Bay folktales. Several years later he introduced Louis le Brocquy to tinkers and their way of thinking as being outsiders. Tinkers would occasionally visit Aran, not to live, but to mend pots and pans and sell holy religious pictures, medals and threads.

149 A gombeen man is a shopkeeper or commercial man who also lends money and earns interest thereby.

150 Barbara Mullen (1914–79), daughter of Pat and Bridget Mullen, was born in Boston and returned to Inishmore in 1932 for the filming of *Man of Aran*. She met and later married John Taylor, who was Robert Flaherty's film laboratory technician, and moved to England. She went on to write of her early reminiscences in *Life Is My Adventure* in 1937 and had a successful acting, dancing and singing career in London.

151 John Millington Synge (1871–1909), Irish author and playwright. Dublin-born and a graduate of Trinity College, Synge spent most of the years from 1895 to 1903 in Germany and Paris. In 1898 on the advice of W.B. Yeats he began a series of annual visits to the Aran Islands (1898–1902), staying on Inishmaan. Learning to speak Gaelic fluently, Synge wrote an account of his time on the islands in *The Aran Islands* in 1901 (published 1907). The experience also inspired three of his major plays, *Riders to the Sea* (1904), *Well of the Saints* (1905), and *The Playboy of the Western World* (1907). He died prematurely in 1909.

152 In 1904 John Masefield suggested that J.M. Synge write a series of articles on the Aran Islands. The following year Synge made an extensive tour of the Congested Districts Board of Galway and Mayo with Jack B. Yeats and the resulting series of illustrated articles appeared in the *Manchester Guardian*. Yeats illustrated Synge's *Man of Aran* (1907).

153 Rivers did publish her book on the Aran Islands, *Stranger in Aran*, in 1946.

154 O'Flaherty never did write his memoir though elements of local lore were included in his short stories.

155 Seán O'Sullivan (1906–64), Dublin-based portrait painter. He studied at the Metropolitan School of Art, Dublin and at La Grande Chaumière and Colarossi's, Paris, 1927–28. He made numerous portraits in oil as well as in pencil. In 1939 he visited Burrishoole and did a large oil portrait of O'Malley, which is still owned by his family. He had also recently completed several pencil portraits of O'Malley, one of which is now in the National Portrait Collection of the National Gallery of Ireland.

156 Maurice MacGonigal (1900–79), Dublin-born artist and friend of O'Malley. He used to visit Achill to paint and stopped by Burrishoole Lodge on his way there in the 1938–41 period. He had served under John/Seán Dowling in the War of Independence and was interned 1920–21. Upon winning the Taylor Prize in 1923, he attended the Metropolitan School of Art (1923–26) and first visited the Aran Islands in 1924. The West became a major theme in his subsequent work. He was a founding member of the Radical Club in 1926. He taught at the Metropolitan School, later the National College of Art, from 1934 to 1969, and succeeded Seán Keating there as Professor of Painting in 1954. He exhibited at the RHA (1924–79) and was an active member from his election in 1933.

157 Harry Kernoff (1900–74) was born in London of Russian-Sephardic Jewish extraction. After his family moved to Dublin, he attended night classes at the Metropolitan School of Art, winning the Taylor Scholarship, which enabled him to become a day student in 1923. He exhibited at the Society of Dublin Painters in 1920s and was interested in modernism, which he studied on visits to London and Paris. He produced stage sets for the Dublin Drama League. A member of the Radical Club and the Friends of Soviet Russia, Kernoff designed the masthead of *Irish Workers' Voice* and visited Leningrad and Moscow in 1930. He exhibited at the RHA from 1926, becoming a member in 1936. His painting turned towards a realist manner from the 1930s onwards.

158 Jack B. Yeats (1871–1957), artist, dramatist. He was born in London, the youngest child of painter John Butler Yeats and brother of W.B. Yeats. He was brought up in Sligo and trained and worked as an illustrator in England, returning to live permanently in Ireland in 1910. From 1899 he exhibited paintings of Irish subjects in Dublin and London. He met O'Malley in 1937. Between 1939 and 1945 O'Malley acquired eight oils by Jack B. Yeats and wrote the exhibition catalogue introduction for the major Jack. B. Yeats National Loan Exhibition in 1945. From 1943 Yeats's work was shown at the Victor Waddington Galleries in Dublin as well as RHA and the Irish Exhibition of Living Art.

159 Cecil Salkeld (1904–69), artist, writer, and dramatist. He was born in India, the son of the poet and actress Blanaid Salkeld. Educated in England and Ireland, Salkeld studied at the Metropolitan School of Art, Dublin from 1919–21, and then in at the Kunstschule, Kassel, Germany, in 1921. He co-edited the avant-garde journal *To-morrow* (1924). He exhibited at RHA from 1929 and was a member of the Society of Dublin Painters from 1927. He lived in Berlin for a year in 1932, painted a three-part mural in Davy Byrne's Pub in 1942 and co-founded the Irish National Ballet School in 1940s. He married Irma Taesler in Germany in 1922. Their younger daughter Beatrice married the author Brendan Behan in 1954.

160 Old Johnston probably refers to James Johnston's father, Patrick O'Flaherty Johnston.

161 The Johnstons had acquired their original lands from an O'Flaherty through marriage, and James Johnston had a middle name of O'Flaherty.

162 Francis MacNamara (1884–1946), poet and landowner. Clare born, Harrow and Oxford educated, he was a close friend of the artist Augustus John. He

abandoned his studies to pursue a literary career and published a book of poetry, *Marionettes*, in 1909. He edited the *Writings of Henry the Eighth* (1924) and translated a volume of *The Lives of Gallant Ladies* by Pierre de Bourdeille (1924). In 1915 he travelled to the Aran Islands and learned Irish. His home in Doolin was burned by the Black and Tans in 1920. In 1936 he transformed Ennistymon House into the Falls Hotel. He wrote book reviews for *The Bell* in 1941. His daughter Caitlin married Dylan Thomas.

163 Liam O'Flaherty (1896–1984), author, was born in the village of Gort na gCapall, just near Kilmurvey on Inishmore. He was the eighth of fourteen children. He married Margaret Barrington, but the marriage broke up in 1932. O'Flaherty was in California for the filming of *The Informer,* based on his 1925 novel, directed by John Ford, when he met Catherine (Kitty) Harding Taylor, who divorced her husband and remained Liam's companion for the rest of his life.

164 Interesting observation by O'Malley who also found an American partner who had had her own life in the arts before their marriage and similarly knew nothing of Ireland's turbulent history before arriving in Dublin.

165 The caravan was brought down by train from Dublin to Galway after Lamb's honeymoon when he and his bride Katharine travelled out to Carraroe in it. In 1928 Lamb brought the caravan over to the Aran Islands on a painting trip. It belonged to his wife who had used it for her veterinary duties in Dublin. (Laillí Lamb de Buitlear, in *Lamb in Connemara at the AVA Gallery,* Adams at Clandeboye, 2012.)

166 Francis Hugh Power (1879–1955) was latterly known as An Paorach. He was born in Plymouth, England, to a Cork father and Scottish mother. After attending public school, he spent time in a seminary in Spain. He went to Dublin in 1906 and became a travelling Irish teacher. He taught in Achillbeg, Co. Mayo, from 1913 to 1922. He joined Sinn Féin, the Irish Volunteers and the IRA in West Mayo. He married in 1923 and lived in Newport until 1945 and then moved to Galway.

167 *A shliocht orthu* meaning 'a sign is on them'. O'Malley's 'signs' could refer to the results of interbreeding on Aran due to the lack of new imported blood lines.

168 Helen O'Malley.

169 O'Malley had spent many months climbing in the Pyrenees in 1925–26, and had written an unpublished memoir of that experience and so was quite knowledge-able about climbing.

170 Blánaid Salkeld (1880–1959), poet and actress. She was born in India, widowed, returned to Dublin in 1910 and became a member of the Abbey Theatre's company and Thomas MacDonagh's Irish Theatre in 1914. Later she became involved in translation of poetry from Russian and was a regular contributor to *Dublin Magazine, Irish Writing* and *The Bell*. She published five volumes of poetry, and her play *Scarecrow over the Corn* was produced at the Gate Theatre in December 1941.

171 The baby was probably Beatrice Salkeld who later married Brendan Behan, who spent time on Inisheer.

172 It appears that the portrait by Salkeld was never completed.

173 Daly's was a thatched pub three doors down from Dr Jim O'Brien's pub with the post office and another house in between.

174 There had been some fishing on Saturdays but by the 1940s the demand for fish had diminished considerably and then the bigger boats started coming to fish in the 1950s.

175 The *Dun Aengus* was the government-run steamer that ran from Galway first to Kilronan, then to Inisheer, Inishmaan, back to Kilronan and then back to Galway. This steamer had started service in 1912 and was still going during O'Malley's last visit in 1956.

176 A *poochawn* is a small sailboat.

177 The Royal Hibernian Academy of Art, Dublin, often known as the RHA or the Academy, was founded in 1823. Its building was burnt to the ground in the 1916 Rising. Later its offices were relocated to 15 Ely Place, the former home of Oliver St John Gogarty, which the RHA purchased in 1939. In 1941 the government withdrew its subvention and the RHA's income was limited to fees and commissions from annual exhibitions. It was unable to replace its exhibition gallery until the 1980s and held its annual exhibitions in the National College of Art premises on Kildare Street from 1917 to the late 1960s.

178 This refers to the fact that the war prevented British art from being sent over to Ireland. Members of the Royal Academy in London were invited to participate in the RHA exhibitions. In addition to wartime restrictions, the withdrawal of the Irish government's subvention that year may also have impacted on the RHA's ability to continue the practice.

179 Guinness stout came in different strengths such as X and XX.

180 Broach meaning to remove the bung or cork and insert the tap to pour the drink.

181 Stan Barry, from Cork, and Viv Barry lived in Galway, and O'Malley stayed with them from time to time.

182 John J. O'Malley was a merchant on the Mall in Westport, Co. Mayo, and later a founding member of the O'Malley Clan Association in November 1953.

183 The Contemporary Picture Galleries, specializing in modernist art, opened in Dublin in 1938. Frequented by O'Malley who mentions a visit there in a letter of 31 January 1941 (*Broken Landscapes,* p. 138). Jack B. Yeats had one-man shows there in 1939, 1940 and 1941. It held a series of important loan exhibitions including the *Loan and Cross-section Exhibition of Contemporary Paintings* (October 1939) and *Six Irish Artists who have Studied at L'Académie Lhote* (November 1940). It closed in 1948.

184 Jack Longford (1911–44), from Leicester, former student of medicine at Trinity College Dublin and Edinburgh, who co-founded the Contemporary Picture Galleries, bringing great flair to the staging of their exhibitions. He died tragically in 1944. (Avril Percival, *The Contemporary Picture Galleries (1939–45)*, Master of Philosophy, TRIARC, TCD, 2006.)

185 Deirdre McDonagh, pseudonym for Moira Pilkington (1897–1970), actress, who was born in Tyrellstown and educated in France. She married T.H. Hinkson, eldest son of Katharine Tynan Hinkson, in 1920 and following the break-up of her marriage in 1929, she returned to Dublin from Kenya and became an amateur actress with the Dublin Drama League. She was distantly related to Jack Longford through marriage. She financed the Contemporary Picture Galleries, which she co-ran with Longford and continued to do so for a number of years after his death. (Percival, *The Contemporary Picture Galleries.*)

186 Daniel Egan ran an art gallery in St Stephen's Green, Dublin, in the 1920s and 1930s that showed work by contemporary Irish artists such as Paul Henry, Grace Henry, Harry Kernoff and Nano Reid. Egan was also involved in staging public lectures and international exhibitions of modernist art in 1920s. The gallery closed c.1940.

187 Ambroise Vollard (1865–1939), French art dealer and publisher, associated with the promotion of modern French art, especially the work of Paul Cézanne, Henri Matisse and Pablo Picasso.

188 Art materials were in short supply during the Emergency. Seán Keating frequented auctions and house clearance sales to obtain second-hand canvases that could be reused. (Éimear O'Connor, *Seán Keating: Art, Politics and Building the Irish Nation* (Dublin 2013), p. 234.)

189 Eugene Judge (b.1910– ) was born in Aughamore, Co. Mayo and was living at Cloonfallagh, Kiltimagh in the 1940s. He studied at the Académie Lhote in Paris in the 1930s. His work was included in the *Six Artists from L'Académie Lhote* exhibition at the Contemporary Picture Galleries in 1940. He had a one-man show there in February 1941. He also exhibited with the White Stag group in October 1940. He exhibited at the Irish Exhibition of Living Art in 1943, 1945 and 1951and at the Society of Dublin Painters in 1948 and 1949. His work was strongly influenced by impressionist and post-impressionist French art. O'Malley included him in his list of contemporary Irish modernists to be interviewed in 1945 but he never acquired his work though his wife, Helen, did.

190 Major D.J. Freyer's house, Corrymore House, Dooagh, is where Captain Boycott, Robert Henri of New York and Paul Henry lived from time to time in Achill.

191 Seán Keating (1889–1977), artist. He was born in Limerick and won a scholarship to the Dublin Metropolitan School of Art in 1911. His mentor there was the painter William Orpen. In 1914 he won the Taylor Scholarship and began exhibiting at the RHA in 1915, becoming a member in 1923 and president (1950–61). Keating first visited the Aran Islands in 1914 with the artist Harry Clarke. He stayed regularly in Inisheer until the late 1950s. *Aran Fisherman and his Wife* (RHA 1915) and *The Men of the West* (RHA 1917) feature idealized portrayals of the inhabitants of Aran, for which Keating and family members posed. In 1927 he illustrated a deluxe edition of Synge's *Playboy of the Western World*, which was commissioned by the Synge family. He later designed sets and costumes for an Abbey production of the play in 1948. The Electricity Supply Board acquired his series of paintings of the building of the hydroelectric scheme on the Shannon in 1929. In 1939 his mural was shown in the Irish Pavilion at the New York World's Fair and he was awarded a prize by IBM for his painting, *Race of the Gael* at the same event. He had several one-man shows at the Waddington Galleries in the 1930s, as well as exhibiting in Brussels, London and New York. He taught in the School of Painting in the Dublin Metropolitan School of Art from 1919 until his retirement as Professor of Painting in 1954. He was an outspoken critic of modernist art. The Aran Islands remained a central theme in his work throughout his career.

192 Austin Clarke (1896–1974), poet, dramatist and novelist. Dublin-born and educated at Belvedere College and UCD (1912–16), he replaced Thomas MacDonagh as

assistant lecturer in English there in 1917. Clarke was strongly influenced by the Literary Revival and the early poetry of W.B. Yeats. He published several books of poetry including *Pilgrimage and Other Poems* (1929), *Collected Poems* (1936), *Night and Morning* (1938), and *Ancient Lights: Poems and Satires* (1955). Earlier volumes reflect on conflicts between Catholicism and the individual and use imagery derived from Hiberno-Romanesque art and architecture. Clarke lived in England from 1930 to 1937 before settling with his family in Dublin where he worked as a reviewer for *The Irish Times* and broadcaster at Radio Éireann. He was made a member of the Academy of Irish Letters in 1939 and was its president from 1952 to 1954. (O'Malley was also a member of the Academy, elected in 1937.) With Roibeard O Faradáin he founded the Lyric Theatre Company in 1944. His autobiography, *Twice Round the Black Church,* was published in 1962.

193   Norah McGuinness (1901–80), Derry-born artist who trained at the Dublin Metropolitan School of Art. She enrolled at the L'Académie Lhote in Paris in 1929, and, after moving to London, was a member of Lucy Wertheim's Twenties Group in the 1930s. She returned via New York to Ireland permanently in 1939. She was President of the Irish Exhibition of Living Art, 1947–72. She represented Ireland with Nano Reid at the Venice Biennale in 1950. In addition to her modernist paintings of the Irish landscape, she was a designer and an advocate of modernism in Ireland. O'Malley owned one of her landscape watercolours, and Helen O'Malley owned two, *Eccles Street,* c.1943 and *Blue Pool* c.1948, as well as others later.

194   Sheila Richards (1903–85), also known as Shelah, was an actress at The Abbey Theatre, 1923–41, and later a member of Helen O'Malley's Players Theatre in 1945.

195   Evie Hone (1894–1955), born in Dublin, studied art in London and in Paris with André Lhote and Albert Gleizes. In 1924 she exhibited abstract cubist paintings in the Society of Dublin Painters and continued to exhibit with the group. In the late 1920s and early 1930s she studied stained glass in Dublin and London and joined Sarah Purser's An Tur Gloine in 1933. She converted to Catholicism in 1937. Her stained glass window *Four Green Fields* was shown in the Irish Pavilion at the New York World's Fair in 1939 where it was awarded a prize. (It now hangs in Government Buildings.) She received many commissions for stained glass for Catholic and Church of Ireland churches and institutions in Ireland and Britain including Clongowes College and Eton College and opened a studio in Rathfarnham after the closure of An Tur Gloine in 1944. Rivers assisted Hone here from 1946 to 1955. Hone was a founding member of the Irish Exhibition of Living Art in 1943. Hone visited O'Malley in Mayo on several occasions and he opened one of her Dublin exhibits in 1945. O'Malley was the first chairman of her memorial exhibition, which opened in 1958 after his death. He had nine Hone works in his collection and Helen O'Malley had even more.

196   Evie Hone was godmother to Etain O'Malley, born in 1940.

197   The Northern Lights or *Aurora Borealis* often occur in September and October and at other times.

198   There were superstitions about not talking on certain subjects while in a currach, such as foxes, or not going out at all if one met a red-haired girl on the way to one's currach.

199 Pat Mullen was outspoken and anti-clerical on some occasions and had even challenged the parish priest on several subjects, and was thus considered 'banned'.

200 The body of Flight Sergeant A. Tizzard from Scotland, an airgunner from the Royal Air force, was found in April 1941 and was buried in Kilmurvey graveyard.

201 O'Malley is referring to the Native Americans whose cultures he was familiar with during his stay in New Mexico in 1929–32.

202 Cathal O'Malley, his firstborn son, was born in 1936.

203 O'Malley in his New Mexican diaries expressed great empathy for the Native American who are asked naive questions and photographed all the time by American tourists. He never liked being photographed unless on occasion by a close friend, such as Paul Strand or Edward Weston.

204 John Collier (1884–1968) had spent the summer of 1929 with Mabel Dodge Luhan in her Taos home, and later became Commissioner of the Bureau of Indian Affairs under President Franklin D. Roosevelt. O'Malley had met him on several occasions in Taos and had photographs of him taken by Helen Golden.

205 The Pueblo Indians lived in settled communities whereas the Navajos traditionally were more nomadic though by time O'Malley visited New Mexico in 1929–32, they were fairly settled.

206 O'Malley may have confused Pat Mullen with Pat Hernon with regard to this story given the occasional tension between Pat Mullen and the parish priest.

207 Frances H. Flaherty (1883–1972) married Robert Flaherty in 1912 and brought their three daughters to live in Aran, 1932–33. She helped him while filming *Man of Aran*.

208 Robert Flaherty had great difficulty with the Aran light while filming. O'Malley was familiar with this light issue as he had spent several years travelling around Ireland photographing medieval Christian churches and had noted in his diaries the best times to take a particular photograph to get contrast from the sunlight.

209 Oliver St John Gogarty (1878–1957) was a classmate of James Joyce at UCD and was later portrayed as Buck Mulligan in *Ulysses*. The reference here could be to his 1937 book *As I Was Going Down Sackville Street*, which included comments on many Dubliners and Joyce. Gogarty got a medical degree and practised in Dublin. He had been kidnapped by the anti-Treaty Republicans and held as a hostage when they thought that O'Malley was going to be executed by the Free State Government in early 1923; however, Gogarty escaped by jumping into the River Liffey and swimming to freedom. Gogarty bought Renvyle House, Connemara, in 1917 and lived there. He left for New York in 1939, dying there in 1957.

210 Holles Street Hospital, now the National Maternity Hospital, Dublin.

211 Dr Jim O'Brien trained as a gynaecologist and had thus possibly spent time at Holles Street Hospital.

212 Leenane village, Killary Harbour, Co. Galway.

213 Ishbel Hamilton-Gordon (*neé* Marjoribanks), Marchioness of Aberdeen and Termair (1857–1939), wife of the longest-serving Lord Lieutenant or Viceroy of Ireland (1886; 1905–15).

214 William Holman Hunt (1827–1910), an English Pre-Raphaelite painter. There is no evidence that Holman Hunt ever visited Ireland. O'Brien may be

confusing him with another artist, possibly the Irish artist Frederic William Burton (1816–1900), whose work shares some characteristics with that of the Pre-Raphaelites. He made several trips to the Aran Islands between 1838 and 1841. One of his best-known works, which was reproduced as an engraving in the mid nineteenth century, was *The Aran Fisherman's Drowned Child* (1841, National Gallery of Ireland).

215 This does not relate to any work by Hunt. He may be thinking of Ford Madox Brown's *The Irish Girl* (1860), which was in Manchester Art Gallery.

216 Ford Madox Ford (1873–1939), English author, editor and critic. He founded and edited *The English Review* in London in 1908, which published the writings of Henry James, Ezra Pound and D.H. Lawrence. In 1923, after moving to Paris, he founded and edited the *Transatlantic Review* whose contributors included James Joyce and Gertrude Stein. Ford was considered to be one of the most perceptive critics of modern English literature and held in high esteem by modernist writers, especially Ezra Pound. He produced several memoirs, but the one referred to here is likely to be *Mightier Than the Sword* (1938).

217 Lamb's wife, Katharine (1900–78), was the younger daughter of Ford Madox Ford from his marriage to Elsie Martingdale. She was the great granddaughter of Ford Madox Brown, the Pre-Raphaelite painter.

218 O'Malley's clachean or claheen might refer to a *criosím* or *racán*, which is a hook or rake on a pole used to collect seaweed.

219 Dummy meaning being both deaf and dumb.

220 Guard or *Garda* meaning policeman.

221 In O'Malley's mind the *Gardaí* represented the government of the Irish Free State against which he had fought in the Civil War. The Local Defence Force was formed during the Emergency. O'Malley wrote an article, 'Renaissance', for *La France Libre* of London in 1946 about how the Emergency allowed Irishmen of all backgrounds to overcome their prior prejudices as they stood to defend Ireland together. See *Broken Landscapes* (Dublin 2011), pp. 406-12.

222 The Pioneer Pledge was taken by those who wished to abstain from alcohol, and was often taken as part of the Catholic confirmation ceremony.

223 Shawls were worn by adult and married women.

224 The Cynthia mentioned here is not Cynthia Smith (b. 1912– ), artist, as could be mistakenly assumed, whose work was included in the Exhibition of Contemporary Irish Painting in 1950 and so was contemporaneous with O'Malley.

225 O'Malley had visited there in the summer of 1926 on his way back to Ireland after spending a year in southern Europe recovering from his war wounds.

226 Henry Adams (1838–1918), American historian and writer. Adams was a member of the distinguished Boston family, grandson of John Quincy Adams, eighth President of the United States. His *Mont Saint Michel and Chartres* was written in 1904 and published first in 1913. In this travelogue, Adams makes encyclopedic references to French medieval architecture, sculpture and stained glass to explain the civilization, social conventions and beliefs of thirteenth-century society.

227 A bawneen is a white woven knitted woollen jersey.

228 Helen O'Malley.

229 Rathmines is a suburb of south Dublin, where the O'Malleys had lived for three years, 1935–38.

230 Gort na gCapall, a village to the west of Kilmurvey where Liam O'Flaherty was born.

231 Bohreen meaning small road or path and derived from *bother*, meaning road.

232 A round knitted bobble or tassel on top of a knitted Aran cap, usually white, *caipín bobailín*.

233 O'Malley wrote the word 'gerleen' phonetically for the word 'girleen' or little girl. Sometimes such a name would stick with the daughter for her lifetime.

234 A tam is a flat knitted beret-style head cap with a bobble or tassel on top and probably comes from the Scottish term 'tam-o'-shanter'.

235 O'Malley refers to the 'West road' in his 1940 Mayo folklore notebooks, now in the National Folklore Commission. Many of the storytellers were along the road leading west from Westport to Louisburgh and in that area.

236 William á Brick O'Malley and Jim Vrdóg were storytellers near Louisburgh, Co. Mayo, from whom O'Malley had taken down folk stories in 1940.

237 Naneen or Annie Mullen was a significant knitter and had a group of knitters working for her. She lived in *tí Naneen*.

238 Seven Churches refers to the ruins of the seven churches in Teampall Bhreanáin in the village of Onaght or *Eoghamacht*, near Kilmurvey.

239 O'Malley included the phonetic pronunciation for *sé scilleacha* or six shillings, there being twenty shillings to the pound.

240 Miss Powell was Violet Powell, an artist. She attended the Metropolitan School of Art. She exhibited in the Dublin Sketching Club, 1912–15, and later worked as a designer with the Gate Theatre. Powell had a joint exhibition with Rivers in the Daniel Egan Gallery in Dublin in May 1936. It consisted of twelve Aran Island scenes made of dolls and props supplied by the islanders, including one of Sebastine by Dara Dirrane. The sets were made by Rivers. Fourteen drawings and engravings were also included. The exhibition was opened by Seán Keating (*Irish Press*, 12 May 1936). Powell continued to make dolls based on real characters on the Aran Islands, selling them as far afield as the United States where she was in 1940–41 giving talks on Irish folklore illustrated by puppet displays.

241 The Show is probably the RDS Spring Show, which had more arts and crafts work displayed.

242 *Bollán,* or bullaum as O'Malley wrote phonetically, refers to a big rock.

243 Teampall MacDuagh, near Kilmurvey.

244 Quern stones were used for grinding corn.

245 The four-metre-high Tuam High Cross was situated in the marketplace in the centre of the town. A fragment of it was kept in the Church of Ireland cathedral where the entire cross is now located. Tuam Cross is dated to the twelfth century through two inscriptions on its surface. Françoise Henry described it as 'in many ways an exceptional monument.' (*Irish High Crosses*, Cultural Relations Committee, Dublin, 1964, p. 70). It was reassembled by George Petrie in the early nineteenth century from medieval fragments that were scattered across the town. The cross was considered by him to be of a late hybrid style, influenced

by foreign designs. Petrie considered the earlier ninth-century crosses to be purer and 'peculiarly Irish'.

246  MacAlister was Robert Alexander Stewart Macalister (1870–1950), distinguished archaeologist, Dublin born, Cambridge educated, Professor of Celtic Archaeology, UCD (1909–43). Author of *A History of Civilization in Palestine* (1912), *Ireland in Pre-Celtic Times* (1921) and *The Archaeology of Ireland* (1928). Bert is probably a colleague of MacAlister.

247  *Cruach Na Cara* or St MacDara's Island lies just west of Mason Island off Carna, Co. Galway. High Island or *Ardoileán* is off Cleggan, Co. Galway. It has remains of a sixth-century church and small beehive nuts. There is a pilgrimage there on 16 July.

248  Dr Denis Coffey, President of UCD. The reference to Royal could be to when the college was part of a royal university or it could refer to the Royal Society of Antiquaries of Ireland.

249  The *Stowe Gospel* refers to the late eight-century Stowe Missal, which was annotated at Lorrhea Monastery in Co. Tipperary.

250  Sometimes chalk would be used to highlight engravings or sculpture to allow for greater contrast. In this case Fr Quinn used chalk to help get a more definitive photographic image. O'Malley's referred to the use of chalk on page A3-37 above.

251  Written by Rev. C.S. Scantlebury (*Irish Messenger*, 1926).

252  Ard Orlean or Ardoileán is High Island, Co. Galway.

253  Françoise Henry (1902–82), French art historian and archaeologist who taught at UCD from 1932, founding the department of art history there in 1965. A student of the eminent art historian Henri Focillon at the Sorbonne, she completed her doctorate on Irish sculpture during the early centuries of the Christian era in 1932. She published articles and books on medieval and Early Christian Irish art and archaeology. O'Malley knew her well, having been a student on the Purser-Griffith diploma in the history of European painting, which Henry ran. He reviewed her *Irish Art in the Early Christian Period* (1940) in the first edition of *The Bell* (Vol 1, No.1), the new literary magazine started by Seán Ó Faoláin in October 1940. She had included O'Malley's image of the South Cross, Ahenny, Co. Tipperary as Plate 39 in her 1940 volume. Henry was involved in the evacuation of museum collections in France at the beginning of the war and later was secretary of the commission for the preservation of works of art in occupied Europe, in London.

254  This notebook ended here in mid sentence and the subsequent diary notebook has not been found, but it might yet turn up, as things do.

## 2: Inisheer, Aran Islands, August 1955

1  O'Malley does not include specific dates in this diary but he did write to Paul Strand from Inisheer on Wednesday, 3 August, which is a day on which the steamer could have arrived there from Galway. O'Malley stayed in the guest house of Colman or Coley Conneely (d.1989) in 1955. Coley married Maura

Sharra in about 1956 and so it was probably Coley's sister, Mary (1898–1987), who, having returned from the United States, helped run the guesthouse. The house is now run by Coley's daughter Una Conneely McDonagh. In this diary O'Malley often included titles for his paragraphs, which was similar to a style he had used in his 450 interviews of veterans of the War of Independence and Civil War. See O'Malley Military Notebooks, UCDA P17b. Some additional paragraphs titles have been added here consistent with O'Malley's own style.

2  This small diary notebook is in NYUL AIA060, Box 10, Folder 13a, measures 4.5" x 2.5" and is handwritten, mostly in ink.

3  Docks refers to dock leaves, a common weed used as an antidote for a nettle sting and usually growing nearby.

4  O'Malley's use of the word steamer or boat is quite confusing and so references have been revised to be appropriate and consistent for the steamer *Dun Aengus*, currachs, turf boats, and trawlers. In 1955 the *Dun Aengus* steamer, which started in 1912, was still running from Galway.

5  A kneeling form is the fixed platform on which one knelt; in modern times it folds up to facilitate the standing position.

6  Braideen or *bréidin* is homespun cloth or tweed.

7  Cormac O'Malley would go swimming with boys of his age – about thirteen years – but none were good swimmers; it was more like splashing, romping and playing.

8  Bitumastic referred to bitumen, which is a tar-like mixture used for roofing and road surfacing.

9  Currachs are made of canvas stretched over a wooden frame of strakes, which is then tarred.

10  The turf boats or *bad na mona* came in from the Carraroe area of Connemara.

11  Tack refers to the additional tack the boats would need to make given the wind direction.

12  Eastern points is probably Trá Crorach.

13  Dried rods of seaweed.

14  Fr Thomas Varley was the parish priest in the 1950s whereas Fr Thomas Killeen was there 1935–48.

15  Probably an expert from the Department of Agriculture.

16  Commons refers to the land held in common among many owners on which they all have an equal right to graze.

17  The lake or *An Loch Mór* is at the eastern end of the island.

18  Probably the village in the middle of the island near *Dún Fornna*.

19  The Dane is Orla Knudsen (1905–70) who lived near the schoolhouse, below *Dún Fornna*. He had been in a Cistercian monastery before arriving on Inisheer. He made crisses and other woven items to sell to support himself and was known locally as 'the Dane'. He is buried on Inisheer.

20  *Muca mara* is the Irish for porpoise, which derives from the Old French, *porpois*.

21  A shelving tank is a cement-roofed structure where rain runs off the roof into a trough for water for the animals.

22  A cock is a small mound or pile.

23  Laid down meaning the keel of the boat had not yet been laid out for its construction.

24 Boxes, or panniers, some lined with a bottom that could be pulled free to allow the load to fall out.

25 This refers to Edgar Degas (1834–1917), *Beach Scene* (Dublin City Gallery/ National Gallery, London, 1877). This is one of the works from Hugh Lane's disputed collection of continental paintings, which had been deposited in the National Gallery, London, before his death in 1915 and which are now shared with the Dublin City Gallery, the Hugh Lane. Lane's codicil revoking his gift of the paintings to London and expressing his wish for them to go to the Dublin gallery was not recognized legally, leading to a long dispute between Dublin and London.

26 Two shillings and sixpence or £0 2s 6d.

## 3: Inisheer, Aran Islands, 10–29 August 1956

1 Probably the Imperial Hotel on Eyre Square where many islanders and island visitors stayed.

2 Due to O'Malley's heart attacks in 1952 and 1953, he was conscious of carrying heavy loads and climbing stairs.

3 Richard Selig (1929–57), American poet who had been a Rhodes Scholar at Oxford, and married the Irish harpist, Mary O'Hara in 1956, returned to the United States and died in 1957.

4 The hold is the storage-holding area.

5 Dr Heinrich Becker (1907–2001), a folklorist from Bonn University. O'Malley suggests that while Dr Becker was teaching German in Dublin during the war, he was a spy for German Intelligence. Dr Becker received his doctorate in 1934, was interested in Irish folklore and language and went to Ireland in 1938 to study them. In 1939 he settled in Rossaveal, Co. Galway, and taught German in Galway. He was a dedicated folklorist, collected and recorded many stories and was well known and liked on the Aran Islands. He returned to Germany in about 1952 and made trips back to Ireland thereafter.

6 The usual phrase is five-card trick.

7 Gretel van Lengerich (1923–2002), Dr Becker's wife.

8 O'Malley was sensitive to being watched or photographed by anyone, a habit he had learned during his earlier IRA military days and had become instinctive.

9 Referring to the recent photographs in the press of O'Malley with the American director John Ford during the making of the trilogy *The Rising of the Moon* in April–May 1956.

10 *On Another Man's Wound*, 1936.

11 *The Sunday Press* ran a weekly series of articles under the banner 'IRA Raids' from September 1955 to June 1956. These articles have since been published as *Raids and Rallies* by Mercier Press in 2012.

12 Poor writing, possibly Laughton or Laughnton.

13 Monsignor John [O'] Hagan, Rector of the Irish College in Rome. O'Hagan approached O'Malley in Dublin in mid 1922 during the Civil War to try to make a peace settlement, and O'Malley later visited O'Hagan in Rome in 1925 and 1926.

14 Fr Peter E. Magennis, Superior of the Calced Carmelites in Rome, was known as
  . the 'General' when O'Malley met him in Rome in 1926.
15 O'Malley was in charge of the Northern Divisions during the Civil War, but he
  does not expand here or elsewhere as to what 'money the [Northerners] would
  gain' by accepting the Treaty in 1921.
16 In 1955 O'Malley has stayed with Coley (Colman or *Coilí Conghaile*,d.1989)
  Conneely; Sean Conneely owned the shop.
17 In 1956 O'Malley stayed at the O'Donnell guest house run by Marie Flaherty
  O'Donnell, whose husband, Patrick or Padraig, had died young in 1951. They
  had two sons (one Patrick) and two daughters (Maire and Brid). The son, Patrick,
  had two children, Micheal Anthony O'Donnell and Padraig O'Donnell, both of
  whom live today on Inisheer.
18 A press is an old term for a cupboard.
19 O'Malley's lack of ability to speak Irish placed him in a position of not being
  able to hear the voices of the islanders in their own language and consequently
  leaves him as an outsider merely observing.
20 Patrick or Padraic O'Donnell had joined the RIC and his brother Michael
  O'Donnell (1888–1952) had joined the Free State National Army.
21 For reference to O'Malley going to Inisheer in 1918 from Clare, see O'Malley,
  *On Another Man's Wound*, p. 127.
22 The two civil servants are later identified as Madge and Teresa.
23 Cakes refers to homemade brown bread.
24 O'Malley wrote 'Inishere' but probably meant Inishmore as he was already on
  Inisheer.
25 Madge and Teresa, the two Civil Service employees, are referred to as 'C.S.' in
  the original text.
26 The round on the Feast of the Assumption refers to an island pilgrimage to
  Liscannor, Co. Clare, which ended in the 1950s.
27 Mother refers to O'Malley's mother, Marion Kearney Malley.
28 Kevin Malley, MD, was a younger brother of O'Malley's.
29 Cathal O'Malley is O'Malley's older son who in 1950 was taken to America,
  with his sister, Etain, by Helen O'Malley from Ring College, an Irish-speaking
  secondary school in Dungarvan, Co. Waterford.
30 Kevin Jacobsen (c.1930–2000), a younger, bearded Dane, had joined Orla
  Knudsen on Inisheer in 1956. Following his Danish family's furniture tradition, Jacobsen made chairs on Inisheer. He established there a group called the
  Followers of Mary and then relocated the group to Spiddal in 1974. He later
  married, had four children and moved to Dublin. He is buried on Inisheer.
31 The Malley family spent their summers up to 1906 in rented houses near Westport
  Quay. Rosmoney, not Rosemina as O'Malley wrote, is on the north-west side
  of Westport. They also summered in Liscarney on the road to Louisburgh past
  Murrisk.
32 The Burren's Cliffs of Moher are due south on the mainland in Co. Clare.
33 O'Malley often had serious indigestion, perhaps a hangover from his forty-one
  days on hunger strike in 1923. He used to take Pepto-Bismol from a small
  yellow-coloured tin container.

34 In some households the cats were spoken to in Irish but the dogs, which had to be licensed, were addressed in English.

35 There were Cromwellian soldiers garrisoned on Inishmore from the 1640s through late eighteenth century.

36 *An Loch Mór.*

37 *An Bóthar Thoir.*

38 Actually the Castle is south east.

39 *Carraig na Finnise.*

40 Waders refers to tall rubber boots, which he would put on to wade out in the water.

41 The bad results probably refer to O'Malley's sensitivity to certain foods.

42 Meaning paintings here, not films.

43 In 1956 the Irish government introduced an import levy on all paintings and drawings executed by hand into Ireland. While those coming from the UK and Canada were given a preferential rate, those from elsewhere were subject to a levy of 60 per cent. In addition the government imposed a 40 per cent tax on all artists' materials brought into the country from abroad. The Republic of Ireland was the only country in Europe to impose a tax on the importation of works of art.

44 Probably a donkey rather than a mule.

45 The islanders appreciated having the Thursday steamer as they would then only have to spend one full day in Galway and seek accommodations for two nights rather than three nights.

46 Material refers to folktales and island stories. James Hamilton Delargy or *Séamus Ó Duilearga* (1899–1980) was a distinguished Irish folklorist and founder and chair of the Irish Folklore Commission, and a friend of O'Malley.

47 O'Malley wrote 'seanakee (sorry)', thus apologizing for not knowing the correct Irish spelling of *seanchaí*, which is such an important aspect of Irish cultural life.

48 Knock pilgrimage, Co. Mayo.

49 People who can speak Irish often wear a *Fáinne* pin to signal their ability and preference to speak Irish.

50 The islanders used to refer to the mainland of Ireland as Éire or Ireland.

51 The Irish government gave each family member a monthly allowance for speaking Irish.

52 O'Malley might have been working on a chronology of events to be included in his military interview notebooks based on newspaper articles from the War of Independence. These notebooks are now in UCD Archives P17b.

53 The recipient of a telegram had to pay if the telegram had been redirected, and in this case, it would have been redirected from O'Malley's flat in Dublin. The telegram was probably from Helen O'Malley who, having divorced O'Malley in Colorado in 1952, had married Richard Roelofs, Jr. in Greenwich, Connecticut on 15 August 1956 and may have asked O'Malley to allow Cormac to visit the United States without telling him the reason. O'Malley would have feared that he might lose Cormac if allowed to travel as he had lost his other two children, Cathal and Etain, in 1950 when Helen had taken them from their boarding school without his permission.

54 Helen Hooker had married O'Malley in 1935 in London, left him and returned to America in 1950, divorced him, and for several years they had been discussing

terms of possible arrangements for their children but there was no final concluding settlement agreement.

55 Helen O'Malley was one of the founders of the Players Theatre in 1944 in Dublin along with Liam Redmond, Gerald Healy and others. It was a repertory theatre company composed of actors who were to write and direct the plays. She helped fund the group initially as well as design their costumes and stage sets. It put on several acclaimed productions in Cork and Dublin. O'Malley had been invited to join their Board, but disputed their essential premise of having actors write the plays, and refused.

56 Helen O'Malley visited Dublin to see O'Malley and Cormac in early September 1955.

57 O'Malley's sketch of two hooker boats in the original diary is not included here.

58 Exercises refers to homework exercises.

59 As of now none of O'Malley's published works have ever been translated into Irish and published.

60 Italian expression meaning sweet idleness or pleasantly doing nothing.

61 Perhaps O'Malley was reflecting on the Native American experiences he had heard of in New Mexico where there were tribal councils who listened to the comments of the pueblo members including their children.

62 The factory was located just outside of the west village and today is the local arts centre, Áras Éanna.

63 A sweet is a dessert such as a custard or jelly.

64 A gateau is a dessert cake made by a cake company called Gateaux, and they made Swiss roll also.

65 In fact, Dr O'Brien later married a Galway matron nurse, but she died before him, and they had no children.

66 The Black and Tans, an auxiliary division of the Royal Irish Constabulary, visited all three islands and raided some houses including the homes of the school-teachers and of Delia and Liam O'Flaherty in Gort na gCapall, where Liam and his brother-in-law managed to escape. Other lads were rounded up and taken to prison in Galway. On 19 December 1920 on Inishmore the Tans fatally wounded Lawrence McDonogh and he died three days later.

67 There had been an RIC Barracks in Kilronan, just next to Dr O'Brien's family house, but it was evacuated in July 1920 when the RIC were recalled to Galway City.

68 Maurteen or Martin O'Donnell or *Máirtín Ó Domhnaill*.

69 O'Malley is talking about how no IRA volunteer would be allowed leave his area without permission.

70 60 fathoms is 360 feet or almost 110 metres.

71 Reference to the spa in Lisdoonvarna, Co. Clare.

72 The enormous lobster was six feet between its claws and weighed fifty-six pounds or about twenty-eight kilos.

73 Bunnies are young rabbits.

74 Liscannor is also in Co. Clare, but on the coast near Lahinch and only a few miles from Ennistymon.

75 Flagstones came from slate, which would have been quarried locally there and used for roofs and floors.

76 A classic of travel literature, *Kabloona* was published in the United States in 1941 and is about Inuit culture, written by French author, Gontran de Poncins.

77 Dr Becker was writing up folklore stories that he had heard in Irish and then transcribed.

78 *Saint Joan of Arc* (London and New York 1936) by Victoria Sackville-West (1892–1962), English poet, novelist and biographer.

79 The Finnis Rocks are a limestone plateau of rocks barely covered by the sea, lying three-quarters of a mile south from Inisheer towards Clare. The Finnis Buoy is there. This passageway is called Finnis Way or *Bealach na Finnise*.

80 Hags Head is on the Cliffs of Moher, Co. Clare.

81 The acetabulum is where the femur meets the pelvis.

82 Patrick O'Donnell, son of Mrs O'Donnell. The full moon was on Tuesday 21 August at 12.39 am.

83 Meaning '*ta se*' or 'it is'.

84 1/2 is one shilling two pence.

85 Probably Michael Conneely of Conneely House.

86 O'Malley remarks about the non-conformity of the three two-storey guest houses in contrast to the single-storey cottages, and yet he must have realized that to house paying guests, the two-storey house was much more accommodating. He wrote in other publications about the ugly nature of modern housing in Ireland. He admired greatly how the Native Americans had adapted to modern life and yet retained their architectural customs. However, he never had to live in the 'old ways', which might not have been too accommodating.

87 Fires probably refers to houses with the traditional open hearth fireplaces rather than the modern oven stoves.

88 O'Malley was reading the Irish newspapers from 1916 to 1924 and making notes on each in a big notebook in order to make a chronology of the facts relating to the military activities by both sides during that period. He often complained of the pain caused by his having to stand at a high desk to read the newspaper.

89 This change occurred after the establishment of the Irish Free State.

90 '*Naomh Muire*' or 'Holy Mary' is the response, halfway through, to the Hail Mary prayer.

91 Sean Conneely's pub had what is known as a snug, where the women and children could sit, drink and wait.

92 The Bretons refer to the trawlers from Brittany, France.

93 Jean McGrail of New York and Kevin Malley, MD of Dublin, O'Malley's younger brother, but neither of these letters have been found.

94 Keating is not Seán Keating, the artist.

95 Coastguard station on Inisheer.

96 The dry battery was needed to operate the radio as there was no electricity on the island.

97 Slumped refers to Cormac actually fainting.

98 The box is the collection box for parishioners to make their weekly contributions.

99 The concept of oats-money originally was for people to give the priest some oats to feed his horse, but in lieu of oats they could give money, and over the years, in places such as in Inisheer where the priest had no horse, it had just evolved into a financial contribution, the amount of which would have been announced from

the pulpit. O'Malley's reference to £60 at Christmas sounds high, and perhaps he might have meant only £6.

100 O'Malley's use of Lucullian does not make sense, but perhaps he was referring to a Lucullian profusion of flowers breeding there.

101 A government grant for building.

102 An egg flip is a combination of hot milk, a fresh egg dropped in the milk and a splash of brandy added.

103 O'Malley was familiar with folktales about seals from Clew Bay and how people should not harm them. The Conneely family name is also connected with seal people and seal stories.

104 Meaning to go to the shop to buy something requested.

105 Message time refers to going to Conneely's shop where there was a phone and a shop.

106 Critter is a dye used for wool.

107 Buckfast Abbey, a Benedictine monastery near Buckfastleigh, Devon, England, was founded in 1018, dissolved in the sixteenth country and reinstituted in the nineteenth century. Their new church was completed in 1938.

108 There were people who did weave on Inisheer, but perhaps Orla Knudsen had met young men who were not interested in such a career.

109 Orla Knudsen had an exhibition in the Little Theatre, Brown Thomas, Dublin in June 1955.

110 The Belfast-born Galway raised actress Siobhan McKenna (1923–86), whom Helen O'Malley brought to London in one of the plays staged by the Players Theatre, and of whom Helen made a bust. McKenna married Denis O'Dea, and her son is Donnacha O'Dea.

111 Siobhan McKenna played St Joan in the play *Joan of Arc* by George Bernard Shaw, published in 1924.

112 This could refer to Helen O'Malley who on occasion helped McKenna as she had become a member of her Players Theatre.

113 O'Malley is talking out loud to Helen O'Malley, who owed him support money at the time for his son, Cormac.

114 Richard Roelofs, Jr, whom Helen O'Malley had just married in Connecticut. The DMP refers to the Dublin Metropolitan Police, which were disbanded or merged into the *Garda Siochana* in 1922.

115 The O'Malleys had a pair of Siamese cats at home at one point, Wang Ho and Wang Hi.

116 O'Malley lived in the Mespil Flats, Sussex Road, in Dublin.

117 For example, if a cow eats some garlic it would influence the taste of the cow's milk in an unsavoury manner.

118 Liam and Barbara Redmond had been neighbours of the O'Malleys in Clonskeagh, Dublin, in the mid 1940s and were well known to them over many years. O'Malley had met them on their honeymoon while on a holiday on Inishmore in 1936. Their oldest child, Helen, would have been nineteen in 1958.

119 Jaquetta Hawkes (1910–66), archaeologist and author; *A Land* was published in London in 1951.

120 Probably *Gift from the Sea* by Anne Morrow Lindbergh, published in New York in 1955.

121 O'Malley had not approved of the Players Theatre in principle because it was to produce plays written by actors rather than playwrights. He had also not approved of the close friendship between Helen O'Malley and Liam Redmond and was particularly concerned here as it was Redmond who had driven the car to facilitate Helen O'Malley's taking two of his children, Cathal and Etain, from their school in 1950.

122 Reference to Helen O'Malley's marriage to Richard Roelofs on 15 August 1956.

123 Reference to Helen O'Malley's possible plans to kidnap Cormac as she had kidnapped their other two children.

124 *The Power and the Glory* (1941) by Graham Greene (1904–91). Greene was a friend of O'Malley's in London.

125 The schoolteacher was Eamon O'Toole, a second cousin of Padraig O'Toole of Bung Gowla on Inishmore. Padraig later married Mary O'Hara, and they have returned to live on Inishmore. Padraig remembered meeting O'Malley on Inisheer at that time.

126 This diary continues in another notebook, which has not yet been found.

## Afterword

1 Susan Sontag, *Reborn: Journals and Notebooks 1947–1963*, ed. David Rieff (New York 2008), p. 164. That dialogue may still be possible in these circumstances is overlooked, as is clear from O'Malley's discussion of Anne Kelly's upbringing by mute parents (see p. 65 above).

2 'The remoteness from a sense of time and from the passage of time is the most extraordinary thing about Aran': Ernie O'Malley to Paul Strand, 26 September 1956, in O'Malley and Allen, eds, *Broken Landscapes*, p. 370.

3 W.B. Yeats, 'The Tragic Generation', in *Autobiographies*, in *Collected Works of W.B. Yeats*, Vol. 3, eds William O'Donnell and Douglas Archibald (New York 1999), p. 263.

4 As Brian O'Doherty notes: '[T]he only way the stereotype [of freedom] could be dignified was by making heroes of those of no fixed abode (still an address of honour in small Irish courts) – those vagrants in motion as much across the country's imaginative as well as physical landscape. Jack Yeats (and Synge – the two bear a comparison that has not been made) faultlessly recognized that a certain dignity is to be purchased through travel, through its conjunction of glamour and loss (other names for promise and regret).' 'Jack B. Yeats: Promise and Regret', in Roger McHugh, ed., *Jack B. Yeats: A Centenary Gathering* (Dublin 1971), pp. 84–5.

5 Ernie O'Malley, 'The Paintings of Jack B. Yeats', in McHugh, ed., *Jack B. Yeats*, p. 69; see also included in O'Malley and Allen, eds, *Broken Landscapes*, p. 395.

6 Máirín Nic Eoin, 'Twentieth-Century Gaelic Autobiography: From *lieux de mémoire* to Narratives of Self-Invention', in Liam Harte, ed., *Modern Irish Autobiography: Self, Nation and Society* (London 2007), p. 137.

7 Máire Cruise O'Brien, 'An tOileánach', in John Jordan, ed., *The Pleasures of Gaelic Literature* (Cork 1977), pp. 26–7, cited in Nic Eoin, p. 137.

# ACKNOWLEDGMENTS

Many people have encouraged me to pursue the publication of the personal diaries of my father, Ernie O'Malley. He wrote diaries to practise writing, starting in France in 1925 and ending in Aran in 1956. I especially want to thank Dr Róisín Kennedy who has willingly undertaken the task of reading between the lines of these diaries and helping to edit them. Her insightful judgment and perspective on the art and other subjects discussed has been critically important in the development of this publication. I also thank Luke Gibbons who has been supportive of these efforts throughout. Antony Farrell of The Lilliput Press was an early advocate and has guided the process for the creation of this volume. I must also acknowledge the Archives of Irish America at New York University, which now has these diaries, for permitting me to proceed, and Rachel Aileen Searcy there.

Though I spent three summers on the Aran Islands, I had only vague memories, but when I read these diaries my recollections were refreshed and enhanced. To come to a better understanding of Aran society, geography and its seafaring ways, I relied on many books, but most importantly on the memories of people who had lived there or were familiar with the background. In this regard I would like to thank Pat O'Toole (recently deceased) and Mary O'Hara, who were not only around with us in the 1955–56 era, but whom I have met separately and jointly on occasions since, and who have always encouraged this publication. Without two transcribers, Cliona de Paor and Christopher Hammond, this volume would never have been initially transcribed.

Let me mention some of the people, among many, who have kindly helped me on this journey – in alphabetical order – David Britton, Tony Conboy, Mary Deedy, Diane Egerton, Carlos Garcia De Alba Zapeda,

Michael Gibbons, Olwyn Coogan Gill, Brid Conneely Hehir, Tresca Hernon Joyce, Margaret Kelleher, Laillí Lamb de Buitlear, Trish Lambe, Una Conneely McDonagh, Alen MacWeeney, John Menton, Kathryn Milligan, Terry Moylan, Paddy Mullen (recently deceased), David and Maura Neligan, Éimear O'Connor, Padraig J. O'Donnell, Gillian Patrick, Dara Redmond, Lucille Redmond, Karen Rehill, Margaret D'Arcy Russell, Jim Street and Bernadette Gill Street, William H. Taft, IV, William H. Taft, V, Mary Paula Walsh, Liam White and faculty members of Glucksman Ireland House at New York University including Marion R. Casey, Hilary Mhic Suibhne and Miriam Nyhan.

Róisín Kennedy wishes to thank David Britton, Diane Egerton, Kieran Hoare, Laillí Lamb de Buitlear, Ciaran MacGonigal, Éimear O'Connor, Jim and Bernadette Street and Ian Whyte as well as the staff at the National Library of Ireland and Cormac O'Malley for his attentive editing skills and for providing access and insights into Ernie O'Malley's diaries and papers.

# GLOSSARY OF IRISH WORDS

| Irish | English | Meaning |
|---|---|---|
| *Aran Mór* | Inishmore | Big Island |
| *báinín* | bawneen | collarless unlined men's jacket of close, woven cloth or wool |
| *bean a'tí* | woman of the house | |
| *bobailín* | bobbelin | tassel on top of cap |
| *bóithrín* | bohreen | side or small road or path |
| *bollán* | bullaun | big rock |
| *braid* | braideen | woven or tweed |
| *crios* | criss | waistband support or belt |
| *criosanna* | crisses | plural of criss |
| *curach* | currach | older term for Curragh |
| *Inis Máan* | Inishmaan | Middle Island |
| *Inis Óir* | Inisheer | Small or South Island |
| *muca mara* | porpoise | |
| *scillinge* | shilling | currency (twenty shillings made a pound) |
| *seanchaí* | seanachie | storyteller |

# INDEX